TWENTIETH-CENTURY
CAUSE CÈLÉBRE

TWENTIETH-CENTURY CAUSE CÈLÉBRE

SACCO, VANZETTI,
AND THE PRESS, 1920–1927

JOHN F. NEVILLE

Westport, Connecticut
London

Library of Congress Cataloging-in-Publication Data

Neville, John F., 1952–
   Twentieth-century cause célébre: Sacco, Vanzetti, and the press, 1920–1927/
John F. Neville.
     p. cm.
   Includes bibliographical references and index.
   ISBN 0–275–97783–8 (alk. paper)
   1. Sacco-Vanzetti Trial, Dedham, Mass., 1921. 2. Trials (Murder)—
Massachusetts—Dedham. 3. Press and politics—United States—History. I. Title.
   KF224.S2N48 2004
   345.73'02523'097447—dc22   2003068722

British Library Cataloguing in Publication Data is available.

Library of Congress Catalog Card Number: 2003068722
ISBN: 0–275–97783–8

First published in 2004

Praeger Publishers, 88 Post Road West, Westport, CT 06881
An imprint of Greenwood Publishing Group, Inc.
www.praeger.com

Printed in the United States of America

The paper used in this book complies with the
Permanent Paper Standard issued by the National
Information Standards Organization (Z39.48–1984).

10 9 8 7 6 5 4 3 2 1

Dedicated to Robert E. Neville
Who kept our family together in its darkest hours

Contents

Preface

Almost all *causes cèlébres* begin political life as well-publicized local trials. Americans often assume that most trials receive mandatory news media coverage. That notion is far from true—only a handful of trials, no matter what their type or jurisdiction, receive news coverage and then only in abbreviated accounts. Very few trials receive national news coverage in the United States or elsewhere in the world, for that matter. Of the small number that are covered by the press and broadcast media, an even smaller percentage become worldwide famous cases: causes cèlébres.

This book studies the press coverage and its relationships with propaganda and public reaction to one of America's most celebrated political cases of the twentieth century. The Sacco-Vanzetti episode began public life as the murder trial of two immigrant Italians accused of killing a paymaster and his security guard in a shoe-company robbery. At trial, however, the issue of their radical backgrounds—both men were anarchists—surfaced and slowly developed, eventually inflating into a worldwide movement.

This case was not born to public life as a notorious cause, but, rather it was laboriously managed and organized to attain that status. Defense committees were formed, money raised, telephone-banks set up; recruiters canvassed neighborhoods, street-corner speakers harangued the curious, volunteers collected signatures on petitions. All of this was done with a view toward getting a new trial. That meant funding appeals; hiring high-priced attorneys; then arranging and staging demonstrations, picketing, speeches, strikes, job actions, press conferences, parties, meetings, leafleting, collections, prayer vigils, fasts, and rallies. None of these is possible without the intercession of money and publicity—in that order. The two became intimately if not inextricably linked beginning in the 1920s.

"Propaganda" is a pejorative term to which no self-respecting organization admits involvement. Propaganda, though, has not always been understood in the modern negative sense. Since World War I, it has unquestionably had a distinctly odious connotation.[1] Before then, however, this was not *always* the case. Until the late nineteenth century, the word usually evoked a less baleful reaction. "Propaganda" was until then a term that was synonymous with "instruction" or "doctrine." In the late sixteenth century, after the Reformation, the Roman Catholic Church sought to retain its lost control over Northern Europe by establishing a Cardinal Prefect of Propaganda.[2] The "Red Pope" was charged with spreading the faith and administering the doctrinal and ecclesiastical offices in non-Catholic countries. He presided over a Commission of Cardinals established by Pope Gregory the XIII. A generation later, Pope Gregory the XV made the commission permanent by creating a sacred congregation, *de fide propaganda.* This ecclesiastical body was entrusted with the administration of foreign missions. The commission eventually became known by its more recognized historical title, "the College of Cardinals," which was established for the benefit of priests and missionaries.[3]

For centuries, the word "propaganda" usually referred to the dissemination of religious dogma, mostly as it related to the Vatican. Later it became associated with organizations and groups and their nonreligious system of beliefs and doctrines. For many generations, though, propaganda usually was linked to the Vatican. And yet, surprisingly, the practice of propaganda had a relatively benign reputation until 1914. With the start of World War I, though, that dramatically changed. For the first time in history, war sparked the planning, coordination, and use of propaganda on a truly international scale. At least to many of more traditional upbringing and sensibilities, those results were uniformly repugnant but surprisingly effective. Government ministries churned out articles, leaflets, posters, advertising campaigns, films, rumors, lies, and myths for the express purpose of fomenting hatred of the enemy. Many on both sides of the Atlantic were repulsed by these results, but propaganda, in both word and deed, would not disappear after the war ended. Like it or not, World War I had seemingly opened a Pandora's box of blithe tricks and clever dissimulations that were here to stay—albeit in a more commercial form.

After the war, propaganda became associated in the popular mind with sensation, lies, and exploitation. As noted, much of this reputation was earned. Both British and German propaganda ministries were responsible for manufacturing and promulgating atrocity stories that usually proved as false as they were outrageous. But propaganda was now as critical to modern warfare as the latest weaponry and communications systems. It was considered a quasi-"scientific" form of mass communication that could no longer be left to amateurs.

In the United States, George Creel oversaw the Committee on Information, a benign-enough-sounding, but powerful, propaganda bureau. For years after the war, there was much public debate about whether government should continue to be involved in something as morally repugnant as propaganda. Many in America were appalled by the very idea of its continued existence in peacetime. A torrent of articles, exposés, and books appeared on the subject throughout the 1920s.[4] Scholarly study of propaganda began as political scientists and sociologists struggled with a moral leviathan that nearly everyone, including government officials, public figures, and private citizens, deplored but also conceded now was an inextricable part of modern existence.

In 1928, Harold D. Lasswell described propaganda as referring "solely to the control of opinion by significant symbols, or, to speak more concretely and accurately, by stories, rumors, reports, pictures and other forms of social communication."[5] Lasswell wrote in an age when just about any form of written persuasion—government agency press release or magazine advertising copy—was likely to be branded as propaganda. He was astute enough, however, to point out that propaganda related only to opinion and attitude management by "direct manipulation of social suggestion." Scholars and academics of the 1920s realized that advertising agencies and public relations firms already had adopted modern propaganda techniques. This prompted an early-American forbear of corporate public relations, Edward L. Bernays, to somewhat defensively claim: "The conscious and intelligent manipulation of the original habits and opinions of the masses is an important element in democratic society."[6] Bernays did allow, however, that government could abuse its ability to manipulate public opinion. While Lasswell was rather pedantic in his analysis of government control of public opinion, Bernays was unapologetically deterministic. He argued that events of "social importance" had to be done with the assistance of systematic propaganda. Bernays, drawing on a background in corporate public relations, noted that propaganda was not, in itself, good or bad but hinged "upon the merit of the crimes urged and the correctness of the information published."[7]

It remains an intriguing but subtle point—one that has escaped the notice of many people distressed by the steady growth of twentieth-century government power and influence. By the late 1920s, the Soviet Union had forged its own extremely powerful and widespread brand of institutional propaganda. Known as the "Comintern," Russian Marxists developed a centrally organized, hierarchically arranged government bureau designed for international effect. With a rigorous system of organization and discipline supporting it, the Comintern attempted to incite revolution much as the Catholic Church had tried to quell reformist rebellion three centuries earlier. The Comintern, however, was structured on a more grandiose scale: global revolution via a first step of propaganda by word. Eventual communist support of this historical episode demonstrates forcefully that Stalin was just as committed to a battle of image and metaphor against the United States as he was spying and subversion.[8] His off-the-cuff comment in 1927 that the Sacco-Vanzetti case proved that America was in a "pre-Revolutionary phase" was revealing if not laughably inaccurate.

Mussolini and Hitler also established formidable fascist propaganda apparti in the 1930s.[9] At first, these formidable instruments were not as worrisome to American government officials, the public, or the news media as were Stalin's propaganda efforts. The concern was not entirely misplaced. Almost by accident, the Comintern discovered in the Sacco-Vanzetti case that it could quite easily incite anti-American antipathy on an international scale simply by noting its defects in the sometimes biased (and mostly provincial) American criminal justice system. It was an unfamiliar experience—the United States was not yet accustomed to being vilified as an unjust brute and spiteful xenophobe. These chapters show that a widely disparate variety of American public officials did not always know *how* to defend themselves on a battlefield of words set against an emotionally charged backdrop of demonstrations and protests.

A century ago, the American public became fascinated with the story of an obscure French army captain, Alfred Dreyfus.[10] Newspaper editors sent reporters to France to cover this morbidly fascinating case, a sensational cause cèlébre involving issues of undisguised anti-Semitism, a fraudulent charge of treason, and reams of inflammatory pretrial publicity. Dreyfus was quickly convicted and sentenced to Devil's Island.[11] The affair eventually returned to split French society into warring camps of Dreyfusards and anti-Dreyfusards. Openly and virulently anti-Semitic newspapers had campaigned for Dreyfus's conviction and a draconian sentence. Framed in a Byzantine plot too complicated for retelling here, Dreyfus was defended by his wife, Lucy, and eventually by the popular French novelist Emile Zola. The publicity-fond Zola then triggered an international cause cèlébre with his blunderbuss article "J'Accuse," a roistering broadside accusing the French army of conspiracy and French officialdom of anti-Semitism against an innocent man.

The American press became fascinated with Zola's attempt to gain a second trial for Dreyfus. American readers, notorious for their unfamiliarity with foreign politics, could not read enough of this exotic case involving high-level conspiracy, cover-up, and betrayal. William Randolph Hearst's *New York Journal* and Joseph Pulitzer's *New York World* competed to relate the latest outrage in the Dreyfus case. There were numerous "interviews" with Lucy Dreyfus. It mattered little to newspaper readers in

America that some of these accounts were outright fabrications.[12] Madame Dreyfus had become a heroine to Americans, who in turn protested Captain Dreyfus's ordeal in record numbers. To American publishers, it was an epiphany worthy of advanced hermeneutics: no angry advertisers, fulminating politicians, or upset clerics—just plenty of readers interested in the travails of a wrongly prosecuted French Jew. Eventually, the political pressure from the United States and elsewhere in Europe overwhelmed the infuriated but compromised French government. Dreyfus was shortly thereafter released from Devil's Island and convicted in a second sensational trial. After worldwide protest against the verdict, he was pardoned in a deal that allowed him to go free. Dreyfus gratefully acknowledged (to an eager Greek chorus of American reporters) the support he had received from the United States.

The Dreyfus case made Americans feel good about themselves as they read about French society and its rather embarrassing defects. More than twenty years later, the French, as well as most of the world, were delighted to return the favor. By then the Sacco-Vanzetti case had become America's Dreyfus case. Although the two cases could not have been more dissimilar, the earlier one had definitely made Sacco-Vanzetti possible. The Dreyfus case had proved to the satisfaction of a cynical post-war world that people could be the victims of government conspiracy and prejudice. It is commonplace for citizens anywhere in the world to conspire against their governments, but when a government office, agency, department, or bureau is accused of "framing" someone, it invariably sticks in the public consciousness for generations.

If one lacks complete evidence of a conspiracy, if it is largely undocumented, then those seeking justice sometimes invoke mythology to fill in the gaps. This does not mean that all defense committees deliberately invent facts, although that does sometimes happen. Warren Susman describes a myth as a utopian unification of the whole, a process that "answers the largely emotional needs of the members of the community and to provide, where necessary, the present and the future in the same instant."[13]

Myths also explain events to those who otherwise would be confused or apathetic without the proffered guidance. For the purpose of this book, they help explain propaganda, as well as define the terms and limits of symbols advanced by trial lawyers and defense committees. This book is about a cause cèlébre, a single, obscure case in which myth was used to generate propaganda and stage-manage globally separate movements dedicated to saving two reputedly innocent men and advance international Marxism. The underlying theme linking Sacco-Vanzetti and the Dreyfus case, and to other causes to come, is conspiracy theory—an alternative to the official explanation of a criminal case. In its narrowest scope, a conspiracy is an attempt by more than two people to commit a crime or perform an illegal action while pursuing a legal purpose. Here, a conspiracy might be defined in its narrowest political sense as an attempt by a government body to break the law before, during, or after a trial or inquiry.

Conspiracies, of course, have been perpetrated and revealed throughout history. Alfred Dreyfus was the victim of a government conspiracy that was revealed by his lawyer, his wife, and a variety of people determined to defend him. The Watergate crisis of the early 1970s partly involved a conspiracy by the administration of President Nixon to conceal illegal activities by a White House-sponsored surveillance team. But other alleged conspiracies have been more imagined than real. A purported plot in the late 1940s to inculcate communist values via fluoridation of municipal water systems in the United States had no basis in fact. Similarly, Senator Joseph McCarthy's sensational compaign against alleged communist control of the State Department in the early 1950s only produced several tormented scapegoats and not the hundreds of traitors he threatened to expose.

Some conspiracies fall into a kind of evidentiary purgatory, where government investigations or investigations conducted years after the event provide a less than definite answer to the question of whether a conspiracy existed. President Kennedy's assassination would seem to fall into this category, as well might the case of Bruno Richard Hautpmann, convicted and executed for the kidnapping and murder of Charles Lindbergh's son in 1932.

Americans have a long history of suspecting conspiracies. Richard Hofstadter has referred to this phenomenon as the "paranoid style" in American politics.[14] By early in the twentieth century it became clear that conspiracy charges would echo farther than ever before—thanks, in no small measure, to the ascent of the international cause cèlébre, the rise of a linked transatlantic news media, the emergence of a global revolutionary ideology, and the institutionalization and commercialization of propaganda. The fact that the Sacco-Vanzetti case took place in the United States was no coincidence: The modern political cause, enriched by propaganda and inflamed by allegations of government conspiracy and wrongdoing, had become a part of the rich fabric of life in the American century. The United States had become the primary locus for cause cèlébres—a host nation where conspiracies are sought out, uncovered, exposed, and promoted.

This is the story of how a variety of disparate people—social reformers, anarchists, communists, socialists, liberals, unionists, reporters, novelists, editors, clerics, crusaders, college students, and death penalty opponents— rallied to defend two obscure, Italian-born anarchists from a suspected government conspiracy to persecute radicals. The result would be a trial, a big case, and, ultimately, an international movement that spawned two novels—Upton Sinclair's *Boston* and James T. Farrell's *Bernard Clare*— two stage plays—Maxwell Anderson's *Winterset* and James Thurber's *The Male Animal*—numerous poems, countless articles, many books, and unending controversy.

ACKNOWLEDGMENTS

I would like to thank several people for assistance on this project. I am grateful for Carol Gissing, of Milwaukee, for accompanying me on a research trip to Boston in 1997 and for providing editing assistance in 2003. I would also like to thank my sister, Sheila K. Neville, of Los Angeles, for her support and encouragement through the years. Gratitude also to my significant other, Devonne M. Baneck, of Milwaukee, for patience and understanding during the lengthy revision and editing process. Thanks as well to Joe Wolf, of Minneapolis, for generously providing a place for me to stay during research trips to the University of Minnesota. I would also like to express my gratitude to the research staffs at Harvard University Law School, Boston Public Library, the State Historical Society of Wisconsin, the Golda Meir Library, University of Wisconsin–Milwaukee, and the Immigrant Historical Research Center at the University of Minnesota.

Secrets: The Galleanisti

We said that in every case of radicals brought to trial, from the
Chicago martyrs to that of Ettor-Giovannitti, the reactionary press has
always been deadly against them—the capitalist press had no more
excuses to keep quiet about our case.[1]
—*Bartolomeo Vanzetti, 1926*

At the 1928 Republican National Convention held in Kansas City,
reporters asked U.S. Senator William E. Borah if his party's presidential
nominee, Herbert Hoover, should consider Governor Alvan Tufts Fuller of
Massachusetts as a running mate. Borah unhesitatingly dismissed Fuller's
chances, saying he would "never do" because the governor was linked
inextricably with the Sacco-Vanzetti case.[2] Borah explained that because
Fuller had refused to grant executive clemency to the Italian anarchists in
1927, the governor would be "obnoxious" to foreign-born American
voters.[3] Political insiders like Borah realized the Republican Party standard-
bearer needed all the immigrant votes he could muster to win the Fall
1928 presidential election. Debating the Sacco-Vanzetti case again in the
press would hardly help Secretary of Commerce Hoover in his quest to
succeed President Coolidge. Hoover needed much help to win in 1928 but
he did not need to relive one of America's most embarrassing cases.
Fuller's name quickly disappeared from conversations at the convention
and he soon retired from political and public life.

In mid-April 1920, a grisly double murder took place on a main street in
a small shoe-factory town near Boston. The homicides in South Braintree

were unusual in at least one respect. A paymaster and his guard were gunned down, methodically executed in daylight before scores of eyewitnesses.[4] Newspaper reports said five men were involved in the robbery: Two gunmen, two "cover" men in the car's backseat, and a driver.

Three weeks later, two male suspects of the crime, both immigrant Italians and dedicated anarchists, were arrested in connection with the murder of the paymaster and guard. Nicola Sacco and Bartolomeo Vanzetti proclaimed their innocence from their arrest in 1920 until their executions in August 1927. Their stories are fused inextricably with Italian anarchism, international communism, various radical sects, massive labor support, New England provincialism, alleged government plotting, and the peculiarly American convergence and synergy of radical and liberal politics that flourished in the 1920s.

But any story of anarchism in the United States must include the watershed Haymarket Square case.

The public hangings of four anarchists in Chicago in November 1887 created headlines worldwide. Known as the "Haymarket martyrs," four men—Albert Parsons, August Spies, George Engel, and Adolph Fisher—had been convicted for the 1886 murders of seven policemen and ten bystanders at a labor rally in Chicago's Haymarket Square.[5] Many more were badly wounded in a bombing that was never solved. One fact about this case remains undisputed among historians and scholars: The executed men had no part in the crime. Nevertheless, the American press took up an editorial cry of cleansing from the shores of the Republic revolutionaries, anarchists, and other radicals.[6] It was a popular stance, and not just in Chicago.

The purge was hardest on anarchists, who had the worst reputation of all the contemporary radical sects: tattered, long-hair, bomb-throwing zealots. The term "anarchist" soon became associated with treason, destruction, and godlessness.[7] The assassinations of President Carnot of France and U.S. President McKinley only stoked the flames of anti-radicalism, particularly anti-anarchism. By 1903, the Immigration Act prevented alien anarchists from immigrating to the United States. The same legislation forbade their naturalization, even if they should slip undetected into the country.[8] All of this made life for anarchists extremely difficult—recruiting native-born Americans into the fold became especially hard. By the turn of the century, most anarchists were foreign-born—many of them did not speak English. By World War I, the largest, most disciplined, and violent anarchist group in the United States consisted of admirers of a spellbinding orator named Luigi Galleani.

Born and educated in Italy, Galleani was an influential and charismatic anarchist in that country during the turbulent late nineteenth century. Forced to flee Italy, he lived for a time in France and Switzerland. After Galleani briefly returned to Italy, he moved to the United States in 1901, not long after President McKinley's assassination.[9] First living in Vermont, then settling in Massachusetts, Galleani resembled anything but the popular stereotype of an anarchist. Outfitted in a frock coat with a flowing mustache and a trim goatee, he had the refined mien of a professor of classical literature. Galleani, however, was not a member of an Ivy Tower set or an intellectual coffeehouse coterie. On the contrary, he was an anarchist *par excellence,* one who invariably urged his countrymen to swift and violent action. He also was the editor of the best-written and edited anarchist newspaper in North America, *Cronaca Sovversiva. Cronaca* was for expatriate Italian anarchists the final word on action-by-deed anarchism in Canada and the United States. Galleani was a prolific writer of great skill and nuance; he was even more highly regarded as a public speaker. Anarchist historian Paul Avrich describes him as a "high priest"—such was his mesmerizing effect on audiences. With piercing eyes and an almost hypnotic tremolo, Galleani could suspend listeners in a state of rapt attention for hours at a time.[10] Still, Galleani was no philosophical anarchist and neither were his audiences. On the contrary, he encouraged the destruction of government institutions as the only way to obtain a just society free of repression, intolerance, and bigotry. But he went further than mere advocacy: In 1905, Galleani published a forty-six-page bomb manual, *La Salutě ě Voi! ("Health Is in You!"),* that was intended to help anarchists "destroy tyrants and oppressors." They endeavored to do just that between 1905 and 1919, when Galleani was deported to Italy. In the interim years there were numerous unsolved bombings that police repeatedly attributed to Galleanisti in various cities across the United States. In one episode, a bomb exploded in a Milwaukee police station in 1917, killing ten detectives. Several years earlier, in New York City, a series of bombings was widely thought to be the work of terrorists linked to Galleani.[11]

After the United States entered World War I, Galleani published an article in *Cronaca Sovversiva* entitled "Matricolati," which encouraged all Italian anarchists in the United States to flee conscription into military service. While he did not overtly urge his followers to resist the draft, the implication was certainly undeniable. In the weeks following publication of "Matricolati," many Galleanisti heeded his pointed suggestion and departed for Mexico. Two of these men, Nicola Sacco and Bartolomeo Vanzetti, were natives of Italy and long-time residents of Massachusetts. In June 1917, *Cronaca* was banned from the mail by order of the postmaster of Lynn, Massachusetts. The effect was immediate and profound: Anarchists now found it difficult to meet and to distribute their literature and newspapers. Adding insult to injury, Luigi Galleani was arrested the same month for conspiracy to obstruct the draft. His followers in Mexico were outraged at the arrest of the brilliant anarchist, as well as by the permanent muzzling of *Cronaca.*[12]

During the Summer of 1917, while still in Mexico, the anarchists launched a plan to seek revenge through a fresh wave of bombings. A well-known and violent Galleanisti, Emilio Coda, exhorted his fellow anarchists: "On your feet, comrades!" Although the major purpose of the bombing was to prepare for a revolution in Italy, men such as Coda, Mario Buda (also known as Mike Boda), and Carlo Valdinoci carried out a series of bombings in 1917 and 1918 throughout the United States. A tightly knit and almost impenetrable cadre of a few dozen Galleanisti assisted Coda and Valdinoci, mostly in East Coast cities. While these new bombings occurred, Luigi Galleani was ordered deported in January 1919 by U.S. immigration officials. Not long after Galleani's deportation order was issued, an anarchist leaflet appeared in various American cities that warned of revenge. Entitled "Go ahead," the circular prophesied: "The storm is within and very soon will leap and crash and annihilate you in blood and fire."[13]

Galleani, however, was not deported until June 1919. Only weeks before his scheduled deportation, a sensational plot to bomb the homes of dozens of prominent public officials and citizens was uncovered by a postal employee in New York City. All told, thirty persons were targeted to receive bombs disguised as gifts from Gimbel Brothers department store. The packages were mailed nation-wide; their recipients included such targets as J. D. Rockefeller and J. P. Morgan, U.S. Supreme Court Justice Oliver Wendell Holmes, Jr., Attorney General A. Mitchell Palmer, Federal Judge Kenesaw Mountain Landis, and Postmaster General Albert S. Burleson.[14] A mixture of U.S. senators, congressmen, and governors comprised the rest of the "hit list." Most of the bombs were intercepted before reaching their intended destinations; however, the maid of a U.S. senator from Georgia had her hands blown off when she opened a package. Although no one ever was arrested for the bombing or other related bombing attempts, postal inspectors, Bureau of Investigation agents, and bomb squad police suspected a small cell of Galleanisti in New York and Massachusetts.

Barely had this news settled on the front pages of newspapers when the Washington, D.C., home of Attorney General Palmer was damaged by a blast. The explosion blew out the front of Palmer's house and shattered windows up and down the residential street.[15] The bomb killed only the bomber, whose various body parts later were recovered as far away as two blocks from the explosion. Police immediately suspected that the dead man was a Galleanisti. They had good reason to conclude as such. An anarchist-style leaflet printed on pink paper, and entitled "Plain Words," was found scattered near the scene. It was signed "Anarchist Fighters." Police also discovered the scattered bits and pieces of an Italian-English dictionary. Although detectives were unable to identify positively what remained of the bomber's remains, anarchist historian Avrich concludes that the dead man was Carlo Valdinoci.

Although Palmer and his wife were uninjured by the blast, the Attorney General would not soon forget this spectacularly gruesome incident. In the following months, Palmer helped coordinate and launch a massive campaign to surround, interdict, arrest, and deport alien political radicals across the United States. This period is popularly referred to as the "Red Scare" and is identified with the immediate post-war period, although its initial phase really began during the later stages of World War I.[16] By the time of the Palmer bombing, this famously extra-judicial phase was well under way. By late 1919, the Justice Department had requested several thousand arrest warrants. By January 1920, a roundup of left-wing radicals began. Many were arrested and detained without properly obtained warrants. By this time, though, public opinion in the United States so opposed political radicalism of any kind that only scattered and mildly worded protests found their way into the press.[17] Galleani, and many of his anarchist compatriots, had long since been deported. More would follow—some leaving voluntarily and with haste. One anarchist who planned to return was Nicola Sacco of Milford, Massachusetts, a shoe-company employee.

Pressure on anarchists during this period was as intense as it was against any radical group or organization. "Philosophical" anarchists, habitués of clubs, restaurants, and cafés, tended to be indiscriminately lumped together with their more militant brethren. The Galleanisti, still relatively numerous for a post-war radical political sect, were almost uniformly extremist in outlook and methodology. In Spring 1920, Italian anarchists in the Boston area learned that the federal police in New York City were holding two of their members. There was a great deal of concern about what might happen. Boston Galleanisti sent Bartolomeo Vanzetti to New York to see what could be discovered about the anarchists—Andrea Salsedo and Roberto Elia. Department of Justice and Secret Service agents had traced the pink paper found at Attorney General Palmer's house to Salsedo's print shop in New York. The *New York Times* described Salsedo as being "high in the councils of the Galleani group."[18] Vanzetti met with Galleanisti in New York and found out that not much could be done for the men, who were being questioned in a Park Row office. Vanzetti later testified that Salsedo's lawyer, as well as the secretary of the Italian Defense Committee, urged him to return to Boston and advise anarchists there to conceal radical literature from forthcoming police raids.

On May 3, 1920, after Vanzetti returned to Boston, Salsedo fell to his death from a height of fourteen stories.[19] Galleanisti immediately attributed the death to murder, claiming that Salsedo had been pushed. The *Times* reported that both men had voluntarily agreed to provide information about their anarchist brethren. Agents had attempted to unravel the 1919 plot against the American government officials and the bombing of the Attorney General's house almost a year earlier. The same report noted that both men had requested protection against "their former confederates."[20] Nevertheless, whatever information Salsedo and Elia had divulged to agents was not enough to produce a single indictment. The Palmer bombing, and the earlier bombing plot, went unsolved. Two-and-a-half weeks before Salsedo's controversial plunge to the pavement of Park Row, in an unrelated incident, a small shoe town, South Braintree, Massachusetts, experienced a rather shocking double murder and robbery. The burglary took place during mid-afternoon on a main thoroughfare before dozens of eyewitnesses and in full view of the Slater & Morrill shoe factory.[21] A paymaster and his guard were shot down in the street by two gunmen, while two other gang members kept eyewitnesses low with covering gunfire. The five gang members then fled by car, one of them firing a parting shot at a railroad-crossing tender. The robbers managed to leave the scene with slightly less than $16,000 of Slater & Morrill's payroll money. Witnesses reported to police that the bandits then sped off in the direction of nearby Brockton.[22]

Payroll robberies of shoe factories and mill towns dotting Massachusetts and Rhode Island were not infrequent in the post-war period. However, execution of paymasters and guards in broad daylight in full view of horrified citizens was quite unusual. The guard, Alessandro Berardelli, died in the street shortly thereafter. The paymaster, Frederick Parmenter, survived the attack, was hospitalized, and seemed poised to recover. Although he died the next morning, Parmenter had regained consciousness just long enough to tell police he did not recognize either of the gunmen.[23]

Two days after the robbery, local police announced they had located the car used in the getaway. Two horseback riders found an abandoned vehicle—a dust-coated Buick, in woods situated near West Bridgewater. The automobile was later identified by a police officer who witnessed the escape and by several other witnesses who recognized a torn curtain on the back window. Massachusetts state police reported that the car had likely been stolen five months earlier from a local man. The Buick had nine gallons of gas left in the tank and lacked number-plates.

This scenario, of course, strongly suggests that the robbers had a second auto waiting in the West Bridgewater woods. The *Boston Sunday Globe* reported that police had found the tracks of two cars on a path leading from the woods. Police theorized that the robbers had eventually escaped to Providence.[24] Some news accounts even suggested that progress was being made in solving the case. The truth was that the gang had seemingly dissolved into the fading afternoon light, leaving behind precious few clues and no discernible trail. That fact that the case also was a double murder had given it extended coverage in the Boston and suburban newspapers.

Outside of eastern Massachusetts, however, citizens and local newspapers expressed little interest about the incident. The crime's unsolved status was, however, an obvious embarrassment to local law enforcement. Moreover, eyewitnesses to the robbery and murders had given widely differing accounts of the action and aftermath. If anything, it was a textbook example for first-year law students: A dozen people can observe the same event from multiple perspectives. Reports differed on almost every crucial point of evidence. For example, description of the gunmen's build, appearance, and clothes varied among accounts in many particulars. There also was disagreement as to when bullets were fired and who had fired them. (Some witnesses reported that a third robber fired shots.) Not surprisingly, even the exact sequence of the crime varied among depictions.[25] Most witnesses did, however, agree that the suspects likely were Italians. Beyond that only one thing was embarrassingly certain: For three weeks police had no suspects to report to the newspapers.

Shortly after the South Braintree crime, Bridgewater Police Chief Michael E. Stewart suggested there might be a connection between the Slater & Morrill robbery and an attempted robbery of another Massachusetts shoe company, L.Q. White, the previous Fall. The December 24, 1919, robbery attempt in Bridgewater failed, and police had yet to make any arrests in that case, too.

Stewart suspected that an Italian anarchist named Ferruccio Coacci was somehow involved in both crimes.[26] Police learned, however, that Coacci had recently been deported to Italy. Still, Stewart's suspicion of Coacci's implication in the crime deepened and led him to suspect another Italian anarchist, Mario Buda, who was also known as Mike Boda. (This was the same Boda who had reportedly helped the late Carlo Valdinochi conduct a campaign of terror by dynamite in 1919.) Based solely on local geography, Stewart had some reason to consider Boda a suspect. Boda lived in the woods near Bridgewater in a house that Coacci owned and had only recently rented out to him. Boda was unknown to Stewart but he immediately became a suspect when Stewart learned that the anarchist owned a 1914 Overland auto. The police chief also knew that vehicle was now being repaired at a local garage. When Stewart inspected a shed next to Boda's house, he found tire tracks for an auto much larger than an Overland. Stewart then learned from interviews with Boda's neighbors that he had been seen driving a "large dark Buick" similar in appearance to the car found by the horseback riders. The police chief also discovered Boda was a former employee of the L.Q. White shoe company.[27] That was not the final coincidence, either. The recently deported Coacci had worked (at different times) for both the L.Q. White *and* the Slater & Morrill companies. When Stewart returned to the ramshackle house, Boda had already decamped. The bald, slightly built but extraordinarily violent ex-bootlegger was next heard from several years later in Italy. But this does not necessarily mean Boda immediately left the United States. In fact, convincing but less than complete historical evidence strongly suggests that he would remain in hiding for one more bombing "outrage." Taking place in New York City, it would be one of the worst terrorist attacks of the American century.

Once Stewart learned that Boda had fled, he hustled to the repair shop that housed the Overland. There he told owner Simon Johnson to contact him when and if anyone had retrieved the car.[28] Johnson agreed to do so when he found out that the auto was part of a police investigation. One week later, Johnson said he received a toll call from Boda. The caller said that he wanted to pick up his car that night. Johnson assured him the auto would be ready the next day, but the bootlegger/anarchist failed to appear as scheduled. One week later, on the evening of May 5, 1920, Johnson's wife, Ruth, answered a knock on her front door in West Bridgewater.[29] Boda reportedly stood in front of her with several other men silhouetted in the backlit glare of a motorcycle headlight. She said two other men approached the house from a distance; reportedly one wore a derby; the other sported a felt slouch hat. Johnson overheard two of the men speaking in what she assumed was Italian.

According to a *Boston Herald* report of May 8, 1920, while Simon Johnson came to the door and stalled the assembled men, his wife went next door to a neighbor's house to telephone a local constable.[30] Boda, however, insistently told Johnson he needed the car that moment. The *Herald* story said Johnson told Boda the car was not yet fully repaired.[31] (In later reports this was amended to Johnson asking Boda if he had current number-plates.) Whatever exactly was said between Johnson and Boda in that conversation, the latter apparently grew wary and decided not to pick up the vehicle that night. Next, the *Herald* noted that Ruth Johnson phoned the West Bridgewater police. A constable in the department somehow learned that two of the men at the Johnson house had boarded a streetcar bound for Brockton.

Brockton police arrested Nicola Sacco and Bartolomeo Vanzetti aboard a streetcar as it pulled into town. Another Italian Galleanisti, Ricardo Orciana, was arrested the next day.[32] Mug-shot photos of Sacco and Vanzetti appeared on page one of most Boston newspapers. Looking somewhat like a British suburban bank clerk, Sacco wore a snappy bowler derby. With a worn, floppy fedora and droopy mustache, Vanzetti resembled a down-at-the-heels day laborer on his day off. Newspapers said neither man had a criminal record in the United States. From the context of the articles, it was apparent that both men were not naturalized citizens. Both were heavily armed at arrest: Sacco had a Colt automatic revolver, a .32-caliber loaded with nine cartridges. Police also found twenty-three loose cartridges in his pocket. Vanzetti had carried a loaded .38-caliber Harrington & Richardson revolver. In addition, he had several shotgun shells in his pockets and a pencil-written draft of a notice for a forthcoming anarchist meeting in the Boston area. The *Herald* account noted that a police search of Sacco's home in Stoughton turned up a rifle and shells "similar" to some recovered near the abandoned car found in the West Bridgewater woods. Vanzetti's room in Plymouth was also searched—police found nothing incriminating, only a radical newspaper. Nevertheless, investigators made it clear that they suspected all three men—Sacco, Vanzetti, and Orciana—of involvement in the Slater & Morrill robbery and murders. They also said that the suspects were "part of a gang" that attempted to rob the L.Q. White company of its payroll in December 1919.[33]

Norfolk and Plymouth County District Attorney Frederick Gunn Katzmann said that the trio most likely would be arraigned the next day on murder charges. Sacco and Vanzetti both pleaded guilty to carrying concealed weapons. They were held without bail pending a hearing. In newspaper accounts about the crime, witness identification of Sacco and Vanzetti sounded *almost* definite. An eyewitness to part of the South Braintree crime said Vanzetti was one of the occupants of the escape vehicle and that he was "quite sure" Sacco was also one of the perpetrators. Further, a Bridgewater police officer claimed the two men were among the gang who attempted the botched 1919 robbery.[34] Both Sacco and Vanzetti denied to police they had anything to do with either crime. Witnesses to the South Braintree crime gathered at the Brockton Town Hall to attempt identification of Ricardo Orciana. Police continued searching for the elusive Mario Boda. It was destined to be an errand in vain: They would never again find him in the United States.

SACCO AND VANZETTI: A BRIEF PORTRAIT

Who were Nicola Sacco and Bartolomeo Vanzetti? It's impossible to form any coherent biographical sketch from newspapers in the aftermath of their arrests. Not surprisingly, outside of their tightly knit anarchist community, they were obscure to the vanishing point. In subsequent months, though, it was learned that both came from different geographical regions of Italy but had grown up in similar socio-economic circumstances. Sacco was born Ferdinando Sacco in 1891 in Southern Italy's Torremaggiore. His family was relatively well off by the standards of local farmers but in 1908, when he was seventeen, Sacco immigrated with his brother to the United States. His brother soon returned to Italy but Sacco remained, working on a road gang and then at an iron works.[35] Sacco married another Italian immigrant's teenage daughter in 1912. Eventually he became an "edger," working in several Massachusetts shoe factories. His longest term of service was at the 3-K factory in Stoughton, where he worked after the war. Sacco was, of course, an anarchist, and he had participated in at least two demonstrations. In 1913, he took part in a strike in Hopedale, Massachusetts. At a solidarity strike in 1916, he was arrested for disturbing the peace on behalf of distant Minnesota strikers. (He was convicted of charges but the conviction was later vacated on appeal by a Massachusetts state court.) After the United States entered the World War, Sacco refused to purchase a Liberty Bond at work and quit in protest. Shortly thereafter, Sacco heeded

Galleani's message and left for Mexico. It was in Monterrey that he initially befriended Vanzetti. The two, along with a group of anarchists, were in Mexico only for several months.[36] Using a false name, Sacco returned to Massachusetts in September 1917. Adopting his mother's name, he worked in several factories in suburban Boston for low wages. Sacco then managed to find employment as a shoe-cutter in the 3-K factory. He made good wages, especially promising for an immigrant of that time. The factory owner, George Kelley, trusted him enough to give him the keys to the factory and make him a part-time watchman in addition to his regular duties. At the time of his arrest, Sacco had set aside $1,500 in savings and seemed poised for middle-class respectability.[37]

Bartolomeo Vanzetti, conversely, likely never experienced material comfort in his life, even on the reduced scale of hard-scrabble New England *petite bourgeoisie*. Partly, this was the result of an immigrant's hard-scrabble existence. A further explanation seems to be that Vanzetti was a drifter, often traveling aimlessly between cities and towns both in Italy and the United States. Born in 1888 in a northern province of Italy (near Villafalletto), Vanzetti was raised in a family that was reasonably prosperous by local economic standards. Still, he left school at thirteen and served an apprenticeship to the owner of a pastry store.[38] Vanzetti then moved to another town, worked for several years as a baker until he quit that job, only to drift from village to town, working what jobs he could find on the road. Somewhere along the way, Vanzetti contracted pleurisy and returned to his parent's home to recover. He regained his robust health, but as he improved his mother became ill with cancer. She died rather quickly, within months of diagnosis. This tragic episode reportedly sent Vanzetti tumbling headlong into a grief that shadowed him the rest of his life.[39]

Like Sacco, Vanzetti also left for America in 1908, settling in New York City. Unlike Sacco, Vanzetti had a more difficult time adjusting to the financial and other hardships of life in a distant and unfamiliar land. At first, he worked as a dishwasher in the posh Mouquin restaurant. Conditions in the kitchen were incredibly unsanitary—shifts often stretched to twelve or fourteen hours. Fearing that he would contract tuberculosis, Vanzetti left the Mouquin after eight months.[40] From there he wandered through Connecticut working odd jobs, living from hand to mouth, much as he had as a young man in Italy. Along the road, he found brief stints of employment on crews in stone pits and brick furnaces; he even worked for a time at the United States Arsenal. After a vagabond existence tramping between towns, sleeping in barns and doorways, he returned to New York City. There he found work at several restaurants, laboring as a pastry chef. By 1913, Vanzetti decided to move to Massachusetts. The going proved every bit as difficult—life in the Commonwealth was just as formidable as in New York. Still, Vanzetti managed to find work as a laborer near Springfield and then found a higher-paying job in the cordage plant in

Plymouth. This factory, where hemp was made into rope, underwent a brief strike in 1916. Vanzetti was active in the strike action but only as a fundraiser. By the time of the strike he had already left the cordage plant and had resumed doing odd jobs.[41] In May 1917, Vanzetti did something few Italian anarchists living in the United States did: apply for American citizenship. This was shortly before Luigi Galleani published his "Matricolati" advice in *Cronaca*. (Technically, Vanzetti was one of the few anarchists in Boston who was actually required to register for the draft.) At any rate, he left for Mexico in the company of compatriots and helped form a cooperative in an impoverished anarchist community in Monterrey. Galleanisti in Mexico were not so much escaping the draft as they were awaiting the word to return to Italy for a revolution, one that they expected would rival the Russian October revolution of 1917. The revolution the anarchists awaited so anxiously never came—at least to Italy. Meanwhile, life in Mexico was much harsher economically than in the United States. It was so bad that most Galleanisti had left Mexico within months of arriving.

True to his wanderlust, Vanzetti returned to the United States, drifting from Missouri to Ohio to Pennsylvania before finally reaching his adopted hometown of Plymouth, Massachusetts. It took him until the end of Summer 1918 to return; the war neared its end. Vanzetti resumed doing odd jobs in the city's Italian community. Mostly, it was as if he had never left New England for Mexico. Vanzetti resumed a close relationship with the Vincenzo Brini family and eventually took up another occupation: peddler. He sold fish, mostly to Italians, along the waterfront in Plymouth.[42] After an armistice was declared, he once again became openly active in anarchistic activities in Boston, attending meetings and lectures, sometimes listening to Galleani's oratorical masterpieces in various clubs and halls. In 1920, Galleanisti leaders sent Vanzetti to New York to see about the fate of Salsedo and Elia. It was to be his final trip as a free man. Contrary to reports in some newspapers, the case against the two Italian anarchists was hardly conclusive.[43] Apparently Frederick Katzmann was in no hurry to seek indictment in the South Braintree case. Because Orciana produced a punched time card for the date of the Braintree murders, he was released and never charged in connection with the case. To local police, however, Sacco and Vanzetti were an altogether different matter. Neither man could document that he had been elsewhere the day of the crime. Moreover, both men had lied about certain topics when questioned by police.[44] The falsehoods were easily detected and later caused immense trouble for them at the Dedham trial. But, for now, the general public knew nothing of this aspect of the case.

Identification of Sacco and Vanzetti by eyewitnesses was, at best, tentative; at worst, it resembled a confused and contradictory process. In fact, Vanzetti would not be charged with complicity in the South Braintree crime until late July, two-and-a-half months after his arrest. Nevertheless, Katzmann and his staff began pressuring several key witnesses into making

more definite identifications. Incredibly, indictment of the anarchists for
the crimes did not come until September 11, 1920.

Sacco and Vanzetti were militant anarchists. How well-known that was at
this time in the narrative is uncertain. Some newspaper accounts noted their
radical background—others did not mention it. Indeed, at this point a New
York socialist newspaper, *The Call,* sent a reporter to Boston to check on
the case. The reporter sent word to New York to drop the idea. "There's no
story in it . . . just a couple of wops in a jam."[45] Given that the excesses of
the Red Scare of 1919–1920 had already begun to ease, this aspect of the
case is sometimes overstated by historians. Still, the residual effects of
publicity can hardly be dismissed out of hand. Both men had just had their
photos spread across the front pages of local newspapers. More seriously,
neither spoke anything resembling fluent English. Both had lawyers but they
lacked the money to retain truly first-rate legal representation. They were
Italian immigrants at a time when that ethnic group occupied the thankless
lower rungs of the urban working classes. Sacco-Vanzetti author Robert
Montgomery notes that when arrested, Vanzetti denied to police his anarchistic background and Sacco equivocated. If there was an issue of radicalism in this, one of the most famous of causes cèlébres, it had yet to emerge
in coherent form. And yet, not all was against Sacco and Vanzetti—hope
remained. Within a day of their arrest, anarchists established an organization to help raise funds for their legal defense. Aldino Felicani, a Boston
anarchist and publisher of *La Notizia* (*The Notice*), an Italian-language
newspaper, helped form a defense committee. Another publisher, Giovanni
Gambera, who edited the Italian weekly *Il Pungolo* (*The Spur*), joined
him.[46] Felicani became treasurer of the group and was joined by perhaps the
most feared and violent Galleanisti in the United States, Emilio Coda. The
best-known anarchist in America, Carlo Tresca, the editor of the newspaper
Il Martello (*The Hammer*), lent his considerable support to the effort.

The June 15 edition of *Il Martello* advised readers to beware of "another
terrible plot." The editorial went on to say that Sacco and Vanzetti were
veterans of a freedom movement and had always been ready to sacrifice
themselves for the cause of anarchism.

"Let us show that the blackest persecution against the 'Reds' has not
broken the ranks of the militants, has not weakened the spirit of proletarian vindication and that all are united to defend . . . by word and deed the
reputation of Sacco and Vanzetti, who may be guilty of political heresy but
not of a common crime."[47]

But would such stirring words translate to immediate action?

Felicani and his associates visited Sacco and Vanzetti at Dedham jail and
assured them that that they were not forgotten. In later years, many of
these anarchists claimed that Sacco's and Vanzetti's politics doomed their
chances for a fair trial. In one respect, though, being Galleanisti seemed to

help them. News of their plight spread quickly through the small but well organized Boston anarchist community and beyond to working-class towns and hamlets throughout New England.

Katzmann faced a difficult choice. Only Vanzetti could be prosecuted for the Bridgewater robbery attempt. (Several witnesses had identified him as the shotgun-toting bandit in that crime.) But there also were numerous Italian witnesses who would swear in court that Vanzetti was delivering eels (an Italian Christmas tradition) in Plymouth on the day of the robbery. If a jury believed them, then Vanzetti, of course, would be acquitted. That would more than likely mean that the case against Sacco and Vanzetti, the South Braintree crime, would collapse. If, however, Vanzetti was convicted, then Katzmann would profit handsomely— potential jurors in Norfolk County would learn of Vanzetti's conviction before the second trial began.[48] Katzmann took a calculated gamble and charged Vanzetti with assault with intent to murder and assault with intent to commit robbery on December 24, 1919.[49] A week later, the *Boston Herald* reported that several witnesses had testified at a preliminary hearing that Vanzetti had brandished a shotgun as he tried to rob Albert Cox, paymaster of L.Q. White shoe company.[50] The judge found probable cause existed and ordered Vanzetti held for the grand jury on $6,000 bail. Vanzetti was indicted three weeks later. His trial began in late June 1920, with Katzmann serving as prosecuting attorney for Plymouth County. Judge Webster Thayer presided, as he would at the more famous second trial. Local attorneys John P. Vahey and James M. Graham represented Vanzetti.

Eyewitnesses at the trial linked Vanzetti to the Bridgewater robbery attempt. The facial features of one of the bandits—high cheekbones and mustache—stuck in the mind of several of the witnesses. Unfortunately for Vanzetti, he possessed just such characteristics. Vanzetti's trial was relatively brief and attracted little attention. Like many criminal defendants, he did not testify in his behalf and, thus, avoided cross-examination. Later this was cited by critics of his lawyer's handling of the trial as a strategic mistake in that it seemed to imply Vanzetti's guilt. Shortly before his execution, Vanzetti bitterly reproved his lead counsel, Vahey, for keeping him from testifying.[51] Such, however, apparently was not the case. Many years later, Graham insisted that Vanzetti was given the option of testifying but he decided to follow his counsel's rather standard procedural advice.

The jurors choose to believe the largely nativist Bridgewater eyewitnesses rather than the foreign-speaking Plymouth Italians. Vanzetti was convicted on July 2, 1920, on both counts of the indictment.[52] A *Boston Globe* report said that Vanzetti shouted "courage" in Italian as he was returned to jail. Two weeks later, Judge Thayer sentenced Vanzettti to Charlestown State Prison for a twelve- to fifteen-year term.[53] Although Vanzetti's trial was not well attended, a small regiment of local police officers appeared at his sentencing. Their presence was not coincidental, as a large number of Italians were present, presumably to show solidarity for their anarchist brethren.

After Vanzetti was convicted, the Sacco-Vanzetti Defense Committee accelerated into high gear. With one defendant already convicted, the task became all the more difficult—more money and volunteers were badly needed. Where before Vanzetti's conviction Italian anarchists had dominated the committee, it now gradually expanded to include native-born Italian-Americans. Political radicals with friends in the labor movement and liberals with connections to the power centers of Boston were now also invited to join the group. The best example of the latter case was Elizabeth Glendower Evans, a philanthropist and wealthy "blue-blood" Bostonian who, for years, had championed sundry liberal causes. Politically, she was a perfect fit for the Sacco-Vanzetti Defense Committee. Evans belonged to the League for Democratic Control and the Community Church; she helped found the New England Civil Liberties Committee (NECLC). Evans also had helped pay the legal expenses of radicals in Boston who had been swept up in the "Red raids" of 1919. Moreover, she became a surrogate mother to both defendants and, in turn, helped infuse the committee with money, volunteers, and a degree of social legitimacy.[54]

The fact that Vanzetti had already been convicted guaranteed that Katzmann would seek indictments against Sacco and Vanzetti for the South Braintree crime. Anarchist historian Steven Avrich notes that Boston Galleanisti were enraged by the indictments. They vowed there would be revenge for this act, retribution so horrific that it would popularize the phrase "mass murder" in the American lexicography of crime. Relying on a documentary historian's version of circumstantial evidence, Avrich concludes that Mario Boda left hiding soon after learning of the indictments. Still a suspect in the South Braintree crime, Boda headed at once to New York City. Once there, he obtained a horse and wagon; the conveyance was then packed full with dynamite and cast-iron slugs. Boda then fixed a timer to a quantity of dynamite in preparation for a trip downtown.

On Thursday, September 16, 1920, just before noon, Boda set out for lower Manhattan, plodding the horse and wagon through heavy traffic. Reaching the intersection of Wall and Broad streets, he left the wagon parked directly in front of the newly opened U.S. Assay Office, just down the street from the J. P. Morgan building.[55] A massive explosion resembling an earthquake killed thirty people outright (three died later); at least 200 were injured, most severely. It was a forbidding, gruesome tableau: When the dust settled, the streets in the vicinity were strewn with corpses, rubble, blood, and severed limbs.

Although an extensive manhunt was mounted, no one was ever arrested in connection with the bombing. Mario Boda had apparently escaped again, this time fleeing the United States for good. (He would eventually resurface in Italy but would never be questioned by American police about the bombing.) Nevertheless, with the Wall Street bombing, Galleanisti had achieved a shattering, ineffably brutal revenge, one whose sheer destruction and carnage had evoked, if not rivaled, classic biblical history's most lurid images of suffering and death.

The Boston anarchists were quite upset by Vanzetti's conviction. They had considered his case difficult but "winnable." In New York City, Carlo Tresca was also outraged that Vanzetti had lost—he considered the conviction the fault of Vanzetti's lawyers. Tresca decided that Sacco and Vanzetti would benefit from the services of Fred H. Moore, a "railroad lawyer" turned "radical lawyer." Moore was a Californian but he had roamed the country for years, often defending members of the Industrial Workers of the World (IWW). His reputation largely was carved from two cases: Ettor-Giovannitti in 1912 and the Kriger case of 1919. The first was a trial involving a murder charge against poet cum labor organizer Arturo Giovannitti and Joe Ettor, an IWW member.

The murder took place in Lawrence, Massachusetts, in 1912. Ettor and Giovannitti had organized on behalf of workers, striking against the American Woolen Company and several other mills.[56] A girl was shot dead in the midst of a large demonstration. The shooter never was identified but a jury acquitted Ettor and Giovannitti of all charges. Seven years later, Charles "Big Bill" Kriger, an IWW organizer, was arrested and charged in Tulsa with dynamiting the home of a Standard Oil executive.[57] Moore defended Kriger, exposing a clumsy attempt to frame his client. Kriger was acquitted and Moore's reputation as a radical defense lawyer soared, perhaps somewhat undeservedly. During the Ettor-Giovannitti trial, Moore befriended Carlo Tresca. In fact, Tresca and Moore had helped coordinate a successful propaganda and fund-raising campaign on behalf of the two men. Now, in the Summer of 1920, Tresca convinced Moore that his talents as a radical defense lawyer were needed again in Massachusetts.

The radical lawyer arrived in Boston without fanfare or advance newspaper publicity in October 1920. A short, stocky, energetic man with a widow's peak hairline, Moore cut a somewhat eccentric figure even among the rather fast company he usually kept. With a slack western image and a proclivity to indulge in partying into the wee hours, he had no trouble attracting attention and new friends. Emotionally, though, he was charismatic, even volatile. Nevertheless, a small, cramped office in Boston was made available to him, as was a modest house in the less-fashionable section of Beacon Hill. With Carlo Tresca's boost, Moore quickly became lead counsel for Sacco and Vanzetti. Two local attorneys, the McAnarney brothers, Jeremiah and Thomas, both respectable suburban Republicans, assisted him.[58] As noted, Moore had arrived in Boston at a considerable disadvantage: Both defendants would be tried together. Moreover, Vanzetti had recently been convicted of attempted armed robbery. Moore was also at another disadvantage, taking on a complex case three months after the arrests had taken place. Not all was hopeless, though. The Sacco-Vanzetti Defense Committee had grown steadily, if not exactly spectacularly, and cash steadily trickled into the group's coffers.

Moore threw himself headlong into the defense effort, immersing himself in fund-raising and publicity efforts. Perhaps because he was a relatively inexperienced trial lawyer, Moore decided early on to present the case to the public as a political conspiracy, a cleverly arranged "frame-up" of innocent political extremists. According to this logic, Sacco and Vanzetti were arrested because as radicals, "Reds," they had walked uncomprehending into a police trap meant for the real culprits of the crime.[59] Moore's ability to raise money and create publicity was almost legendary. He worked tirelessly at both pursuits, sometime neglecting the tedious detail work of trial preparation—reviewing depositions, affidavits, and police reports. Moore knew that his efforts to present Sacco and Vanzetti as victims of a conspiracy would get nowhere without funding and the press coverage it could generate.[60] Emphasizing his flair for public relations, Moore attracted the services of several energetic, left-leaning writers: John Nicolas Beffel, Arthur Shields and, later, Mary Heaton Vorse, to assist him in writing pamphlets and articles. Another journalist, Eugene Lyons, a part-time reporter for the *Boston Telegram,* helped Moore with propaganda, even traveling to Italy to seek publicity there in Fall 1920.[61] Once there, Lyons spoke with anyone he managed to buttonhole: socialists, anarchists, communists, syndicalists, village mayors, and journalists.

Moore had instructed Lyons to find "certain witnesses and evidence."[62] Lyons was not notably successful on either count but he did manage to write several articles on the case for *Avanti!*, a socialist newspaper. Lyons also succeeded in persuading a member of the Italian Chamber of Deputies to mention Sacco's and Vanzetti's upcoming trial in an address. It meant almost nothing then; strikes and political turmoil had convulsed Italy that year. But in terms of an effective international propaganda campaign, Lyons had sewn proverbial dragons' teeth. Wisely, the former Columbia University student had kept his message simple: Two Italian anarchists were arrested for their political beliefs and charged with crimes they did not commit. This was the message that Moore wanted to spread throughout the world. But Italy, and the rest of Europe, were not yet ready to elevate Sacco-Vanzetti to the level of a global cause cèlébre. (Thanks to a delay, their trial could not begin for another six months.) Moore realized that the American mainstream news media would likely not be very helpful in diffusing his conspiracy theory, either. He decided to target radical and foreign-language newspapers in the United States and solicited radical and mainstream international coverage in whatever countries would have him. Moore assigned most of the "foreign desk" to Spanish anarchist Frank Lopez, who wrote articles on the case for newspapers in South America, Cuba, Spain, and Mexico. After his Italian sojourn, Lyons arranged publicity for left-wing, labor, and foreign-language newspapers in the United States and radical papers in England.[63] Moore also could indirectly count on the reporting skill of Tom O'Connor, a former news service writer. O'Connor worked more closely with Aldino Felicani, but his journalistic experience proved valuable in later years when he wrote about the case for various American opinion journals, pamphlets, and newsletters.

To outsiders it might have seemed a pretentious, if not downright grandiose, propaganda strategy. At first, the conspiracy allegation probably seemed quite far-fetched but several years later, Moore's audacity yielded rich dividends in news coverage. Whatever expertise Moore lacked as a defense lawyer, he readily grasped the two most important maxims of any cause: a simple, comprehensible message and a reasonably plausible, tack-sharp accusation of conspiracy that ignites resentment and indignation. Far easier said than done. It would take many years for that to occur—but in a way that prompted millions to question whether the United Stated cared at all for justice when the poor and politically radical faced police charges. Moreover it was a question that would be repeated many times in the next two generations.

Fred Moore had a brilliant, capacious, and rather uneven intellect. Although his mind was arguably first-rate, Moore also had several serious character defects. For one, he was a heavy drinker, a "binger," who sometimes disappeared, often at critical times, for several days at a stretch. Secondly, he was what a later generation might describe as a womanizer. Married several times, his marriages predictably were short-lived as Moore invariably fell in love with his latest secretary. But Moore's problems hardly were confined to his love life. He was given to quarreling with anyone who questioned his strategies and decision making, including his clients, colleagues, and members of the defense committee. Worst of all, Moore gradually became a drug addict during the years he represented Sacco and Vanzetti.[64] Despite all this, the wayfaring lawyer succeeded in advocating his clients' cause in the court of world opinion to an extent not witnessed since the Dreyfus case.

Shortly after Christmas 1920, a woman in her twenties named Angelina De Falco approached Sacco-Vanzetti Defense Committee Treasurer Aldino Felicani. De Falco described herself as a friend of Frederick Katzmann. De Falco, who sometimes worked as an Italian language interpreter for lawyers in Dedham, spoke to Felicani about Sacco's and Vanzetti's legal representation. According to Sacco-Vanzetti author Francis Russell, De Falco talked about them a great deal, apparently heedlessly, even wildly.

She allegedly shocked Felicani by offering to assist in freeing Sacco and Vanzettti for a large sum of money. (The amount has varied through the years in innumerable retellings between $25,000 and $50,000.)[65] Felicani said that De Falco explained that for a good deal of cash District Attorney Katzmann could be bought off, along with his assistants and the jury foreman. Allegedly, a staged trial would be held and the two anarchists would be acquitted—provided that the money was delivered on time. Felicani said De Falco also insisted that certain lawyers, including Percy Katzmann, brother of the local prosecutor, would have to be hired by the defense. In this scenario, Frederick Katzmann would then recuse himself from the case to avoid any appearance of impropriety. Felicani discussed the incredible offer with committee members, weighing its credibility and risks. Felicani had several more meetings with De Falco. Eventually, Moore was alerted to De Falco's seemingly outrageous proposal. While Felicani and the Italians on the committee pondered the offer, Moore had De Falco arrested for soliciting legal business without a law degree.[66] Although De Falco had served as an interpreter for Percy Katzmann and Norfolk County Clerk of Courts Francis Squires, both men testified that De Falco had acted of her own volition. Frederick Katzmann testified that he had never met De Falco before seeing her in court.[67] De Falco, however, was acquitted of unlawfully attempting to solicit law business, although the trial judge upbraided her behavior as "imprudent and unwise."

The De Falco incident, seemingly no more than a tempest in a teapot, should have dissolved into historical trivia. But instead it grew into legend, into what might be described as the second sustained myth of the Sacco-Vanzetti case. (The first was Fred Moore's far-fetched but shrewd claim that his clients were political victims.) Felicani, his anarchist brethren, and the "Americans" on the defense committee were certain Frederick Katzmann had orchestrated De Falco's offer. Generations of conspiracy buffs, radicals, authors, college students, and several historians have cited the De Falco incident as "proof" that Nicola Sacco and Bartolomeo Vanzetti had been framed in a conspiracy involving the federal government and local law enforcement. By the time of the executions in August 1927, though, the incident already had been inflated into highly visible international propaganda. Today, it is all but certain that Frederick Katzmann had nothing to do with De Falco's overture. His brother, Percy, more than likely was the naive victim of a conniving poseur. (De Falco was convicted ten years later of offering to arrange for payment a man's release from prison.)[68]

Aldino Felicani and the Sacco-Vanzetti Defense Committee members believed that DeFalco merely did Frederick Katzmann's bidding. In a day when petty corruption and graft were more common in local law enforcement and criminal justice systems, DeFalco's seemingly outrageous offer, though possible, was far more likely improbable. The Italians on the defense committee were anarchists, disposed to view any form or level of government with contempt and suspicion. The offer of an extravagantly expensive bribe convinced them that Fred Moore's conspiracy hypothesis was true beyond doubt. To them, it provided the missing pieces to a puzzle, the "unification of the whole" that validated the view that the ruling class needed to make a victim of the immigrant radical. Sacco and Vanzetti may have been victims of too hard work, too little pay, and inadequate opportunity; also, victims of discrimination in their trials. According to surviving historical evidence, however, there are few, if any, facts suggesting they were victims in any political sense involving a coordinated police and government conspiracy.

The fact that immigrants of radical beliefs had been persecuted in the "Palmer raids" of 1919 and 1920 provided Fred Moore and the Sacco-Vanzetti Defense Committee a historical coincidence of rich potential. Many people outside of that tightly knit, heterogeneous circle could be convinced that both men had suffered the same fate as the victims of the far-flung Justice Department arrests and detentions in late 1919 and early 1920. Propaganda (in this context, an argument based on certain political values) could be cut to fit the exigencies of the arrests and upcoming trial. Recalling that myths are not blatant falsehoods so much as a need to create an idealized reconstruction of tragic or painful events, in this view one can create a myth to fit a preconceived notion, believe it fully, and yet not be responsible for inventing any consequential historical lies or distortions. It is a paradox of the modern cause cèlébre, perhaps beginning with Sacco-Vanzetti: the bigger the case, seemingly the fewer the overt lies. Yet, minor deceptions and slight falsehoods, if developed properly, can be just as effective in driving propaganda as can major distortions and outright prevarications.

Fred Moore was able to gain a delay of the trial's start. The date was moved back from March to late May 1921. Moore put the extra time to good use. For one, he promoted Eugene Lyons to publicity director of the defense committee. (In Moore's charge, anyone capable of writing a press release was made publicity director of something or another.) Significantly, Moore soon succeeded in the biggest coup of his four-year representation of his clients. In February 1921, the NECLC announced in a circular-letter that evidence against Sacco and Vanzetti was "unsubstantial."[69] The letter noted that the immigrant anarchists were being prosecuted because they were "active and influential radicals." The American Civil Liberties Union (ACLU) soon joined its regional stepchild in supporting Moore and the defense committee. It was a stunning public relations victory, one whose implications were at first not altogether apparent. Author Robert Montgomery notes in his 1960 book, *Sacco-Vanzetti: The Murder and the Myth,* that Moore had to overcome the initial reluctance of NECLC Executive Committee Chairman John S. Codman. Montgomery says Codman was pressured into registering his doubts about the case "before there was any evidence that any civil liberty was in peril."[70] Once again, historical timing played a crucial role in this case. The liberal and radical communities of Boston, embarrassed about the excesses of the Palmer raids and their enfeebled response to them, rallied to protest an allegedly unfair trial given two obscure Italian anarchists. Another, and perhaps more ingenious, myth that Moore invented about his clients was the labor issue. Realizing the tremendous resources that organized labor could muster behind Sacco and Vanzetti, the California lawyer quickly decided that his clients not only were victims of a government conspiracy against radicals but that they also were labor martyrs. On its face this was quite preposterous. Anarchist *labor* heroes? The concepts are polar opposites on just about any spectrum of political analysis anywhere, as they certainly were in 1921.

Still, it became yet another example of Moore's brilliant audacity. Although it was a contradiction in terms, it was not quite a lie. After all, both men had at least once participated in strikes. It may only have been once but that was sufficient enough for Moore to inflate their images into latter-day Haymarket martyrs.

Of all the myths surrounding the Sacco and Vanzetti case none was more fertile than this one. Nor was any other more effective—in the United States or elsewhere. As with other decisions that Fred Moore made, the labor myth would take several years to germinate. When it did flourish, however, it would blossom spectacularly, spreading worldwide. In bringing labor to his side, Moore assured himself of huge rallies, the support of numerous labor newspapers and organizers, the backing of nervous trade leaders and powerful political bosses. He also left the garden-gate open for communists to enter the case should they choose to do so. For the time being, they were indifferent to the plight of the anarchists, but their attitude would eventually (and spectacularly) change.

Fred Moore had elevated his mythology of the case to a level that could not be ignored by the international press. (The American press, however, was still unimpressed or indifferent, depending on one's point of view.) Although Sacco and Vanzetti sat in jail awaiting trial, unprepared for life behind bars, they now had powerful friends fighting for their freedom in both word and deed. This time deed meant fund-raising and distributing pamphlets, not dynamiting houses and issuing revolutionary ultimatums. The case seemed poised on the brink of respectability.

The first article on Sacco to appear in a national publication was John Nicholas Beffel's "Eels and the Electric Chair." It ran in Herbert Croly's *New Republic,* then a bellwether liberal opinion journal popular among liberals, college students and faculty, and intellectuals. Beffel's article can be summed thusly: (1) Vanzetti did not receive a fair trial at Plymouth; and (2) the chance of a fair trial at the forthcoming Dedham trial was imperiled because of the Plymouth conviction. Beffel reiterated Fred Moore's hypothesis that both men were arrested and charged because of their radicalism and a conspiracy among prosecutors, police, and the Justice Department to convict local Reds.[71]

Beffel's piece was an excellent representation of motivational propaganda: Not quite libelously false, it was, however, indiscriminately inaccurate in detail. Referring to Vanzetti's trial, he charged that the defendant's lead counsel would not let him testify "unless he would agree to conceal that he had radical beliefs about the economic conflict."[72] Beffel was right about Vanzetti not taking the stand but almost surely he was wrong about who had made that decision. Beffel also said that after their arrests Sacco and Vanzetti had been forced to endure mob anger in various small-town police stations as potential eyewitnesses tried to identify them. It was a stirring accusation enlivened by vivid imagery. It also was distorted beyond recognition from the known facts. Beffel's source of information? Bartolomeo Vanzetti, whom he had interviewed at Charleston state prison. (Sacco, meanwhile, passed his time at Dedham jail reading Victor Hugo's *Les Miserables*.) Beffel concluded his pessimistic article on a sanguine note, hoping that Moore might convince the jury of Vanzetti's innocence of charges in his first trial. In that case, then, both men would have to be acquitted—or so logic seemed to dictate.

Beffel's *New Republic* piece had followed "Are They Doomed?," a pamphlet about the case written by Art Shields. The pamphlet circulated mostly in the Boston area, raising sporadic interest and not very much money. Although it is cited in most books on the cases, it appears to have had little effect in 1921. As with almost everything else in this case, its value would come in later development.

More volunteers showed up at the cramped offices of the Sacco-Vanzetti Defense Committee. The small, leased house Fred Moore lived in on Beacon Hill filled evenings with a variety of radicals, anarchists, artists, free-love advocates, flappers, professors, journalists, unpublished novelists, bohemians, no-accounts, hangers-on, and those who savored the promise of bootleg liquor and raptures of the flesh. Not all, however, were Greenwich Village bonhomie. By the time the trial began, the Italian anarchists began to loathe Moore. Although anarchists were political radicals, excluding religious practice, they were quite traditional in the conduct of their private lives. The jaded libertine atmosphere and frequent hip-flask bacchanals at Moore's house disgusted them. More crucially, the Californian had also alienated Judge Webster Thayer even before the trial officially began. (One of his clients, Sacco, was also increasingly resentful of the role Moore played in his defense.) His co-counsels, the McAnarney brothers, were concerned enough about these circumstances that they asked Moore to step aside as lead counsel. Moore refused, barely listening.

THE TRIAL BEGINS

Somewhat more than a year after their arrests, the Sacco and Vanzetti trial began in Dedham courthouse. A small town that doubled as a Boston commuter suburb, Dedham had a handsome, if somewhat forbidding, granite courthouse and well-kept, large grounds dotted with shrubs, large shade trees, and nearby stately Victorian homes. If it superficially resembled a picture postcard New England town, the view was at least somewhat misleading. Socially, it was a town "in transition," and quite appropriate in at least one sense for the trial. Dedham had conspicuous "old-money" gentry, a modest-size middle class and a large working class, mostly populated by a hard-scrabble immigrant Italian population. The Italians, most noncitizens, lived in the swampy lowland of Dedham with its wrong-side-of-the-track appearance.

When the trial began on May 31, local and state police clearly were expecting trouble; spectators were searched as they entered court.[73] The *Boston Herald* reported that uniformed police and plainclothes detectives were "scattered throughout the courthouse."[74] Outside, state constabulary patrolled the grounds and vicinity on horseback and motorcycle. Outfitted in olive drab uniforms with bandoleers, the state police lent Dedham the look of a town under martial law. The all-too-obvious anxiety of regional and local law enforcement may well have influenced the local populace. It was well known, for instance, that Judge Thayer and District Attorney Katzmann had received many hostile letters, some of them containing death threats. A rumor had spread about town that various anarchists and "wobblies" (IWW members) would closely follow the trial. Adding to the tension, spectators, reporters included, entering the courtroom were searched for weapons. But outward appearance, no matter how ominous, was at least somewhat misleading. By the time the defendants walked into the courtroom accompanied by "a miniature police-parade," Dedham's streets near the courthouse were almost vacant. Jury selection for the Sacco-Vanzetti trial proved about as easy as an election recount and even less popular. The exasperated trial judge was forced to exceed the 500-man-limit jury pool. Various interpretations of this circumstance were offered in the local press. A Boston newspaper reported that many excluded or excused jurors were sixty-five-years or older, suffered from illness or disability, or simply opposed capital punishment.[75] Judge Thayer ordered sheriff deputies into the surrounding towns to locate more potential jurors from among the lodge meetings, band concerts, pool halls, and factories. All of this took time, effort, and added complications. Not incidentally, it was also quite expensive. Newspaper reports pointedly noted that it already was the most costly jury selection process for a capital crime in the state of Massachusetts.

When the Sacco-Vanzetti jury was finally impaneled, jurors were taken on a ninety-five-mile trip through Norfolk and Plymouth counties.[76] This was a tour of various towns along the route of the far-flung crime of which the defendants stood accused. The jurors returned to the courthouse dust-caked and sunburned, looking to bemused reporters like extras in a D. W. Griffith motion picture.

Just as the jury selection process ended, the second nationally distributed article on the case appeared in the *New Republic.* "Foreigners," penned by Elizabeth Glendower Evans, was a lengthy and more rational sequel to Beffel's article. Beffel more or less was a leading voice of radical Massachusetts, at least as far as Sacco and Vanzetti were concerned. In contrast, Evans was the symbolic representation of liberal, old-money, establishment Boston. With impeccable social pedigree and a sharp pen, she let interested liberals know that Vanzetti's first trial resulted in a "grave miscarriage of justice" that required their intervention.[77]

Thematically, Evans's article differed little from Beffel's December 1920 piece. It did, however, emphasize that the Vanzetti jury had ignored the testimony of many Italian-born eyewitnesses—that the defendant could not have committed the Bridgewater crime. Evans, however, carefully avoided the canard that Vanzetti was not allowed to testify. Instead, she focused on Fred Moore's fiction that Vanzetti was a despised Red and that hysteria from the Palmer raids had infected the judgment of the jury. Evans told the *New York Times* that she would attend the forthcoming trial as an "observer" for the League for Democratic Control, of which she was secretary. "We propose to stand by Sacco and Vanzetti as a second stands by a duelist. With the Italian Embassy we propose to see that every ethic of justice is observed. If it is not, we can multiply our voices a million fold to spread the news across the land."[78]

For its part, the *Times* coyly tweaked Evans with the headline "Reds Will Defend Alleged Slayers." Although she surely exaggerated the interest of the Italian government in the case, Evans nonetheless adroitly represented the angst of the reawakening post-war intellectual. It was a rally cry that would not be heeded *en masse* for several years but, nonetheless, a political tocsin had been sounded among the far-left and those of a liberal inclination that had not been heard in at least several years.

A week and a half after the trial began, *Boston Herald* reporter Elizabeth Ellam fired the first salvo against the propaganda efforts of the Sacco-Vanzetti Defense Committee. Part nineteenth-century sob-sister, part New England scold, Ellam decried the public loss of memory about the case's forgotten victims. "Every so often in criminal history comes a case before the courts in which the real vital issues seem to be completely obscured by the mass of motives and reasons and the allegations from about it, in an attempt to befog or befuddle the minds of the people as to the real case on trial. Such was the case when Ettor, Giovanitti and Caruso were on trial in Lawrence eight years ago. Such was the case when Thomas H. Mooney was tried for the bomb outrages of California on Preparedness Day five years ago. Such is now the case of Nicola Sacco and Bartolomeo Vanzetti."[79]

Ellam's point—that radicals obscure the sanctity of tragedy with tawdry displays of propaganda—was if nothing else, unique. Her caveat most certainly tweaked the collective noses of liberals and radicals who visited Fred Moore's leased Beacon Hill house. To them, the Sacco-Vanetti case was the marriage of New England's nativist intolerance and an officially sanctioned conspiracy. To Ellam, Moore and the defense committee had launched a case built upon a mythological foundation of misplaced perceptions. It was a simple matter of engaging the right sentiment for the wrong reason. Sacco and Vanzetti were to be pitied because of their roughshod immigrant displacement and a harsh life in the New World, not their alleged political oppression and violated civil rights.

Ellam said the forgotten victims of the case were the widows of Berardelli and Parmenter; as well as Nicola Sacco's wife, Rosina; their son, Dante; and their infant daughter, Inez, born while Sacco awaited trial in Dedham jail. Noting that "two sorrowing women were deprived of the love, the protection and the care" of their husbands, she observed that several children were left orphans without the support of fundraising. Ellam took no position on guilt or innocence, which, in any case, to her seemed entirely beside the point. She did, however, assume the men guilty of getting involved with the wrong element. That, of course, did not make them guilty in the legal sense, merely worthy of compassion, understanding, and a certain detached fascination—like lepers on an alms collection mission. It was a viewpoint some of the Americans on the defense committee privately held. Six years later, tens of thousands of Americans would share essentially the same opinion. Even in 1921, though, some Boston anarchists and a few tight-lipped friends and underground contacts began to whisper that Sacco was guilty and Vanzetti, while legally innocent of the South Braintree crime, knew of Sacco's involvement. The Italian anarchist code of silence would eclipse this little-known aspect of the case for several decades. It would not end until the early 1980s when an aging, soon-to-die Galleanisti finally confided the unconfirmed rumor to his college professor son.[80]

Ellam's article, which featured a portfolio of pen-and-ink sketches of the major figures of the trial, was unusual in two respects. It ran *after* the trial began and was the first report to implicitly question the claims of Fred Moore. She doubted that the defendants were "labor agitators" and "philosophical anarchists."[81] Ellam said that Sacco and Vanzetti should only be convicted "if their hands are stained with the blood of the two men." She assured readers that the defendants could count on a fair trial, pointing to Judge Thayer's handling of a difficult 1919 case. "Those of us who knew Judge Thayer in the Bessie May Sheels case in Lawrence, two years ago, know that these friends of liberals and radicals . . . can rest perfectly secure in the fact that every right of the defendant is being protected."[82] With a trace of admiration, she recounted the fund-raising efforts of the defense committee in "Italian colonies from one end of the country to the other." She said the case was now described as the Mooney case of New England and attracted propaganda "of the most startling kind." In 1921, the American public was far better acquainted with that case than with Sacco-Vanzetti. It was well known that Mooney and Warren Billings were imprisoned for a crime that virtually the entire radical community and a growing number of liberals and college students said they did not commit. Across the United States, newspaper columnists, university presidents, judges, and politicians said publicly or privately confided that one or both of the Mooney-Billings team was likely innocent.

Such was not yet the case with Sacco-Vanzetti, whose trial was just beginning. The location, for one, was hardly synonymous with international publicity. Dedham is located near Boston but in population size, it was far from being a city. Rather, it was a sleepy suburban village with a couple of factories, some quaint old houses, a few handsome churches, and a nice-looking courthouse square. There were reporters from all the major Boston newspapers and a stringer from the *New York Times* but, then again, this was a local robbery and murder trial. Many years later, critics of the prosecution and jury sometimes pointed to the allegedly pernicious effect of pretrial newspaper publicity surrounding the case. Although it certainly was well known among locals that Sacco and Vanzetti were radical anarchists, the Boston newspapers seldom made reference to their controversial political values.

Sacco-Vanzetti case author David Felix notes that no Boston area newspaper referred to the deportation of the anarchist Ferruccio Coacci or the revolutionary-style circular found on Sacco at the time of his arrest. Too, there was no known attempt by the local press to link the Boston Galleanisti to the Wall Street bombings in September 1920.[83] (Local police had suspected a link shortly after the arrests, although one was never definitively established.) Aside from one or two purple sentences in Ellam's *Boston Herald* article, there was nothing that could be said to bias the jurors against the defendants, assuming any of them had even read the article. (As required, the jury had been instructed by the judge not to read about the case.) Once the trial began, a *Boston Globe* reporter, Frank P. Sibley, provided coverage of the trial that was sometimes discernably sympathetic to the defense. His editors at the *Globe* made no effort to curb or quell his reportage. Indeed, several years later Sibley would help furnish the Sacco-Vanzetti Defense Committee with its best publicity director, Gardner Jackson, a former *Globe* reporter.

This does not mean Sacco and Vanzetti were tried in an atmosphere of judicial equanimity free of anti-immigrant and anti-radical biases. Indeed, historian James Joll notes this was a time when many citizens of Massachusetts feared and despised anarchists, who had amassed a reputation as wild-eyed bomb-throwers.[84] The early 1920s were a particularly unfortunate time to be linked to a militant group with strong ties to Europe.

The Trial

The news media often use the celebrities and prominent public figures attracted to a courtroom spectator's section to measure a trial's popularity and importance. By this crude yardstick, the Sacco and Vanzetti trial was, at best, a modest success. Present were Elizabeth Glendower Evans; Mrs. Lois Rantoul (representing a Boston-based church organization); Mrs. Cerise Jack, wife of a prominent Harvard University professor; and a lone international figure (a minor one at that), the Marquis Agostino Ferrante, a monocle-wearing Italian counsel in Boston.

Presiding over this esoteric assemblage was Judge Webster Thayer. Graduated from Dartmouth University in the 1880s, he had been a reasonably successful lawyer and then served many years as a judge. In his early sixties, Thayer was gaunt with a clipped white mustache and dark sepulchral eyes behind pince-nez glasses; he wore the stiff, white collars and ties that recalled small-town judges of an earlier age. An unabashed patriot given to hackneyed speeches from the bench that sometimes sounded as if they were *American Legion* editorials, Thayer was disgusted with the "radical" international publicity the case had attracted. (In fact, as noted, he had already received several death threats.) Thayer enjoyed talking about the case outside the courtroom. The judge was fond of expressing off-the-record opinions to reporters during lunch breaks, a habit that would return to haunt him with a vengeance in this case.

For newspaper reporters, the heart of the trial began with identification of the physical evidence. This included an extensive cataloguing of the victims' clothing, the bullet holes, etc.[1] The first witness for the Common-wealth, Shelley Neal, was an agent for the American Railway Express at the South Braintree train station.

First witnesses often set the tone for many big trials. Neal could only be said to do so in the negative sense, at least for the prosecution. Examined by Assistant District Attorney Harold P. Williams, he testified to being on duty April 15, 1920, when the payroll destined for Slater & Morrill arrived from Boston at 9:25 that morning. Neal described the appearance of the iron payroll box: two feet long, a foot-high, and a foot-and-a-half wide.[2] The payroll was to be delivered directly to the business office of Slater & Morrill, then to the nearby Rice and Hutchins Company factory. Shortly after the payroll was taken to the business office, Neal testified that he noticed a "newly varnished Buick" parked in front of Slater & Morrill. He said that he saw the same car again at a little past 3:00 that afternoon. This happened before the express agent said he heard the sounds of gunfire.[3] Neal's testimony was quite dramatic, although it was designed for nothing more than identification of the so-called bandit car found in the West Bridgewater woods. Unfortunately for the prosecution, however, Neal's identification broke down under cross-examination. Neal had not seen the number-plates of the auto in question. Fred Moore's questioning of Neal revealed contradictions of prior statements made by the eyewitness. Neal also admitted that his identification of the Buick could also have applied to cars of another make. All told, Neal had made a poor impression as a wit-ness, forgetting his earlier statements and testimony.[4] The second prosecu-tion eyewitness, Mary E. Splaine, was a Slater & Morrill bookkeeper who witnessed some of the crime from a second-story business-office window.[5] From her perch, Splaine testified that she saw Nicola Sacco leaning outside the getaway car. Splaine made a better witness than Neal, but Moore was again able to get the witness to back away from a positive identification. (Splaine, in fact, had been less than certain in identifying Sacco at a prelimi-nary hearing shortly after the latter's arrest.)

To make matters worse for District Attorney Katzmann, the next prosecu-tion witness also reneged on his identification of Sacco. Lewis Wade, a shoe-maker at Slater & Morrill, testified that he had identified Sacco as the mur-derer of Allesandro Berardelli, shortly after Sacco's arrest. On the witness stand, though, Wade quickly developed second thoughts. He told Moore: "Well I ain't sure now. I have a little doubt. Well, my best judgment is this: If I have a doubt, I don't think he is the man."[6] The Boston Globe gleefully played up Wade's embarrassing volte-face, featuring an eight-column, full-page headline: "Witness Fails to Identify Sacco; Wade Has Changed His Opinion."[7] The next prosecution witness also wound up embarrassing Katz-mann. Louis Pelser developed uncertainty during cross-examination about his identification of Sacco. Unlike Wade, though, Pelser did say that Sacco was the "dead image" of the gunman he saw that April afternoon in 1920.

Beyond that, Pelser would not be more conclusive, at least on the witness stand. He was the third consecutive prosecution witness who had retracted or modified certain identification. The trial was less than a week old; yet, perhaps surprisingly, Sacco's and Vanzetti's case looked far from hopeless.

The trial received its first jolt of drama when prosecution witness Lola Andrews identified Nicola Sacco as a man she had spoken with near the Slater & Morrill factory the afternoon of the crime.[8] This proved too much for Nicola Sacco, who shot out of his chair in the prisoner's cage and shouted: "I am? Take a good look. I am myself." Sacco's unexpected outburst spiked the quiet hum of courtroom routine like a spray of ice water. The courtroom fell silent as the defendant hovered for a second, a smile on his face. Heads and eyes swiveled his way as tension mounted. At the direction of the bailiff, Sacco abruptly sat back down. Spectators blinked, not sure if they had heard him right or if they had imagined something. Meanwhile, Vanzetti remained in his seat, on the other side of the witness cage. Sacco's interruption was out of keeping with his usual courtroom demeanor. News reports said that he rarely spoke, and then usually only to his wife or to Vanzetti. Williams resumed his examination of Andrews. Under cross-examination Andrews, though strenuously challenged by Moore, fared better than the preceding prosecution witnesses.[9]

The trial continued quite uneventfully. After the first week, attendance sharply dropped; the spectator section was soon half-empty. Still, the *Boston Herald* decided to enliven its copy with an injection of potboiler judicial mystery. "Looking across the courtroom of Dedham yesterday into the eyes of three witnesses on the stand, Nicola Sacco smiled three times, lips curving and eyes twinkling as each one identified him as having been in South Braintree on the day of the murder of Parmenter and Berardelli and the theft of the Slater & Morrill payroll. What the true significance of that smile may be, whether that of a guilty man seeking to disguise his inward feelings or that of an innocent man confident of acquittal, cannot be guessed until the jury returns a verdict."[10]

Sacco's outburst had prompted local police to even greater concern about security. Spectators were again frisked for weapons as they entered the courtroom. The trial continued with a steady parade of often dubious or diffident eyewitness identifications. Once again, the defense team did a creditable, if not always successful, job of shaking the various accounts. John W. Faulkner pointed to Bartolomeo Vanzetti as a disembarking passenger on a commuter train that stopped at South Braintree the morning of April 15, 1920. A railroad crossing-tender, Michael Levangie, then testified that Vanzetti was in a car that sped off shortly after the crime occurred.[11]

Under cross-examination, however, Faulkner was unable to provide descriptions of any other passengers on the train but Vanzetti. Testifying with some embarrassment, Levangie denied earlier statements to police that plainly contradicted his courtroom identification of Vanzetti. A bookkeeper,

Frances J. Devlin, testified that she spotted Sacco from the second-story business-office window. Unlike her colleague Mary Splaine, Devlin said she actually saw Sacco fire a gun while inside the getaway auto. On cross-examination, however, Devlin admitted that she could not make a positive identification of Sacco at a pre-trial hearing in 1920.[12] Another eyewitness, real-estate owner William Tracy, testified that he had seen Sacco near a drugstore in South Braintree before the shootings. Nevertheless, Tracy wavered on cross-examination just enough to cast doubt on his account: "Well, I would not be positive, but I would say to the best of my opinion, it's the man Sacco."[13] Confusing the issue even more was Louis De Beradinis, a cobbler, who identified Sacco as a bandit who had pointed a pistol at him from the getaway car. Under cross-examination, the witness allowed that the bandit was light-skinned and fair-haired, unlike Sacco who had dark hair and a swarthy complexion. Piano-tuner Harry Dolbeare testified that Sacco was one of five "tough-looking" men he had seen riding around town in a car several hours before the crime occurred. Dolbeare's view of Sacco was only a profile glimpse, however, and he was unable to identify any of the auto's other occupants.

The state's procession of eyewitnesses and witnesses continued, though the remainder were mostly secondary in importance. Austin Reed, a Brockton shoe factory worker, testified that he saw Vanzetti at a railroad crossing in Matfield the afternoon of the crime. Reed claimed that Vanzetti yelled at him to lift the gate: "What the hell did you hold us up for?"[14] Next, a sixteen-year-old girl, Julia Kelliher, provided identification of the getaway car, which she said she saw speeding through Brockton Heights. Similarly, Francis Clark, a bakery wagon driver, said he saw the escape car drive past him in North Stoughton. Carlos Goodridge identified Sacco as the bandit who pointed a revolver at him as the car sped past a pool hall Goodridge patronized.[15]

Next, Ruth Johnson testified that she had seen Nicola Sacco the night of May 5, 1920. Johnson said she also saw three other men, one named "Mike" Boda; she noted the other was called "Orciana."[16] The third, she thought, had a mustache. Nevertheless, Johnson could not identify Vanzetti positively as the man with the mustache. At the same session, the now infamous "bandit car" was admitted into evidence. There then was a brief but intense clash between defense and prosecution about whether the jury should be allowed to view the car. Judge Thayer allowed the jurors to inspect the auto that had been discovered by horseback riders in the woods off Manley Street in West Bridgewater.[17]

This time it was Bartolomeo Vanzetti's turn to jolt snoozing court spectators from their collective reveries. He became infuriated with the testimony of one of the police officers who had arrested him. Brockton patrolman Michael J. Connolly testified that Vanzetti had tried to draw his pistol after arrest. This testimony prompted Vanzetti to leap to his feet and shout "liar."[18] (Connolly said that he was acting on orders to locate "two foreigners" who reportedly had attempted to steal a car in Bridgewater.)

The next day's session featured what seemed the most mundane testimony of the trial. A Slater & Morrill worker, Frank L. Loring, said that a cap recovered at the crime scene allegedly belonged to one of the defendants. (Later in the trial it was said to be Sacco's cap.) A dark-colored cap was then introduced into evidence along with the revolver found on Nicola Sacco. During the trial, the cap was only a sidebar and would be forgotten about for years. But several years later, it would eventually become the most famous *chapeau* in American jurisprudence, even inspiring a lengthy editorial by the *New York World* in August 1927. But this would be six years later. Six years of the forgotten or vaguely remembered, six years of argument and counter-argument, six years of investigations and theories, six years of appeals (legal and otherwise) and impassioned debate and propaganda.

The widows of Parmenter and Berardelli made their appearances on the witness stand the next day. Hattie Parmenter and Sarah Berardelli identified the murder-scene clothing of their late husbands. In addition, Berardelli testified that her late husband carried a .38-automatic revolver similar to the one found on Bartolomeo Vanzetti. Like so many other prosecution witnesses, however, she could not make a positive identification—in this case, of a weapon. Three employees of the Iver Johnson company swore that Alex Berardelli had repair work done on his .38-revolver shortly before he was killed.[19]

George Kelley, superintendent of the 3-K Shoe Company, testified about the whereabouts of his employee, Nicola Sacco, on the murder date. Kelley was called as a prosecution witness. His testimony, however, corroborated some of Sacco's alibi, namely that the defendant had been in Boston in the afternoon of the murder. Kelley said that Sacco had just learned of his mother's death and wanted to visit his father while the elder Sacco was still alive. Kelley said the younger Sacco took off work to obtain a passport from the Italian Consulate in Boston.

Perhaps the most controversial testimony of the trial took place June 21, 1921, although, as with so much else surrounding the case, it would not become controversial until well after the trial. That day, the prosecution introduced its firearms experts, Captain William H. Proctor of the Massachusetts state police, and Charles J. Van Amburgh, a former U.S. Army ordnance officer. Proctor testified that bullet number three, the one that killed Alessandro Berardelli, was "consistent with being fired from" the revolver found on Sacco after his arrest.[20] Van Amburgh noted that he "was inclined" to believe that the Colt automatic found on Sacco fired so-called bullet number three. Proctor said that the remaining five bullets fired into the victims came from a Savage automatic.

This portion of the testimony was crucial to the prosecution, inasmuch as the eyewitness identifications had been, at best, a mixed success. Nevertheless, the defense managed to reveal that Proctor, though he had testified in hundreds of trials as a firearms expert, was indeed not always surprisingly expert on the topic. When asked by Fred Moore to disassemble the Colt automatic while on the witness stand, Proctor failed. Embarrassed, he explained that he was not an expert about the inside of a handgun. His expertise, he said, was confined to bullets fired from a revolver. To make matters worse, Proctor then conceded that he was unfamiliar with other makes of pistols that made rifling marks similar to that of a Colt.[21] Under cross-examination, Van Amburgh conceded that scratches on bullets allegedly fired through the Colt could have been caused by other makes of pistols. (The scratches were caused by rust pitting in the corner of the barrel grooves.)

Proctor's and Van Amburgh's testimony took place at a time when ballistics analysis was just emerging from its infancy. Judges, prosecutors, and defense attorneys struggled with complicated evidence they understood chiefly in outline. For their part, reporters had no technical understanding of the issues at hand and, instead, focused on the sensational and obvious. Such was the case generally in courtrooms across the country and, specifically, in Norfolk County's Sacco-Vanzetti trial. As it turned out, the fate of the defendants would hinge on the jury's interpretation of the ballistics evidence. After presenting sixty-one witnesses, the prosecution ended its case, saving the firearms evidence for last. (The defense had yet to introduce its experts in this still-developing specialty.)

The notoriously muggy heat of a New England summer settled upon Dedham like a visitation of an Old Testament plague. By mid-June, the courtroom sweltered. With air conditioning several years in the future, only palm hand-fans and folded newspapers provided relief from the soaring temperatures. In concession to the oppressive heat, Judge Thayer, usually a stickler for judicial decorum, nonetheless allowed men to remove their suit coats and vests. Jurors availed themselves of the rare opportunity to slouch in shirtsleeves and braces, as if they were sitting on a front porch.

The defense opened its case with testimony from a crime-scene eyewitness. Frank Burke, a professional glassblower, testified that he saw the escape of the getaway car but did not recognize Sacco and Vanzetti among those in the vehicle. Burke said he was close enough to the fleeing auto to see the occupants, one of whom pointed a revolver at him.[22] Another defense eyewitness, laborer Emilio Falcone, testified in Italian that he did not see the defendants at the crime scene. Falcone swore that neither Sacco nor Vanzetti was among the bandits in South Braintree that day.

Three other eyewitnesses to the crime also testified that the defendants were not present that day at the crime scene. One, John Sullivan, contradicted the testimony of prosecution eyewitness Michael Levangie.[23] According to a newspaper account, District Attorney Katzmann was only partly successful in getting two of the witnesses to qualify their accounts. On cross-examination, another eyewitness said Sacco and Vanzetti *might* have been among the bandits but said he didn't think that they were at the scene.

At the next day's session, another defense eyewitness testified that she did not recognize either defendant as a bandit who held a gun on her. The testimony of key prosecution eyewitness Louis Pelser was then challenged by several defense eyewitnesses.[24] The *Boston Herald* noted that jurors heard the name of the Sacco-Vanzetti Defense Committee in court for the first time. The monotonous drone of witnesses, exhibits, and arguments continued apace. The reference likely meant little to them, unless they had already read Elizabeth Ellam's account of the case in the *Herald*.

Defense firearms expert James E. Burns said that his tests revealed that bullet number three was not fired from Nicola Sacco's revolver.[25] A ballistics engineer at the U.S. Cartridge Company, Burns said that he was "unable to determine" whether the bullet was fired from a Colt or from a pistol of another make. The next trial day, J. Henry Fitzgerald, test and proof-maker at the Colt Patent Firearm Company, noted that his tests showed that bullet number three was not fired from Nicola Sacco's Colt. Fitzgerald also said that the revolver found on Bartolomeo Vanzetti had not been repaired shortly before the murders, as prosecution witnesses had testified.

Oddly enough, the ballistics testimony of the defense was mentioned only in passing in the press. What did catch reporters' attention was the appearance of a defense witness, Harry Kurlansky. Kurlansky testified that eyewitness Lola R. Andrews had told him that the prosecution had pressured her into a positive identification of Sacco and Vanzetti.[26] He also said Andrews told him that she did not recognize either one of the defendants from the crime scene. Andrews wound up causing Katzmann almost as much grief as Sacco and Vanzetti and all their anarchism, radical allies, and liberal supporters combined. After the trial it would be said many times that the prosecutor had manufactured a case against Sacco and Vanzetti by pressuring tentative and ignorant eyewitnesses like Andrews into perjured identifications. Given the behavior of some prosecution witnesses under cross-examination, there is likely some truth in this claim, although it would later be developed into a sweeping hypothesis of conspiracy. Katzmann was used to the rough-and-tumble of provincial criminal trials, most of which received little or no publicity. He had little or no idea that his professional judgments (some of which were poor) would be put under a microscope, examined closely, and then used against him in the greatest peacetime cause célébre of the twentieth century.

The next day's court session featured the testimony of two alibi witnesses for Bartolomeo Vanzetti. Both swore that Vanzetti was in Plymouth, not South Braintree, on the day of the crime.[27] Joseph Rosen, an itinerant peddler, and Mrs. Alphonsine Brini, Vanzetti's former landlady, testified that Vanzetti had spoken with them late on the morning of the crime.

In an unusual development several days later, the deposition of Giuseppe Andrower, former Italian consulate employee, was read into the trial record. (The diplomat had since returned to Italy where he gave a deposition.) Andrower swore that Nicola Sacco had visited the Italian consulate in Boston on the afternoon of April 15, 1920. He placed Sacco in the consulate office at about 2 P.M. about an hour before the crime occurred in South Braintree.[28] In another deposition (filed as cross-examination), Andrower said that he could not specifically recall another person visiting the consulate after April 15, 1920. Two more witnesses, Felice Guadagni and Antonio Dentamore, also swore that they saw Sacco in Boston on the afternoon of the murders—Guadagni at a restaurant and the latter at a banquet. On cross-examination, however, their explanation for recalling that specific date was challenged with some success by the prosecution.

Bartolomeo Vanzetti took the witness stand on July 5, 1921. After a brief biographical statement, the defendant testified that he was peddling fish in Plymouth the day of the crime.[29] He then described a visit to his friend Nicola Sacco several weeks later, shortly before their arrest. Vanzetti said that he was carrying a revolver the night of his arrest to protect himself because "it was a very bad time." The witness also described a political pamphlet that he wrote that police found on Sacco after their arrests. Vanzetti testified that he had visited the house of Simon and Ruth Johnson, accompanied by Ricardo Orciana, Mike Boda, and Sacco, to pick up Boda's repaired car. Vanzetti said that Boda and the other men left because the car did not have a current number-plate. The witness explained that the car was to be used to collect radical literature from various friends. It was to be put in a "proper place," apparently the house of a friend in Plymouth. He then described his arrest and detention on May 5, 1920.

Frederick Katzmann's cross-examination of Vanzetti began with questions about the witness evading the draft in 1917. Vanzetti readily conceded to the prosecutor that he fled to Mexico to avoid the draft. Katzmann then asked the witness about his alleged lies to police and the district attorney. Vanzetti was also asked where his friends intended to take Boda's car the night of May 5, 1920. His answers to this and to follow-up questions often verged on the implausible. Katzmann's relentless cross-examination revealed that Vanzetti and his fellow countrymen had intended to visit Vittorio "Pappi" Papa that evening in Plymouth. Vanzetti conceded, however, that he did not know where Papa lived.[30] The witness claimed that he and his friends were going to visit the houses of various Italians to collect radical literature. Where? He testified that they would travel to Haverhill, Sales, Bridgewater, Brockton, Plymouth, and "many other places." Geographically and logistically, his explanation could hardly have made less sense. The towns Vanzetti mentioned were scattered throughout suburban Boston in a wildly looping orbit that would have taken until early the next morning to complete. (Then, too, the defendant did not help his cause when he refused to say whom he was visiting in the various towns.) Vanzetti's testimony only took a day but his credibility as a witness was badly damaged by the seeming illogic of his responses. The defense looked to Nicola Sacco to repair the damage done by his fellow Galleanisti and codefendant.

Nicola Sacco's English was not nearly as accomplished as his compatriot's command of the language. Nevertheless, Sacco decided to testify in English, although an Italian language interpreter was available. *Boston Globe* reporter Frank Sibley suggested in a report that this was a mistake, as the defendant often had difficulty expressing himself in English.[31] At any rate, Sacco's appearance once more filled the court, which had been only half-filled for several weeks. For some unknown reason, many of the new spectators were women. The hot weather continued; courtroom walls and floors beaded with moisture during the long afternoon sessions. The atmosphere was so close that one reporter described it as "deadly." Judge Thayer allowed extra recesses as jurors mopped their brows with one handkerchief after another.

Sacco's initial examination was rather uneventful: The usual biographical details went undisputed. Then he described his journey to West Bridgewater the night of his arrest, explaining that he, Vanzetti, and four other Italian anarchists had set out to collect radical literature from friends who lived in hamlets scattered throughout suburban Boston. Sacco said he carried a gun that night because he had planned to go into the nearby woods and discharge all of the bullets he had at home before leaving for Italy. He said that his plan was thwarted when a friend, Orciana, showed up and distracted him so much that Sacco absent-mindedly stuck the gun in his waistband.[32] Sacco swore that he did not shoot or attempt to shoot anyone in South Braintree on April 15, 1920. The witness said that he thought that he had been arrested weeks later because he was a political radical.

On cross-examination, Katzmann quizzed the defendant about his evading the draft during World War I. Sacco admitted his flight to Mexico with other Galleanisti and the use of an assumed name. Nevertheless, he was far less clear about the aborted automobile trip that was supposed to have taken place the night of his arrest (the planned trip to collect radical literature). Like Vanzetti, Sacco's answers were characterized by evasion and unexplained details. Like his comrade, Sacco did not seem to know exactly where he was going that night. Similarly, he was also at a loss to explain the late start of the rather mysterious venture.

Both defendants had no doubt made a less than positive impression on the jury. Their alibis accounting for their actions the day of the crime were certainly plausible enough but their explanations for their behavior the night of their arrest repeatedly strained credulity. Too, their reasons for carrying concealed weapons brought scant credibility to that pregnant topic.

The hot spell that had plagued prosecution, defense, judge, jury, and a sparsely populated spectator section finally broke. Rain fell as thunder-claps boomed overhead in unrehearsed theatricality. Suddenly the court-room became "delightfully cool" in contrast to the steam-bath oppression of recent days. Katzmann decided to give Fred Moore his wish to inject his clients' radical politics into the record of the trial transcript. The district attorney asked Sacco about a statement he had made during examination about his immigrating to the United States because he "loved a free country."[33] (The trial transcript records Sacco actually said "like.")

Katzmann's question was a gauntlet thrown down. Sacco responded with a lengthy response that struck most reporters as rehearsed. The entire answer is too long to quote in entirety here, but the following provides an indication of just how intent Moore had been in introducing the risky subject of anarchism into the seemingly apolitical venue of a murder-robbery trial.

When I was in Italy, a boy, I was a republican so I always thinking republican has more chance to manage education, develop, to build some day his family, to raise the child and the education, if you could. But that was my opinion; so when I got to this country, I saw that this was not what I was thinking before but there was all the difference because I been working in Italy not so hard as I been working in the country . . . I could see the best men, intelligent education, they had been arrested and sent to prison and died in prison for years and years with getting them out, and Debs, one of the great men in this country, he is in prison, still away in prison, because he is a socialist. He wanted the laboring class to have better conditions and better living, more education, give a push his son if he could have a chance some day, but they put him in prison. Why? Because the capitalist class, they know they are against that because the capitalist class they don't want our children to go to high school or to college or Harvard College . . . What is war? The war is not shoots like Abraham Lincoln's and Abe Jefferson, to fight for the free country, for the better education, to give chance to any other peoples, not the white people but the black and the others, because they believe and know they are mens like the rest, but they are war for the great millionaire. No war for civilization of men. They are war for business, million dollars come on the side.[34]

This remarkable statement, an impassioned, sometime stirring, occasion-ally inchoate speech, was in reality a carefully crafted legal strategy.

Doubtless it was meant to impress the jury, the press, and the public that the men on trial really had been arrested for being dangerous radicals, not armed robbers and murderers. There was no going back now: The subject was politically and legally revealed. Instead of retreating or ignoring Sacco's ungrammatical fulmination, Katzmann took ample advantage of the opportunity. The next day's *Boston Globe* headline described his cross-examination as a "grilling." At the very least, that was an understatement. Katzmann's blunderbuss questions about draft-dodging and radicalism and Sacco's rambling, militant speech had nothing (or next to nothing) to do with the crimes charged. Defense counsel made objections, but Judge Thayer upheld the district attorney's line of questioning. The effect was devastating to Sacco (and Vanzetti) who now appeared radical as well as anti-American. That wasn't all, though. The district attorney also queried the defendant about other unpleasant facts surrounding his arrest. Sacco conceded that he had lied to police the night of his arrest and again the next day when Katzmann questioned him. In perhaps the most visual incident of the trial, Sacco then tried on the so-called "murder cap." The witness insisted it was not his and did not fit properly. The *Globe*'s Sibley noted that the cap fit, albeit somewhat snugly. (The incident provided Boston newspaper cartoonists fodder for the next day's editions with at least one depicting Sacco sitting in the witness case with a child-size cap perched atop his head.)

Nevertheless, in the end Sacco's testimony was a stunning backward blow to the defense. He simply left unexplained several misrepresentations and contradictions. His punishing ordeal on the witness stand lasted several days and did nothing to compensate for Vanzetti's own bumbling testimony. More importantly, neither Sacco nor Vanzetti had presented the jury with anything resembling an alternative scenario to rebut the prosecution's aggressive case against them both.

Katzmann had scored a yeoman victory in odd circumstances: an internationally famous murder-robber trial that would exact a tremendous personal price. Although the convictions would be repeatedly upheld in appeals courts, the case would return many times to haunt him. Fred Moore, Sacco, and Vanzetti and their numerous defenders would claim that a jury biased against their political convictions had convicted them. More than seventy years later, that is a topic that is still debated. Nevertheless, given the poor quality of their witness-stand performances, it is difficult to deny today that the anarchists' testimony at the Dedham trial did nothing to help their chances of acquittal. There have been many "trials of the century" in twentieth-century America. The Sacco-Vanzetti case has long been considered one of a deserving few arrayed in this rarefied strata, but closer inspection suggests that is true only in the sometimes distorting retrospective lens of history. If the Sacco-Vanzetti case was the "trial of the century" in 1921, it could only be said to claim that mythical title in Massachusetts or perhaps only Norfolk County. Elsewhere, its notoriety would not spread until well after the trial ended, but eventually it would serve a unique place in history.

In 1926, Vanzetti bitterly asserted that the press had maintained a "conspiracy of silence" about keeping the public informed about the case.[35] This was a blithe reference to the alibi story of Celestino Medeiros, small-time professional criminal cum convicted murderer who stepped from the shadows of jail and said Sacco and Vanzetti were innocent of the crimes for which they were convicted.

Vanzetti felt that the American press, unlike radical newspapers in Europe and Latin America, had ignored new evidence that could lead to a new trial. He also claimed that the press had been unfair to him before the trial started, thus infecting the impartiality of the local jury pool. But thanks in part to Fred Moore's pre-trial public relations juggernaut, the press (consisting of the Boston newspapers and several suburban weeklies) handled trial coverage mostly with kid gloves. One can spend days pouring over news accounts of the trial and only find misspellings of minor witnesses' names and a few other minor inaccuracies. In fact, the news accounts of the trial are so devoid of editorial slant that authors who wrote of the case in the 1960s and 1970s refer to newspaper articles almost as much as the more authoritative trial transcript. This was not always the case in many major trials of the 1920s. In the years to come, tabloid "jazz-journalism" would mar the conduct and coverage of, among other well-known cases of the era, the Mills-Hall, Ruth Synder, and Bruno Hauptmann trials. Still, Judge Thayer was of the opinion that the defendants were receiving too much friendly publicity. Although it would not be known until 1927, Thayer privately told reporters during the trial that Boston newspapers had an obligation to state that Sacco and Vanzetti were getting a fair trial.[36]

In a way that he had likely not intended, Thayer had a point. Fred Moore's strategy of asserting a political conspiracy against his clients had perhaps ensured a certain level of objectivity by the press. In the end it probably had no effect on the jury but, then again, Vanzetti knew or suspected that the Sacco-Vanzetti Defense Committee would make no progress without the coverage of the Boston press. Several reporters who had covered the trial did not feel the defendants received a fair trial. Journalistic conventions prevented them from saying so in print but in later years, 1926 and 1927, the Sacco-Vanzetti Defense Committee had the benefit of reporters surreptitiously volunteering promotional ideas and services.

But the press (in this pre-television and mostly pre-radio day), at least in one way, was guilty of blindness. Why was there no effort to track down the other members of the bandit gang? And what happened to the nearly $17,000 of payroll money? Though the fact had gotten lost in the shuffle of recent events, not a cent of those funds had been recovered. Further, had the local police and prosecution concealed information that could have been helpful to the defense? Whatever the answers to these questions, reporters failed to attempt to even answer one of them.

The evidentiary phase of the trial ended with a whimper, not a bang. Secondary witnesses shuffled to and from the witness stand like minor characters in a Russian play. Rosina Sacco, Nicola Sacco's wife, testified that her husband had kept socialist literature in their home. Sacco's erstwhile employer, George Kelley, said that he did not recognize the cap that Sacco had tried on earlier in the trial. (Actually, *two* caps had been entered as evidence but Sacco only tried on one during the trial.)[37]

During summary, Moore asked the jury to deliver an "American verdict free of all prejudice." The *Boston Daily Globe* report of Moore's summary said that the California defense lawyer had mentioned "feeling like an alien in New England."[38] Moore melodramatically used his own outsider status to implore jurors to consider the plight of men "who are really aliens." Katzmann had already raised the issue of "consciousness of guilt," a legal way of saying that certain actions result from guilty behavior. Moore explained that his clients' lies to police and prosecutors resulted from fear of arrest and prosecution as radicals and draft-resisters. On this point, Jeremiah McAnarney was more blunt than his colleague. He claimed that "you would not kill a dog on the identification evidence in this trial." Interestingly, the *Boston Evening Transcript* reported another McAnarney comment: that the Commonwealth had not questioned any Italian or Spanish eyewitnesses to the crime.[39] McAnarney's implicit point was that the prosecution was exceptionally prejudicial in its review of evidence, a theme that would resurface many times in future years.

Katzmann told jurors the idea that Sacco and Vanzetti had acted guilty because they were draft-dodging radicals was "absurd."[40] He said that the strongest argument against the defendants was their own testimony. Noting that both men had enough ammunition when arrested to kill more than thirty people, he scoffed at the idea that either man was a philosophical anarchist.[41]

The next morning a bouquet of pink gladiola adorned Judge Thayer's private desk. Newspaper reporters buzzed among themselves, then noted in their articles the front-row presence of Italian Consul, Marquis Agostino Ferrante, and vice consul, Silvio Vitale. In fact, every seat in the court was taken that day. Rumor quickly spread among the press corps that Thayer's charge would be of "interest and importance."[42] As expected, the charge to the jury was quite long. As was his custom, Thayer swathed his instructions in purplish hues, a trait he had cultivated during many years on the bench. ("Let your eyes be blinded to every ray of sympathy or prejudice and let them ever be willing to receive the beautiful sunshine of truth, reason and sound judgment.")[43] He urged jurors to think of themselves as performing a duty similar to that of American soldiers on a battlefield in France. More significantly, he included a reference to the "consciousness-of-guilt" phrase. This simple juridical phrase would prove quite controversial and would resurface on appeal more than once.

The jury retired to consider a verdict at 3:00 in the afternoon of July 14. Shortly thereafter reporters noticed that the jury had gone for dinner. By 7:30, an impatient throng had gathered on the court house steps, Judge Thayer included.[44] Just before 8:00, jury foreman Walter Ripley notified a sheriff's deputy that a verdict had been reached. Frank Sibley of the *Boston Daily Globe* said word spread "magically" throughout Dedham. Citizens dashed through the cool summer evening air to find a seat in the quaint, dark-paneled courtroom. Sacco and Vanzetti arrived shortly before jurors filed back into the jury box.

Both defendants were found guilty on two counts of the indictment. In an unguarded moment, a newspaper report said lawyer Thomas McAnarney made a face suggesting despair. Vanzetti's beetle eyebrows knit in consternation. Sacco searched the individual faces of the jury, then shouted in Italian: "Sonno innocent!" Then he said in English: "You kill two innocent men."[45] Rosina Sacco furnished the deadline-conscious reporters with the melodramatic angle they craved as she ran to the prisoners' cage and threw herself at her husband. "What am I going to do? I've got two children. O Nick! They kill my man!"

Police rushed to separate husband and wife. Twenty-five officers escorted the defendants on the grim procession back to Dedham jail. Sentencing was then suspended until the appeals process was complete. Later Vanzetti was returned to Charlestown state prison; Sacco stayed at Dedham jail, pending sentencing.

Why did the Sacco-Vanzetti jury find the defendants guilty? If a 1950 newspaper interview of surviving jurors is credible, both the identification testimony and the prosecution's ballistics evidence convinced the jury of the defendants' guilt. The *New Bedford* (Massachusetts) *Standard-Times* published a lengthy article on the Sacco-Vanzetti trial on November 12, 1950.[46] The article featured the only known comments on the case by jurors made to any publication or author. Juror Seward Parker professed surprise at the fact that the case had become an international cause cèlébre. "I can't understand why the trial went around the world. They talk of Reds being involved in it, somehow. There never was a mention of Red in the courtroom or among the jury. I never could see where the idea of prejudice was picked up." Juror George A. Gerard thought that accusations that the jury was biased against the defendants were ridiculous. "If they say the country was witch-hunting those days it must have escaped me. I don't remember all the radical talk. I always thought it was propaganda only."[47] In 1950, former Norfolk County District Attorney Katzmann refused comment on the long-ago trial to the *Standard-Times*. In fact, he never spoke publicly about the case after the trial ended in 1921.

The history of Sacco-Vanzetti is often described as a case study involving intolerance, propaganda, conspiracy, legal institutions gone adrift, misguided use of capital punishment, political in-fighting, ideological warfare, and Yankee intransigence. It is all this and more, but first and last, it is very different people and their secrets. The secrets of the Galleanisti were to them as obligatory as the dank catacombs were to early Christians. The Sacco-Vanzetti Defense Committee had its secrets, as did the communists. The Justice Department, too, had official documents on the case it would not permit to be publicly revealed (although not nearly as many as its critics would later assert). To a great extent, though, it was the secrecy of Galleanisti revolutionary zeal, bound by feudal anarchist loyalty, that kept the truth of the case, whatever it is, from emerging. It will likely never fully emerge, but by the early 1980s enough had come out to make many realize that some historians had been mistaken in describing this jumbled episode of robbery, murder, and radicalism as the American Dreyfus case. But this new information about the case was also coldly shocking: It appeared to confirm that at least one of the defendants had been legally innocent.

The Sacco-Vanzetti trial was mostly forgotten—at least in the United States. Several months would pass before news about the defendants again appeared, and then only in local newspapers. By then the appeals process had already started.[48] The Sacco-Vanzetti Defense Committee also established and reinforced lines of communication throughout the world. Fred Moore had failed in the courtroom but, not surprisingly, he was determined to succeed in the battle for post-trial fund-raising and publicity. Here his instincts on the subject of both topics were usually accurate. In fact, there was no other way to finance appeals. Although the American press soon forgot Sacco and Vanzetti, newspapers in Europe and Latin America, sensitive to the plight of immigrant foreign nationals in North America, at times gave the case extended coverage. Surprisingly, Moore's fund-raising efforts were not snuffed out because of lack of publicity in the United States. Thanks to his powerful organized labor connections, he raised money at a level that would have seemed unattainable only a year before. Just when it seemed Moore would never again get significant publicity in this country, Sacco and Vanzetti were struck anew by public relations lightning.

Appeals and Cocaine

Although fund-raising went reasonably well, Fred Moore's ambitious publicity campaign in America foundered during the Fall of 1921. The only references to the case, other than reports of bombings and violence linked to Sacco-Vanzetti partisans in Europe and Latin America, were two articles in two relatively low-circulation magazines. It was just as well: Both reports proved somewhat embarrassing to the defense committee, as well as to Moore. An article by Clarence Skinner in the *Survey* largely emphasized the fairness of the trial.[1] Boston lawyer Arthur Warner's piece in the *Nation* bluntly dismissed the notion that Sacco-Vanzetti was another Mooney case and noted that the anarchists were not "labor leaders."[2] Although Warner did not doubt the innocence of the Italian radicals, he rather pointedly noted that "they were of too little importance to be persecuted by any powerful interests."[3] It was one of those thoughtlessly embarrassing revelations misguided friends and allies seem to make—and at the most inopportune time.

Just when it seemed that the Sacco-Vanzetti case would suffer the dubious distinction of being famous internationally, but limited at home to news coverage in Boston and its suburbs, a week-long series of articles on the case appeared in the *New York World*. Written by reporter Samuel Spewack, the series began just before Thanksgiving. Spewack's series was syndicated by the Press Publishing Company and appeared in many major American daily newspapers. Fred Moore could not have planned or timed the release of the articles any better. The fact that Spewack's reports sometimes depicted the Sacco-Vanzetti Defense Committee as communist toadies and zealous propagandists hardly mattered. This was that rare case in which any publicity, no matter how negative or distorted, seemed to be better than nothing. The series had its debut November 20, 1921, with the headline "Kindle Red Uprising From Murder Trial."[4]

Spewack traced the propaganda efforts of the Sacco-Vanzetti case to a small, sparsely furnished office on Hanover Street in Boston. It was here that he said a Spanish carpenter, a former Columbia University student, and an Italian newspaperman coordinated publicity efforts on behalf of the world's two best-known anarchists.[5] According to the article, Frank Lopez, Eugene Lyons, and Aldino Felicani produced propaganda on an Olympic scale that would have made any wartime government agency proud.

From this humble setting, from these obscure personalities, sprang a movement that rocked the capital cities of Europe, penetrated into Moscow, swept South America. Bombs were placed in the home of Myron T. Herrick, American ambassador in Paris, and that of the American counsel general in Lisbon. Anti-American demonstrations were held in Rome, in Stockholm, in London. Mobs stormed the American embassy in Brussels. Threats were made against representatives in Havana, Lima, Buenos Aires. Boycotts of American goods and general strikes were declared in Uruguay. This is at best a faint etching of the known effects of the forces set into motion by these three men. Their equipment consisted of several typewriters, a mailing-list, a little money and the phrase: "Save Sacco and Vanzetti." Here was a Dreyfus and Mooney case in one. The Italian radical papers flashed headlines appealing for two members of their race. It was discussed in the Chamber of Deputies. Scores of mass meetings and demonstrations were held. Coupled with this, always, were the political beliefs of the men. Every syndicalist paper—in France, in Italy, in South America—spread this latest iniquity of America . . . across the front pages: "Save Sacco and Vanzetti."[6]

Spewack noted that the defense committee produced an Italian-language newspaper, *L'Agitation,* to help popularize the notion that Sacco and Vanzetti had been tried for their anarchist views and involvement in labor strikes. Spewack said the simple message was that what happened to Sacco and Vanzetti could easily happen to other immigrant radicals. "Propaganda," he said, "flamed across two continents." He noted, much to Fred Moore's delight, that certain "disinterested" trial spectators felt that the evidence against the defendants had been "flimsy." Spewack also added that supporters of the men seemed sincere in their belief of innocence.

In fact, he indulged in more than a little hyperbole in describing Lopez, Lyons, and Felicani as master propagandists. He did not exaggerate, however, the effect that the case, really the radical representation of the case, had on Europeans. Twenty people were killed when a bomb exploded in a street demonstration in Paris in late October that year.[7] On that same day, two squadrons of cavalry charged at surging street crowds. A hand-grenade was thrown into the residence of U.S. Ambassador Herrick. The ambassador was not injured, but suddenly the case was big news everywhere—except in the United States. Spewack laid the blame for these incidents on French radicals and on French anarchist newspapers, especially *La Liberation*. Other radical newspapers and periodicals had agitated for the release of Sacco and Vanzetti and urged that protesters storm the American embassy.[8] The second article in the series said that "scores" of meetings were held throughout Paris each day. Although Spewack had exaggerated the propaganda networking and influence of the American Sacco-Vanzetti Defense Committee, there was little hyperbole in his description of a city in siege. Ten-thousand French army troops reportedly guarded Paris. Sacco-Vanzetti "committees of action" were said to have sprung up Minerva-like, almost overnight, throughout the city. The left-leaning newspaper *La Libertaire* announced a "grand meeting" of various political groups, including the Union of the Syndicalists of the Seine.[9] Eugene Lyons told Spewack that the street violence in Paris was "too well organized to be spontaneous." Fred Moore's Sacco-Vanzetti publicist for English-speaking countries attributed the turmoil to the Third International. "They saw an opportunity to get back at America," he said with a candor that still resonates many years later.

But even the ebullient Lyons had underestimated the popularity of the cause. *La Cas Sacco-Vanzetti* was hardly confined to Gallic Bolsheviki storming Parisian barricades. French authors Anatole France, Romaine Rolland, and Henri Barbeusse appealed to Americans to support the effort to secure a new trial for the Italians.[10]

Street demonstrations and picketing were not confined to France. Spewack said that Italy's big cities had their share of turmoil, fights, and broken shop windows. Portugal, Holland, Great Britain, Mexico, Switzerland, Uruguay, Belgium, Russia, Puerto Rico, Cuba, and Algeria also had noisy protests and rallies, most in front of United States embassies and consulates.[11] By late October, the protests had reached a crisis stage. It was then that the Italian Minister of Foreign Affairs promised the Italian public that he would file a plea of mercy with the American government should Sacco and Vanzetti be sentenced to death. Italian radicals were somewhat less than mollified by the offer. The left-wing newspaper *Umanita Nova* was particularly contemptuous of what it described as the pusillanimity of the Italian government. "It means simply that the Italian government wants to divert the attention of the people and smother the national conflagration by making it think there is no immediate danger of the electrocution of Sacco and Vanzetti. We are here to repeat that Sacco and Vanzetti were convicted principally because they were Italians—just as Negroes are condemned over there or revolutionaries condemned by the Czar principally because they were working men."[12]

Spewack made an especially salient point in his next installment. In the United States, politically radical groups at first ignored the plight of the anarchists, while a small group of Boston intellectuals and Galleanisti rallied to their side.[13] It was only after the trial that supporters of the convicted men expanded to include leftist and far-left groups. The left fringe of organized labor made its not inconsiderable financial contributions sheepishly, and mostly at arms' length. The United Mine Workers of America; the Chicago Federation of Labor; and the Central Labor Unions of Boston, Pittsburgh, and Detroit; as well as the Amalgamated Textile Workers of America; the Cloak and Shirt Makers Union; the International Association of Machinists; the Brotherhood of Painters; the Fur Workers Union; and the United Brotherhood of Carpenters and Joiners supported the Sacco-Vanzetti defense movement with varying degrees of enthusiasm. All had newspapers of one type or another providing editorial support for the cause, although not every labor union unquestioningly accepted Fred Moore's "labor martyr" mythology. (Oddly, though, Spewack implicitly did—early in the series he referred to Sacco and Vanzetti as "the two labor leaders.")[14] Still radicals, liberals, and left-leaning labor unions formed the bulk of the proffered support. Spewack said that various Italian-American societies, including the Sons of Italy and the Italian Chamber of Labor, had made donations to Saccco-Vanzetti Defense Committee coffers.

Nevertheless, given that it was now an international movement, the success of the campaign in the United States was barely modest. About $60,000 was raised, most of it to retire debts and expenses from the trial. Spewack implied that the defense committee's propaganda campaign had envisioned only mixed success stateside. That was unquestionably true. Until his series appeared, only the foreign-language and labor presses, quite large but relatively limited in political impact, paid any heed to the case in the United States.

The *New York World* reporter probably did not know that his own series would help place the Sacco-Vanzetti Defense Committee on the not terribly well-known map of American causes célébres. Spewack was generous (and impartial enough) to include in one of his articles the view that not everyone who observed the trial was convinced of the prosecution's case against the defendants. In fact, there were respected high-society people, "Brahmins," who accepted without much in the way of explanation that the case had been a frame-up. Spewack would not know for several years that his series was the first news that most Americans had of the peculiar double murder and payroll robbery trial from New England.

Spewack had indeed exaggerated the international propaganda influence of Lopez, Lyons, and Felicani. He attributed to this unlikely triumvirate near mythological propaganda abilities that they clearly did not possess. Still, the publication of the series on the Sacco-Vanzetti movement was a publicity shot-in-the-arm for the defense committee. It literally could not have bought the kind of coverage received from *The World*'s syndicated columns. Before the series, a handful of American newspapers featured editorials condemning the violence of European radicals acting on behalf of the Sacco-Vanzetti movement. The *Baltimore Evening Sun, New York Herald, New York Telegram, Buffalo Times, Cleveland Plain Dealer,* and *Washington Star* cautioned their readers against the malign intent of the radical left in championing an international case.[15] Without more background and an interpretive framework, however, the editorials likely meant little to readers. The truth was only a handful of Americans outside of Boston knew anything about the Sacco-Vanzetti case.

Even before the *World* installment ended, a powerful article from French author Anatole France appeared in the *Nation.* An open letter to Americans (presumably liberal and left radicals), France's message indicated his understanding of the case was limited, if not one-sided. Though unmentioned, obviously the hoary ghost of the Dreyfus case hovered behind France's every sentence. "In one of your states, two men, Sacco and Vanzetti, have been condemned for a crime of opinion. It is horrible to think that human beings should pay with their lives for the exercise of that most sacred right, the right which we ought to defend, to whatever party we may belong."[16]

While France may have lacked a detailed knowledge of the trial, his understanding of the underlying issues driving the propaganda campaign was plain enough. He warned that an "iniquitous" sentence could easily make worldwide martyrs of the men. Americans, in that case, would be forced for generations to bear the brunt of international outrage. "Fear to make martyrs. It is the unpardonable crime, which weighs upon generation after generation."[17]

Shortly after France's article appeared on newsstands, the American ambassador to Italy accurately noted that the Sacco-Vanzetti case was outside the scope of consideration of the U.S. federal government. Richard Washburn Child quickly washed his hands of the matter, at least politically speaking. The Italian Sacco-Vanzetti Committee would have none of it. Issuing a statement from its headquarters in Rome, the organization quickly asserted that its countrymen had been convicted on the basis of insufficient evidence. The press release was short and to the point, although it lost something in an awkwardly phrased translation. "The castle of lies of the American politics will fall like the famous castle of paper. The workmen of the world are following the case of Sacco and Vanzetti . . . and await to see them restored to liberty and to see justice done."[18]

To borrow a show-business expression, in the space of just several weeks the case had become a cause cèlébre with legs—far-reaching international legs. Spewack's syndicated series in the *New York World* introduced most Americans to this quirky, soon-to-be volatile case. Spewack predicted a forthcoming propaganda war that would rival, if not exceed, that of the Mooney case. Several nationally distributed American magazines, including the *Survey,* the *Outlook,* and the *Literary Digest* also featured articles on the burgeoning cause. The *Outlook* described the attempted assassination of Ambassador Herrick as "Red Terror."[19] Eugene Lyons penned an article for the newsmagazine the *Survey* about the support of the foreign-language press in the United States for Sacco-Vanzetti.[20] The *Literary Digest* ran an even-handed account of the case and trial in early December. (Unlike many other American newspapers and periodicals, the *Digest* opined that the convicted men's alibis were supported by "reputable witnesses.")[21]

The stage seemed quite well set for a decision on the first appeal for a new trial. On Christmas Day 1921, Boston newspapers reported that Judge Thayer had denied Fred Moore's motion for a new trial.[22] The motion had been filed in October and argued later that month. With over 4,000 pages of trial transcript and record to review, Judge Thayer took ample time to reach a decision. The document was twenty-eight pages long—then an unusually long holding for a provincial trial court. The judge was careful to note that the Commonwealth's Supreme Judicial Court gave him the ability to set aside a verdict only for "extraordinary cause"—that instance obtained, he said, only when jurors were obviously mistaken or had in some way "abused their trust." Thayer then quickly established that because no abuse or mistakes had occurred, he was "powerless" to over-turn the verdict. He defended his mention of "consciousness of guilt" to the jury, noting that the defendants had lied to police after their arrests. He also dismissed the appeal on the basis of jury prejudice against the defen-dant's political radicalism, noting that the defense had introduced that sub-ject into the trial transcript.[23]

Judge Thayer's decision likely came as no great surprise to Fred Moore and the Sacco-Vanzetti Defense Committee. It was highly unlikely that a thoroughly traditional and politically conservative judge like Thayer would overturn a jury verdict against foreign radicals, unless he must. Spewack had analyzed the case from several different perspectives but he neglected to answer the crucial question, "why?" As in *why* had the Sacco-Vanzetti case suddenly been elevated to an object of universal interest and outrage? Much of the answer seems to be that the message was simple and credulous; the timing, clearly, had been fortuitous. After all, had not many innocent people been swept up in Attorney General Palmer's Red raids? Had not an American gone mad with hate for foreign radicals framed two anarchists it could not otherwise legally convict? That message had reverberated among a resentful European populace suffering in the midst of grim post-war reconstruction. Also, it was a plausible and painfully embarrassing scenario that could likely not be refuted by a single American official abroad.

The success of the Russian revolution, and its attendant spread of the revolutionary discipline and *esprit de corps* throughout Western Europe, provided an opportunity to challenge the corruption of the United States.

What was surprising about the case was not that its disarmingly simple propaganda message had captured the interest of so many, but that it was so hastily planned and amateurishly coordinated and implemented. The violence in France and elsewhere was plotted at the local level using the small-scale guerrilla tactics of street theater, not the sweeping strategy of global protest. As of yet, the Comintern had no real long-term interest in Sacco-Vanzetti. That would come several years later and would occur in such a way that comparison would make the events of 1921 seem like a playground scuffle among schoolchildren at recess.

The American government abroad—the ambassadors, consular chiefs, and *charge d'affairs*—could not argue the merits of the case with anyone: Practically no one knew the first thing about the "American Dreyfus case." In November 1921, the State Department sent a circular telegram to embassies and consulates overseas about the Sacco-Vanzetti case. The telegram contained inaccurate information that proved, at best, marginally helpful.

Thayer's ruling was far from the end for Sacco and Vanzetti—there were at least several major grounds for appeals. Also, the defense was well aware of the judge's off-the-bench comments and eyebrow-raising conduct during the trial. Meanwhile, news dispatches about the case were something less than earth shaking. After New Year's 1922, the *New York Times* reported that the General Council of United Labor Bodies had sent a telegram to President Warren Harding requesting the release of all "class-war prisoners." Massachusetts Governor Alvan T. Fuller received a telegram from the same group; not surprisingly, it strongly recommended a new trial for Sacco and Vanzetti.[24] Several weeks later, the Workers Defense Union, another New York City labor union with far-left ties, announced in a press release that the Italian anarchists had been convicted because of a "prejudice against the defendants as radicals and foreigners."[25]

Two months passed without any news of the case. Just when it seemed that it would slip into oblivion, the *New York Times* featured a long article on the case in its Sunday edition of March 5, 1922. The headline read, "Are Sacco and Vanzetti Guilty?" Researched and written by Louis Stark, the labor reporter had obviously cribbed notes from Samuel Spewack's *New York World* series. Unlike Spewack, however, in somewhat self-serving tones, Stark announced that he was writing a "fair and unbiased" report of the case.[26] In doing so, he interviewed three newspaper reporters, twelve "conservatives," and a "Red." (The term then was used quite loosely to describe a leftist radical and was not necessarily linked to a member of the Communist Party.) Stark described this sundry and somewhat curious assemblage as representing "the important figures on both sides."

Like Spewack, Stark emphasized that the prosecution's case was built upon eyewitness identification coupled with ballistics testimony. Stark also noted that Bartolomeo Vanzetti was placed at the scene of the crime by only one witness.[27] He also made clear that testimony was divided evenly between the defense and prosecution witnesses: Almost every major point was couched in diametric opposition. Even the ballistics testimony was split down the middle in a neat cleft of legalistic counterbalance. Stark explained that Judge Thayer's controversial "consciousness-of-guilt" instruction allowed jurors to interpret the behavior of the defendants as indicating either guilt of committing murder and robbery or fear of being exposed as militant radicals.[28]

Stark's lengthy article was not a series but it did appear in the Sunday edition of America's most respected newspaper. It was, as Stark had claimed, an even-handed if unremarkable report, more digest and interpretation than fresh revelation. To his credit, Stark did not impart as much significance as Spewack did to the Sacco-Vanzetti Defense Committee publicity efforts. For the *Times* reporter, the popularity of the case overseas resided in its symbolic richness—not bombastic press releases typed in a tiny office in Boston's North End. Perhaps the most interesting thing that came out of Stark's interviews for his article did not appear in print until 1938, eleven years after Sacco and Vanzetti were executed. It was only then that Stark told of Judge Thayer's suspicion that the *Times* sought to covertly assist the propaganda juggernaut that had attached itself to the Sacco-Vanzetti movement. (The judge's comments to Spewack were almost certainly off-the-record.)[29] Nevertheless, Thayer was almost certainly right in a way that he had likely not intended. Indeed, the free publicity was incalculably valuable to the defense committee. Two big-circulation American newspapers had made sure that news of the case had reached many cities, villages, suburbs, and distant hamlets throughout much of the country. This does not mean that everyone who read of the "radical Italians" took the case to heart. In fact, such was far from the case. Ordinary Americans would not sit up and take notice of the case until 1927. From 1922 until then, a wide variety of liberal, labor, and radical groups—odd bedfellows for the most part—championed the Sacco-Vanzetti movement in the United States. But for a case that has long been associated with political radicals in search of a fight, there was relatively little emphasis on propaganda at home. As Sacco-Vanzetti author Robert Montgomery notes, fundraising was the primary objective before and after the trial.

Propaganda was almost an afterthought in this country and for good reason. Unlike Europe, the United States of 1922 had a small labor press, an ever-smaller radical press, and a large but hopelessly balkanized foreign-language press. Also, unlike that of many European countries, the mainstream press in America lacked a coherent liberal voice after World War I. No newspaper columnists and commentators were yet interested in an obscure case that featured as principles two Italian radicals from an anarchist sect widely suspected as responsible for the then single-most despicable act of terrorism in American history. The one or two writers who defended Sacco and Vanzetti did so for the *New Republic* and the *Nation*, both public opinion journals favored by intellectuals, liberals, and college students. Behind the scenes, a steadily escalating tension rose between Moore and certain members of the defense committee. The California lawyer often spent lavishly, hiring old friends, cronies, and acquaintances to run errands and perform chores; he traveled extensively, checking out the most farfetched rumors about the case, even journeying to the federal penitentiary in Atlanta to run down a lead.[30] All of this created a financial strain on the defense committee and only served to infuriate the prickly Galleanisti. Hardworking and frugal, the anarchist Italians deeply resented Moore's spendthrift ways, his addiction to cocaine, his womanizing, his bohemian parties, and his inclination to disappear for several days running.

Not all was bad news, though. Shortly after Stark's articles appeared, news from Italy lifted the spirits of Sacco and Vanzetti. In mid-March, the Socialist Deputy Leon Mücci argued on behalf of his countrymen in the Italian Chamber of Deputies. Mücci claimed that the anarchists were innocent by virtue of "all circumstances."[31] He also cited the recent agitation in Europe on behalf of Sacco and Vanzetti as testament to their worthiness. Mücci accused the Italian government of "subservience" to America and pointedly questioned the Italian undersecretary of foreign affairs about what the government had done on behalf of the imprisoned Italians. Undersecretary Tosti Valminute rather defensively explained that everything that could be done had already been done.[32] He noted that the Italian Ambassador to the United States, Rolandi-Ricci, had made diplomatic intercessions on behalf of Sacco and Vanzetti in Washington. Valminute explained that it was "impossible to interfere with the courts of another country."[33] This point, lost in the shuffle of inside-page news dispatches, would arise many times in the future. For Europeans, it was the single most difficult to understand issue of the case. Many disbelieved the notion that someone as powerful as the President of the United States could not reverse what appeared, on the surface, to be a patently false conviction.

Nevertheless, the case seemed to have assumed a political life of its own in Europe. Three days after the Mücci statement appeared in the American press, the U.S. legation in Sofia received letters threatening to bomb the building it occupied if Sacco and Vanzetti were executed. The American minister turned the letters over to Bulgarian police and the incident was duly noted and forgotten. The Sacco-Vanzetti movement was not so much a cause cèlébre as it was an offbeat political jigsaw puzzle that emerged a single piece per week. The question was, "Would it coalesce into a coherent image or would there be several years' worth of unrelated pieces?" No one knew for sure but the betting odds seemed to be against the anarchists. Simply put: Not enough Americans cared about the case to make a difference to either defendant or the defense committee despite a vaguely sympathetic article in the November issue of the *American Bar Association Journal*.[34]

Overall, 1922 and 1923 were difficult years for Sacco and Vanzetti. Both men struggled to adjust to the harsh monotony of prison life—Vanzetti in Charlestown State Prison and Sacco in Dedham County Jail. Nicola Sacco, who angered easily, was as angry with Fred Moore as he likely had been with anyone in his life. He complained that the American lawyer seldom listened to his concerns and suggestions. A sensitive, sometimes volatile man not given to compromise, Sacco developed a seething contempt for Moore. Vanzetti was somewhat more kindly disposed toward Moore but he also had had disagreements with the Californian. It was a tense situation that had only one positive side: No matter how bad things got, negative publicity could easily be kept to a minimum. In the sensational, unforgiving, fly-by-the-seat-of-your-pants world of 1920s jazz journalism, only a judge's ruling or a death sentence would stir any interest. Fred Moore still had support from most of the Americans on the defense committee, but he had lost the trust of at least one of his clients and virtually all of the Italians.

Sacco and Vanzetti returned to Judge Thayer's courtroom in late 1923. By this time a respected and politically conservative Boston lawyer, William G. Thompson, assisted Moore in researching and writing appeals. Two hearings, the first in late September and the second in late November, were noticed in passing by the press but eventually cast a shadow on the case that would linger in memory for half a century. In late September, the defense attorney introduced affidavits attacking the state's case against Sacco and Vanzetti. As part of its motive for a new trial, the defense included Albert Hamilton, a "firearms" expert from New York. He testified that Sacco's pistol did not fire the crucial bullet number three, as a prosecution expert had testified at the trial. Hamilton's testimony, though, was hardly a reason for a new trial. Five weeks later, however, another more surprising revelation emerged from the same courtroom. Thompson had read in court from an affidavit submitted to the defense by Captain William Proctor. As prosecution witness, Proctor had testified that the pistol found on Nicola Sacco at his arrest was "consistent" with having fired the bullet that killed Alessandro Berardelli. Proctor's after-trial affidavit, however, stated that he had told prosecutors before the trial that he did not think that bullet number three was fired by Sacco's Colt automatic. On its face, this appeared to contradict his trial testimony. Had Proctor really switched positions on this crucial issue? No one will ever know for sure. In a *deus ex machina* redolent of an Agatha Christie murder mystery, Proctor died shortly after giving the deposition. These incidents were reported locally and in the *New York Times* but were soon forgotten—at least for now. Eventually, though, both affidavits would figure prominently in the propaganda campaign to save Sacco and Vanzetti. For the time being, though, the issues were too obscure to excite much interest, let alone passionate outrage.

In their 1948 book, *The Legacy of Sacco and Vanzetti,* G. Louis Joughin and Edmund Morgan criticized the press in the United States for its failure to probe beneath the state's somewhat disjointed presentation of the case. As noted, reporters inexplicably never investigated the absence of any official explanation of what became of the stolen payroll money and the state's failure to locate the other members of the gang. There were also several other quirks in the prosecution's case (i.e., weakness of eyewitness identifications, variations in the alleged escape route, etc.) that were never probed. But it's also odd that Fred Moore and the defense team did not aggressively challenge these defects. Obviously, several interpretations can attach to such behavior, but the fact remains that Moore and his colleagues seemed to ignore this aspect of the case. Also, as noted, the defense's presentation of an alternative scenario cogently explaining what really happened at the crime scene during the trial was virtually nonexistent. That situation would not change for several years. Clearly, Fred Moore had to gingerly sidestep this issue. Does it mean that Sacco and Vanzetti were guilty? No, at least not by itself did it mean or imply guilt. But it strongly suggested a desire to avoid revisiting a topic perhaps best left alone. This eventually developed into a corollary for the modern cause cèlébre: Do not delve too deeply into the details of a case or the inner workings of a defense committee. In order for a cause to succeed, it must be convincing. Too much information can douse interest, or worse, prompt doubts. In 1922, the Sacco-Vanzetti movement was growing but not convincingly enough in the country where it mattered most to its success. No matter how effective the propaganda movement was in Europe, and elsewhere, it could not reach a crescendo without the participation of a sizable cross-section of the American public. For that, several essentials were necessary. One, a successful publicity and propaganda campaign in the United States was a *sine qua non;* two, leadership of prominent liberals to help attract middle-class volunteers was equally crucial. Radicals, a helpful but reluctant labor movement, and a handful of dilettante liberals would not be enough to form a protest movement in America. Finally, the committee required a new head legal counsel, one who was skilled at drafting appeals and arguing them in court. It would also require that he explain clearly and credibly to his publicists what really had happened on April 15, 1920.

By 1924, it was apparent that Fred Moore would either be fired or forced to resign. Moore delayed as long as he could the inevitable and did not quit until it became obvious that he would be fired. Finally he withdrew as head counsel and departed after Nicola Sacco wrote him an angry letter, threatening him with violence. (Sacco had never forgiven Moore for signing papers allowing the anarchist to be briefly committed to the Bridgewater State Hospital for the Criminally Insane in 1923 after a botched suicide attempt.)

Moore's position as head case counsel, not surprisingly, had been tenuous for many months, if not years. Three Italian-American anarchist associated newspapers—*Il Martello, Il Protestario,* and *L'Adunata dei Refrattari*—had published a statement from the Italians on the committee calling for Moore's head. Elizabeth Gurley Flynn, a Communist Party member and companion of Carlo Tresca, entered the case to push Moore out the back door.

Ironically, as Flynn plotted to get Moore fired, the latter tried to push the *Daily Worker* into more Sacco-Vanzetti coverage of a kind that would not compromise his unnamed confidential sources. (The *Worker* was largely run and edited by nonjournalists, who either ignored or disdained the niceties of professional ethics even on the somewhat reduced scale practiced by the radical press.) Party leader Earl Browder assured Moore in July 1924 that the *Worker* was under financial pressure and needed to compete with the capitalist press through "drastic action." In a somewhat less than cerebral phraseology, Browder described this badly required material as "hot stuff."[35]

Moore's attempt to prod more coverage out of the *Worker* is instructive. The newspaper offered a view to readers that obviously was dictated by party leadership. But the party's directorate remained unconvinced that Sacco-Vanzetti was going to last and it was not entirely cynical in thinking so as a matter of fact. Many causes often peter out after several months of feverish international popularity and debate. To the communists, or at least to the leadership of the fierce if usually undersized and rather discombobulated American party, this cause cèlébre seemed to fall into that category. Besides, asking Socialists and Marxists to take to the streets to defend the honor of anarchists was a rather risky proposition. (Anarchists, after all, are pledged to attack, subvert, and destroy any form of government.)

Finally after Judge Webster Thayer dismissed five motions by Moore to have the trial verdict vacated, Moore agreed to quit.[36] The motions had been based on several affidavits, including one by the late Captain Proctor. Thayer described the documents as "weak, unsatisfactory and unconvincing." The *Worker* did run a brief, front-page editorial in late October condemning Thayer's decision, characterizing the trial of Sacco and Vanzetti as the result of "manufactured evidence and perjury."[37]

Broke, hooked on cocaine, and deserted by most of his libertine friends, Fred Moore resigned in November 1924. In reality, his leadership had ended many months before when William G. Thompson became head legal counsel for appeals. Years later, Moore confided to novelist Upton Sinclair that not long before he left Boston, Moore learned that Nicola Sacco had indeed committed robbery and murder and that Bartolomeo Vanzetti may also have been guilty.[38] Moore's off-the-record aside had been whispered for years but was often dismissed out-of-hand as the bile of an embittered former counsel. Still, others reportedly said the same thing privately—including Tresca, the most respected anarchist in America.[39] Moore's comments to Lewis have been re-told many times in a large case literature. Often forgotten, however, is Lewis's recollection of Moore readily conceding that neither anarchist had ever admitted to him guilt of any crime.

Whatever the truth, this much is certain: Moore gathered his few possessions and drove back to California, leaving the case in the hands of Thompson. By then he had received the then hefty retainer of $25,000 from the Sacco-Vanzetti Defense Committee. Thompson made no secret of his contempt for his predecessor's handling of the trial, particularly Moore's cross-examination of prosecution eyewitnesses. In truth, the well-regarded Boston attorney had some reason to be upset. Thompson had agreed to an unenviable position, inheriting a once-sensational case that had long since cooled off. Moreover, he was left to do battle in an unusually awkward posture. While few in the United States knew or cared about Sacco-Vanzetti, the world awaited new and startling revelations reminiscent of the Dreyfus case. Thompson and his assistants had to find enough new evidence to force Judge Thayer to declare a new trial. That was a task far easier said than done. As noted, Moore had traveled extensively, investigating almost every lead that came to his attention. Was there anything remaining? Would Thompson uncover some nugget of evidentiary gold that would compel a new trial? It was an odd, even extraordinary, situation few outside the Italian anarchist community even knew existed. Most of the Italians on the committee disliked and distrusted Moore, declining to confide in him. Nevertheless, if Moore had told Lewis the truth, the question lingers: Did they want their lawyer, who truly believed his clients innocent, to discover that Sacco was guilty and that Vanzetti knew of Sacco's guilt? It remains a tantalizing, but ultimately unanswerable, question eighty years later.

Deus Ex Machina: Zola Redux

After Christmas 1924, the Sacco-Vanzetti case slid into the tepid bathwater of news media obscurity. That was not particularly the fault of anyone on the defense committee. A new and overtaxed head counsel had no time for coordinating a public relations campaign. In early January 1925, news came that Bartolomeo Vanzetti had been transferred to the Bridgewater Hospital for the Insane, reportedly suffering from hallucinations. Newspaper reports declared Sacco had also been confined two years earlier for similar behavior, an oblique reference to Sacco's unsuccessful suicide attempt.[1] The situation was very difficult. Neither man had reckoned on being in prison so long, if at all. Several months went by before Vanzetti was sent back to prison and declared sane. By the time he had recovered and was returned to Charlestown prison, a parade of 1,500 demonstrators in Boston had demanded a new trial for the anarchists. The meeting was taken seriously enough by city hall that the acting mayor of Boston spoke to the assemblage.[2] The parade was a joint production of the Workers' (Communist) Party and the Amalgamated Clothing Workers of America. But just in case there was any doubt as to whose idea the production was, Sacco and Vanzetti were declared "victims of class persecution." No less a figure than party chief Benjamin Gitlow was on hand to ensure the smooth functioning of the day's choreographed agitation-propaganda.

Nevertheless, the Sacco-Vanzetti Defense Committee was conspicuous by its absence. This was by design, not inadvertence. The Communist Party in the United States had cold-shouldered the Sacco-Vanzetti cause for years. Finally, American communists began to take notice of the case late in 1925. Why so late? The answer has little or nothing to do with anyone in the United States, communist or otherwise. In 1925, the director of communist agitation-propaganda in Western Europe was a small but dynamic man who bore a passing resemblance to the motion-picture star Charlie Chaplin. His name was Willi Münzenberg. In his Berlin office, Münzenberg had received his marching orders from Moscow: Foment an international propaganda campaign that would disgrace the United States in the eyes of the world. Münzenberg's idea was at first rather vague. He would publicize some well-known case that would contradict the popular notion of America as the land of immigrant opportunity.[3] Historian Stephen Koch explains that unlike most major nations of Western Europe in the 1920s, the Communist Party in the United States was undersized, underfunded, unfocused, and generally unimpressive. Neither Stalin, nor Lenin before him, had ever thought seriously of fomenting revolution in America. The best that could be done was to try and showcase the United States as a sort of New World capitalist quagmire. For that, Münzenberg needed a political case that would help the party in the United States gain stature by leading worldwide condemnation of American bigotry, arrogance, and corruption. In Koch's words, Münzenberg "surveyed his options in search of a case that would humiliate America in the eyes of the proletariat foreign-born."[4]

For a 1920s Marxist revolutionary, Münzenberg cut an unusual if ideologically contrary figure: garbed in tailor-made suits, he also was barbered and manicured daily. He lived in a well-appointed flat in an upscale neighborhood and was chauffeured about the city in a limousine. Despite his outward elegance, though, Münzenberg was a shrewd, tough, and highly intelligent propagandist. When the Sacco-Vanzetti case attracted his attention in 1925, the once hot cause had long since cooled to room temperature. Münzenberg ordered American party leaders, notorious for their lack of initiative, to get behind the Italian anarchists and reinvigorate the case. That would not be easy—a defense committee dominated by dedicated Italian anarchists and pushy American liberals blocked the way. But Münzenberg could not resist what he suspected could well become a propaganda bonanza. Whatever his faults, Fred Moore had milked a lot of international attention from the case from 1921 to 1923. Then the case quickly fell victim to mismanagement and the plodding pace of American appeals courts.

Despite its moribund state, Münzenberg liked what he saw of the Sacco-Vanzetti movement: a judge accused of prejudice, a prosecutor alleged to have been offered a pretrial bribe and a jury infected by rabid post-war xenophobia. He instructed party leader James Cannon, head of the American International Labor Defense (ILD), to give the case his special attention. A political off-shoot of the international Red Aid, the ILD had recently been formed in Chicago to call attention to cases of political injustice.[5] Cannon later wrote to socialist leader Eugene Debs that the former's stewardship of the Sacco-Vanzetti case was a source of intense pride. "The protest movement for Sacco and Vanzetti is becoming deep and strong. The most inspiring thing about it is the unity of forces in the fight . . . The movement is growing along these lines everywhere. Our aim is to keep it on this track, to make the fight for Sacco and Vanzetti a real united working class fight."[6]

The Sacco-Vanzetti Defense Committee did not exactly abandon itself to transports of ecstasy to learn that it was to share stewardship of the case with the communists. By now, Mary Donovan, an Irish-American and a Massachusetts state social worker, had given up her job to devote her energy to the Sacco-Vanzetti Defense Committee. She knew enough to know that there was no working "with" the Communist Party—either you worked for them or not at all. The defense committee immediately distanced itself from the party and warned its leaders to keep to their side of the fence.[7] Cannon and the American leadership could have cared less. The objective of the ILD was to establish its own defense committee, grow in size, and eventually force the original committee off the road.

None of this meant, however, that Münzenberg actually wanted to "save" Bartolomeo Vanzetti and Nicola Sacco. From a purely cold-blooded ideological point of view, that would translate to nothing less than failure driven by incompetent case management. In order for America to be properly shamed in the eyes of the world, Sacco and Vanzetti would have to be electrocuted or hanged. Prison sentences for the anarchists would spell political and propaganda disaster. (The death sentences Sacco and Vanzetti received were not imposed until April 1927.) This meant that Münzenberg had to gamble that the trial judge would not back down under unrelenting international pressure and sentence the Italians to prison. He took the gamble and directed Cannon to begin agitation on behalf of Sacco and Vanzetti.[8] The latter had an unenviable assignment. Cannon was not only to wrest the defense of Sacco and Vanzetti from an already entrenched committee, he also had to invigorate and expand the American party on the backs of two anarchists. And none of it would work without Judge Thayer's cooperation. As noted, Münzenberg and Cannon needed Thayer to sentence Sacco and Vanzetti to death. Without executions, the Sacco-Vanzetti movement might metamorphose into another Mooney case. Tom Mooney and Warren Billings were convicted and sentenced to death for their alleged participation in a bombing in San Francisco in 1916. Their sentences, however, were commuted to life in prison under the principled but nervous stewardship of President Wilson. Soon after the commutation was announced, the Mooney case lost much of its drive and sputtered for many years. Although that case achieved near legendary fame among the radical left in the 1930s, some liberals and many middle-of-the-road American citizens avoided it as if it were political leprosy itself. You could not have an international cause cèlébre without the participation of ordinary Americans—without the bolstering and affirmative presence of the middle class. All of those college students, ministers, law professors, business executives, housewives, and small-town managing editors were needed to trip the light-fantastic of international propaganda. That seemed all but impossible in mid-1925. Then, just before Thanksgiving, a convicted murderer with no seeming connection to the case changed the odds in favor of the world's most famous Galleanisti.

At the heart of every debate about Sacco and Vanzetti lies the spectral presence of Celestino Medeiros. On November 18, 1925, Medeiros was an inmate at Dedham jail. On that day he sent a note to Nicola Sacco by a jail messenger. The message was short and to the point: "I hereby confess to being in the South Braintree shoe company crime and Sacco and Vanzetti was not in said crime."[9] Medeiros had already sent a note to this effect to the *Boston American* but the newspaper did not publish his ostensibly shocking revelation. Prior to sending both notes, Medeiros reportedly had asked a jail trustee for a pamphlet about the Sacco-Vanzetti case. Reportedly, he had previously tried to tell Sacco the same thing in a brief encounter while the two men were let outside their cells, but Sacco ignored him. (Sacco had been warned by other Gallieanisti to be wary of police spies in jail.) William G. Thompson found out about this extraordinary new development and immediately left for Dedham to interview the inmate. Thompson interviewed Medeiros in the rotunda of the Dedham jail the day after Nicola Sacco received the note.[10]

The convict explained to Thompson that he could no longer bear to watch Rosina Sacco and her children visit their falsely imprisoned husband and father. Medeiros's account apparently impressed Thompson sufficiently enough that he retained the services of Herbert Ehrmann, a young Boston lawyer and Harvard Law School graduate, to check out the convict's account. Ehrmann then set out to verify Medeiros's incredible confession: that a gang of professional thieves led by an ex-convict had committed the South Braintree crime, not Sacco and Vanzetti.

Medeiros was born to a poor, large family in Villa Franca in the Azores. While still a child, his parents immigrated to New Bedford, Massachusetts, exchanging one place of poverty for another. Partially blind as a child, Medeiros was epileptic; he also was afflicted by "worms" from birth.[11] Nevertheless, these disabilities did not stop him from maturing into a physically robust young man with a keen talent for bloodletting and sundry forms of lawbreaking. His special fondness was for firing handguns, which he sometimes trained on stray flies. Medeiros also occasionally trained his sites on human targets. He had survived several gunfights with spoken-out-of-turn colleagues or those who tried to impose unbidden on him their views or values. Nonetheless, in November 1924, he graduated

from minor felon to major criminal stature when he shot to death an elderly and unarmed bank clerk in Wrentham, Massachusetts. Medeiros was
soon convicted and promptly sentenced to death. It was during his appeal
for this conviction that he confessed to a rather minor role in the South
Braintree crime.

Ehrmann wrote several years after the executions that when Thompson
hired him to verify Medeiros's story, at first he thought he was being sent
on a futile mission. Much to his surprise, though, Ehrmann discovered that
a local gang fit the general physical contours of Medeiros's seemingly far-
fetched story. While questioning police in Providence, mention of a Joe
Morelli, leader of a local Italian-American gang, came up almost immediately.[12] A couple of days later, Ehrmann returned to Rhode Island again,
this time with his wife Sarah, who assisted his efforts. While he was busy
talking to Morelli's former defense lawyer, his spouse checked the list of
federal indictments in the local U.S. district court. What she discovered
eventually changed the history of the case. The list revealed that the Morelli
gang, led by paterfamilias Joseph Morelli, had been the subject of a fifteen-
count indictment in 1919 for robbing freight cars of merchandise shipped
from the Rice & Hutchins and Slater & Morrill factories in South Braintree. Loosely composed of several brothers and others, the Morelli gang
had been indicted and convicted for stealing shoes in Providence from the
same factory that Sacco and Vanzetti were convicted of robbing.[13]

Unfortunately for Ehrmann and Thompson, Medeiros refused to identify any other members of the gang. Even more notably, he was already
under sentence of death for murder and, furthermore, had a background
that included robbery, rum-running, smuggling, confidence games, and
working as a bouncer in a roadhouse brothel. His credibility as a witness
was about as low as human nature and the Commonwealth's criminal justice system allowed. Still, Medeiros's confession fell into Thompson's lap
as a legal deliverance of almost spiritual dimensions. Why? For the first
time since their arrests, Sacco and Vanzetti could advance a coherent alternative scenario to counter the prosecution's account of April 15, 1920.
Had Medeiros made his confession before the trial, the outcome of the
Sacco-Vanzetti case might well have been different. Herbert Ehrmann
naively expected that once the prosecution learned of Medeiros's confession, it would accommodatingly request the convictions be vacated.[14] To
his dismay, he learned that the district attorney's office dismissed the
account as nothing more than an outrageous tissue of jailhouse lies, the
desperate machinations of a convict seeking to avoid execution by confess-
ing to a crime he did not commit.

Nevertheless, this new development gave the Sacco-Vanzetti Defense
Committee tremendous hope. Moreover, it infused it with seemingly
renewed propaganda possibilities. Accepting a definition of propaganda as
an argument backed by powerful political symbols delivered via the mass

media, the committee had an impressive new weapon at its disposal. Thompson analyzed the Sacco-Vanzetti case from just the opposite view. Fred Moore had sought publicity for any angle he could think of that might raise additional, badly needed funds. Thompson was far more cautious in his approach to his defendants' plight. He did not seek publicity after Celestino Medeiros's confession, although that would seem perfectly reasonable. Thompson, of course, was interested in securing a new trial but he was not naïve. Medeiros's confession well might be fraudulent, the work of a conniving career criminal languishing in a jail cell. Ehrmann had done an outstanding job linking Medeiros to the Morelli gang of Providence but his explanation of the information he had uncovered was merely a working hypothesis. Thompson was too good a lawyer to assume that a judge would order a new trial solely on the basis of a convict's affidavit. There was another and more formidable obstacle: Judge Thayer would decide whether or not to grant a new trial.

For Herbert Ehrmann, the discovery of the Morelli gang and its sordid past was an epiphany that rang across his lifetime. Moreover, it was vindication, proof positive that Sacco and Vanzetti had never been involved in the South Braintree crime. The young lawyer said he had set out on the road to Providence half expecting that Medeiros's story would be a convict's tale worthy of Dashiell Hammett's detective narrative *Continental Op*. What he learned from the Providence police and his wife's research convinced him that Medeiros had mostly told the truth. As noted, not everyone agreed with Ehrmann. Francis Russell believed that Ehrmann had uncovered several coincidental but unrelated facts about Medeiros and then ingenuously concluded that his client was being entirely truthful.[15]

In any event, it was all a moot point: Medeiros had refused to provide Thompson with an affidavit until after he found out if the state of Massachusetts would grant him a new trial. It was only after Medeiros had been convicted for the same murder a second time that he agreed to provide Thompson with the affidavit. That document—a curious amalgam of police station confession and jazz-age pulp detective story—helped re-ignite the case. Too lengthy to reproduce here, it told a simple story of a Rhode Island gang pulling off a daring payroll robbery of a Massachusetts shoe company. The crime sounded familiar enough: A paymaster and his guard were murdered in broad daylight. The gang, taking the payroll to a distant woods, switched cars, and returned to Providence.[16] Although Medeiros refused to identify other members of the gang, defense lawyers quickly ascertained that Joe Morelli, and one Tony Mancini, had killed Frederick Parmenter and Alessandro Berardelli. That was the essence of the Ehrmann hypothesis and there was some interesting circumstantial evidence to support it, too. Several criminal partners of Medeiros eventually provided affidavits supporting his claim to have participated in a robbery that included murders.[17]

Perhaps most intriguing was evidence that Medeiros had acquired and spent a large sum of money in Spring 1920. Then there was the striking resemblance of Joe Morelli to Bartolomeo Vanzetti: The two looked like brothers, at least in side-by-side photos. Moreover, Providence police noted the Morelli gang often used a Buick touring car similar to the one seen by eyewitnesses in South Braintree. Also, several members of the Morelli gang were at liberty on the date of the crime. But not everything in Medeiros's affidavit lined up squarely. For instance, he could not recall many basic details of the crime; too, his description of local geography was badly flawed. Further, Medeiros's chronology of events was sometimes transparently contradictory. Still, the fact that Thompson could now argue a case from an alternative perspective made a tremendous difference. The distinction would not so much be in the courtroom as it would be in the streets and in newspapers.

Thompson had urged the state of Massachusetts to look into the Morelli gang's alleged involvement in the South Braintree crime. Although there has been much written about the Norfolk County district attorney's office refusal to investigate the Morelli gang and its whereabouts in April 1920, no one ever mentions the Boston press's lack of interest in the fascinating trail Ehrmann and his wife uncovered in Rhode Island. What several enterprising reporters might have learned following up on the trail of the proprietarily biased Ehrmanns is interesting to consider. At least several Boston reporters had allegedly developed a bad conscience about the Sacco-Vanzetti trial. Yet, after the Medeiros affidavit was filed and became public knowledge, no reporter bothered to investigate. No one bothered to step forward to sift through the incredible details that the Ehrmanns recovered from the Providence police, Joe Morelli's former defense lawyer, and the local federal district court. The truth is that no mainstream editor would dare assign a reporter to cover this story. Sacco-Vanzetti was now "radical" political property, both in the United States and in Western Europe. Editors of American newspapers were not going to extend beyond obligatory coverage (i.e., court rulings on various motions and appeals). To go any further would be to risk giving aid and comfort to communist propagandists. But the way things had recently been arranged in Berlin, there was some truth to that rather pregnant fear.

News of Medeiros's confession swept through the Sacco-Vanzetti Defense Committee in Boston in Spring 1926. By the time that William Thompson had filed a motion for a new trial, euphoria among defense committee members had replaced lassitude and defeatism. The feeling that there might just be a fighting chance helped buoy sagging spirits. In any event, the Medeiros affidavit could not have been delayed any longer. On May 12, 1926, the full bench of the Massachusetts Supreme Judicial Court denied Thompson's request for a new trial.[18] A newspaper report said the holding "closed to them the last door of legal appeal from death in the electric chair." That certainly was not true. In fact, the case of Sacco and Vanzetti was about to re-ignite. Volunteers were again queuing up at defense committee headquarters in Boston's North End. The Communist Party front group, ILD, added thrust to the movement in a separate but determined effort.

Whatever resistance the imprisoned anarchists had in accepting help from the Workers' Party evaporated in May 1926. Late that month, a somewhat sheepish-sounding Bartolomeo Vanzetti wrote an open letter to the *Daily Worker* acknowledging party support.[19] Thanking the ILD for helping provide the "solidarity with all," Vanzetti also obliquely referred to the gaping ideological difference between anarchism and 1920s Marxism. "If I delayed so much it is because I was embarrassed to you on account of our different views on (a) very delicate and important matter which I would, or rather, which I shall not hide to you. But the last stabbing of the Massachusetts State Supreme Court does not have me enough time nor breath enough to discuss things. They are preparing the fire on which to burn us alive. Only the revolutionary workers, the people, can give us life and freedom."[20]

Vanzetti's statement, unendorsed by Nicola Sacco, was, if nothing else, extraordinary. An anarchist, a militant anarchist, thanking communists for assisting in his defense was akin to a Protestant minister in Northern Ireland inviting a Catholic bishop to address his congregation. But by 1926, international anarchism was atrophying, dying a rather painful and slow death. Locked away in prison, Sacco and Vanzetti could not be particular. Just to keep abreast of the current communist line, Vanzetti read the *Daily Worker,* along with several "capitalist papers." The Sacco-Vanzetti Defense Committee, a non-communist organization, could hardly control the movement outside the perimeters of its own network. That would be too risky—the movement needed as many volunteers as possible. Under whose roof they would enter the fray became a major anxiety for the defense committee. Those European communists were now aroused to battle-pitch and deployed for action. In Paris, a poster circulated showing five figures hanging from separate gibbets. It read: "Chicago, November 11, 1887. Like the five martyrs of Chicago, Sacco and Vanzetti are innocent. Save them."[21]

In July 1926, the German Reichstag, represented by President Paul Loebe, sent a radiogram to Governor Fuller protesting "the imposition of the death sentences."[22] The fact that the death sentences would not be imposed for another nine months was unusual and, at least in this case, somewhat paradoxical. The Sacco-Vanzetti movement in Europe likely would not catch fire without the naked provocation of death sentences. From Willi Münzenberg's point of view, that meant developing propaganda pressure points on American public opinion regarding the case. A propaganda campaign that focused on the drive for a new trial and neglected to dwell on the asserted unfairness and barbarity of death sentences would inspire little interest. But a topic of conversation that featured the United States government executing foreign-born radicals would be an unavoidable political trip-wire, and a top-shelf agenda-setter.

During Summer 1926, the Sacco-Vanzetti Defense Committee benefited immensely from the inclusion of former *Boston Globe* reporter Gardner Jackson. Born and raised in Wyoming, he was tall, shaggy-haired, and strikingly handsome. Jackson was an unusual cultural blend of Ivy League and Western liberal: cowboy boots with Harris Tweed sport coats and gabardine slacks. A friend and colleague of *Globe* reporter Frank Sibley, Jackson was a perfect fit for the job of committee public relations director.[23] In fact, his arrival was nothing less than a godsend. Jackson lent badly needed organization, direction, and leadership to a rudderless, balkanized propaganda effort and he also became a symbol of sorts for those reporters who had guilty consciences about the outcome of the trial.

Jackson's arrival at committee headquarters signaled a shift in attitude and membership. Because of deportation and defection to Italy among its membership, the committee had lost a segment of its anarchist population. Americans, many of them middle class, college educated, and politically liberal, mostly replaced them. Several Irish-Americans, including Mary Donovan and the writer Tom O'Connor, joined Jackson in the cramped office in the North End. Of the newcomers, though, the latter proved to be the most valuable. His friendship with Marion Denham Frankfurter was crucial in obtaining the assistance of former Harvard Law School Dean Felix Frankfurter.[24] Moreover, Jackson had connections to wealthy liberals and celebrities—Broadway stars, novelists, playwrights, artists, poets, even Boston Brahmins—from which his mother's family descended. His ability to lure prominent public figures and the celebrated would pay rich publicity dividends in the months to come. But, for the time being, Jackson revamped the public relations effort into a streamlined juggernaut featuring regularly published bulletins and a steady flow of press releases that focused on forthcoming events and actions.[25]

Concomitant with Jackson's arrival was the emergence of the flamboyant, respected, and publicly popular Felix Frankfurter. A long-time Harvard Law faculty member, he resembled a prematurely middle-aged, overworked bookkeeper in a Dickens' novel. Short, squat, and interminably pale with dark circles magnified by pince-nez glasses, Frankfurter nevertheless was a dynamo whose mere presence in the midst of the Boston Saccco-Vanzetti movement was something of a propaganda coup. As a highly regarded establishment liberal, to that section of the political spectrum he was very nearly above reproach. Moreover, he had worked in 1917 on President Wilson's Mediation Commission, a panel that pointedly concluded that radical Tom Mooney's conviction for alleged complicity in the 1916 Preparedness Day bombing in San Francisco was not properly obtained.[26] Middle-class citizens, political moderates, liberals, even some conservatives, would listen to such a man. When Frankfurter stormed into Walter Lippmann's *New York World* office in Summer 1926, the syndicated columnist listened and almost immediately modified his position on the case. Frankfurter, unlike many law professors, did not shrink from public attention, either. On the contrary, he had enough sense of celebrity and drama to inject himself into the front ranks of the case at a crucial time. He had worked quietly behind the scenes for several years while his wife helped raise funds among Boston's liberal upper-middle classes and the 1920s radical chic wealthy. Her husband, however, did not step into the spotlight until Gardner Jackson had imposed structure and discipline on the publicity arm of the Sacco-Vanzetti Defense Committee. (By this time William Thompson had guided several appeal motions through the Massachusetts state judiciary.)

His front-and-center presence did much to boost international interest in the case. More significantly, he helped legitimize participation in the movement for thousands of politically moderate Americans. Frankfurter's public emergence was especially fortuitous: Modern propaganda was more refined than the lies, myths, and bombast of World War I. Streamlined by advertising, public relations, and marketing strategies, it now relied on persuasion more than jingoistic slogans and ethnic stereotypes. Who better than a respected law school professor (from Harvard no less) to argue on behalf of two persecuted radicals? Frankfurter's wife prodded him into his remarkable contribution to a cause that desperately needed an established figure of national stature. Once there, though, he needed no additional coaxing. It was Frankfurter who had become the Emile Zola of the Sacco-Vanzetti case, not Fred Moore or William Thompson.

Moore had made Sacco-Vanzetti a legitimate cause cèlébre but he was not well enough known or trusted to fill the role of patron. John Dos Passos was a gifted intellectual and writer but he was too radical and not yet well enough known outside dramatic, artistic, and literary circles. Frankfurter fit the role of sponsor in much the same way that Zola had thirty years earlier in the Dreyfus case. There were as many differences as similarities between the two men, but both had sought relief from what they described as a corrupt and conspiratorial government. Both sensed that that they could make the politically extreme palatable to ordinary citizens. Both knew that this could only be accomplished through extensive daily press coverage. Frankfurter was not quite as well known in the 1920s United States as Zola was in late 1890s France. But he was a recognized presence in the nation's most respected law school and had influential friends both in and out of government. His article, published in the February 1927 *Atlantic Monthly,* was the American equivalent of Zola's "J'Accuse," the famous shot across the bow of the Army and the government of late-nineteenth-century France. Although Frankfurter's article did not have the immediate impact of "J'Accuse," it gradually attracted worldwide support. Interestingly, though, Zola and Frankfurter had used similar strategies in preparing their respective articles. Both decided to make them as hard-hitting and attention getting as possible. Zola even went so far as to intentionally attract a libel suit on behalf of the French government. Libel law in 1920s America was more liberal than that existing in 1890s France, at least as it concerned public officials. Although Frankfurter had less to worry about than Zola in terms of libel prosecution, he had to present his accusations as dramatically as possible. A mass movement might force the governor of Massachusetts or the Supreme Judicial Court, or even the federal courts, to review the convictions. In 1898, Zola fought to present evidence favorable to Captain Dreyfus at the novelist's libel trial. Zola thought that the resulting publicity might redound to his client's advantage.[27] The move backfired, however, when prosecutors constructed such a tightly drawn indictment against Zola that the contents of "J'Accuse" were excluded from the libel trial.[28]

Nevertheless, Zola had succeeded in getting Captain Dreyfus's name back into newspapers. In fact, he had succeeded beyond his wildest dreams: The case quickly became a national obsession. It then developed into an international cause cèlébre, the first truly modern transcontinental case in history. *Le Cas Dreyfus* became especially popular in the United States, where the Yellow Press found a political soap opera custom-fitted to its unapologetic, sensational character. But it was in France that the case became a national obsession, tearing asunder the very fabric of that nation's social structure. Debate about it raged seemingly everywhere— among family, friends, colleagues, and strangers in the streets; in cafes, at church, and at work. A slanderous anti-Semitic campaign against "Dreyfusards" lent an inquisitorial caste to the affair. (Major French newspapers often spearheaded this vicious movement.) Frankfurter never faced the ferocious backlash that Zola did, but the American and his wife struggled to bring focus to Fred Moore's briefly successful but ultimately scattershot approach to publicity seeking.

Most importantly, Felix Frankfurter lent a badly needed imprimatur to Herbert Ehrmann's "Morelli" thesis. Celestino Medeiros's confession may or may not have been truthful, but the fact that a towering figure in American jurisprudence took his side in the affair was the best news that Sacco and Vanzetti had since their arrests.

The *New Republic* thought that there now was enough doubt surrounding the convictions in the Sacco-Vanzetti case to warrant a new trial.[29] The standard of the Commonwealth for a new trial was that new evidence be "grave, material and relevant." The article said that Thompson was endeavoring "to find the real criminals." The editors sounded a note of caution, delivered almost *soto voce,* asserting that "misrepresentation is

the fate of all celebrity, especially of causes cèlébres." Bartolomeo
Vanzetti, hostile as he was to the mainstream press, was delighted with the
New Republic's position. In a June 13, 1926, letter to patron Alice Stone
Blackwell, he rhapsodized about the journal's "splendid editorial." Now
fluent, if not remarkably articulate, in English, Vanzetti clearly yearned for
a new journalistic zeitgeist, something to transcend the seamy, tabloid jazz
journalism that defined the 1920s. "Oh, if everyone who wrote on our
case would have such a capacity and treated it so well as that writer, how
much better it would have been for us. The indolence, the incapacity, the
inexactness of those who have willingly or half-willingly wrote on our
case, has always caused much disgust, and, often indignation and wrath to
me."[30] By then, though, Thompson and Ehrmann had struggled mightily
to corroborate any of Celestino Medeiros's compelling but decidedly
helter-skelter confession. It was not easy—there was already another complicating factor. By Summer 1926, it was obvious the Communist Party
was now anxious to make its mark on the movement.[31] This new facet of
the campaign scared away some supporters, including a few local politicians. The mayor of Boston, for example, refused to grant a public-meeting
permit to any group supporting Sacco and Vanzetti. In a statement that
probably made Gardner Jackson alternately cringe and seethe, a Massachusetts congressman condemned such assemblies as a "Moscow plot."
While the Sacco-Vanzetti movement struggled to regain lost momentum in
the United States, it quickly revived in Europe. Willi Münzenberg's decision to promote and agitate in behalf of the case in Western Europe had
proved quite successful. By July 1926, U.S. Ambassador to France Myron
Herrick had already received two death threats. The letters to Herrick had
been traced to "international anarchists," though by then anarchism was,
politically at least, a spent shell.[32] The *New York Times* noted that meetings and street demonstrations in Paris sometimes attracted as many as
10,000 people. Fiery speeches against the American government and
courts were coordinated and conducted by the indiscreetly named International Communist Aid Society. Meanwhile, in Boston, William Thompson
petitioned for a new trial on the basis of the Medeiros confession. (The
recent emergence of a heretofore unrecovered 1920 Pinkerton Detective
agency report on conflicting eyewitness accounts of the South Braintree
and Bridgewater crimes also added thrust to the legal effort.)

The Sacco-Vanzetti Defense Committee reported that Medeiros had been
"implicated" in the South Braintree crime and that neither Sacco nor
Vanzetti was a member of the gang that committed the crime. In any event,
fund-raising for the anarchists was said to have accelerated noticeably in
recent weeks. It has been estimated that the defense committee amassed an
extraordinary $300,000 in its six years of operation. How much of this
sum had already been spent under Fred Moore's rather erratic leadership

was not publicly revealed. During Summer 1926, a hearing was set for the new evidence. Unfortunately for Sacco-Vanzetti partisans, the date was set for September 15. Because Celestino Medeiros was scheduled to be executed for first-degree murder on September 5, 1926, Thompson appealed to Governor Fuller to grant the prisoner a respite so that he could testify at the upcoming Sacco-Vanzetti hearing. Fuller refused, at least until Trial Judge Thayer formally requested that the governor grant the stay. By now Medeiros had become a minor celebrity in his own right, a sort of sideshow to the political center-stage attraction.[33] The *Times*'s Roland Gibson mentioned him in a mid-September column about the case and its peculiar mark on Massachusetts history. "In all the annals of crime it would be difficult to find any case that had wider reverberations than this. In itself it is a case that would have ordinarily been disposed of with little comment, but the radical affiliations of the defendants and a suspicion of the labor movement that they have been "framed" have stirred up protests in every corner of the world."[34] Gibson's point was well made. It was something of a miracle that the case initially had become an international cause in the early 1920s. Now that it was on its way to regaining, if not surpassing, its old status was incredible, if not historically unprecedented. Citing evidence in support of his argument, Gibson pointed to bombings of the U.S. Embassy in Buenos Aires and the American legation in Uruguay. Massive demonstrations in Mexico, Germany, and France on behalf of the anarchists had raised worldwide recognition of the case after a five-year hiatus. The last words of French novelist Anatole France were said to be a warning to the United States: "Fear to make martyrs of the two Italians."[35] France had offered substantially the same advice in 1921. That he extended it again in 1926 seemed unusual, almost comically redundant. But no matter how compelling the final words of a French author, the Sacco-Vanzetti movement required greater participation by Americans. As things stood by Summer 1926, that expected development obviously was not happening. It was one thing to have enough money to finance an appeal and plenty of volunteers to hand out leaflets on street corners. It was another to have your cause dominate the conversations of most people in the nation. It was one thing to have purely routine news coverage of your clients' appeals and motions. It was another to have syndicated columnists and big-name wire service reporters calling headquarters to arrange interviews. No matter how passionate debate throughout the world became, it would mean little without commensurate action in the United States. That would not be easy. The political calculus of the matter was relatively easy to understand: Most Americans did not like to protest in the streets. It made them feel like radicals and radicals occupied the margins of both culture and politics in the United States.

In mid-September, William Thompson appeared before Judge Thayer to read the Medieros confession into the record. He also had filed an additional sixty-two affidavits. The state countered with twenty-seven affidavits.[36] The hearing, it so happened, was far from dramatic—in fact, neither Sacco, Vanzetti, nor Medeiros appeared in court. The report, however, indicated startling good news for the Sacco-Vanzetti Defense Committee. Thompson said that two former Department of Justice agents from the Boston office had filed affidavits indicating that, in their considered professional opinions, Sacco and Vanzetti had not participated in the South Braintree crime. Thompson then requested access to all Department of Justice files pertaining to his clients' case.[37] (He cited a letter from U.S. Senator William Butler of Massachusetts to U.S. Attorney General John G. Sargent that suggested the same thing.) This was truly sensational news. The agents, Fred J. Weyand and Lawrence Letherman, had signed affidavits claiming that when they worked for the Bureau of Investigation in Boston, they concluded that "professional highwaymen," not anarchists, were responsible for the crime committed on April 15, 1920. Letherman and Weyand also described a close working relationship between Frederick Katzmann and Boston federal agents. According to their accounts, as many as a dozen agents had been assigned to the case, some as spies, in the months before and after the trial. Thompson, Ehrmann, and the Sacco-Vanzetti Defense Committee claimed the files of the Justice Department would furnish evidence that would help free Sacco and Vanzetti. Nevertheless, not surprisingly, Thayer turned down Thompson's request for a new trial.[38] Thompson had asked for a new trial so that his clients could challenge information that might have been used to convict them. Thompson and Ehrmann strongly suspected that Katzmann had worked out a deal with federal agents to frame their clients. From a purely cold-blooded, legalistic point of view, it was an intriguing argument. There was something else to consider—as propaganda it was another richly sensational development. Celestino Medeiros might have conjured his confession out of thin air but here were two former Bureau of Information officers saying what Sacco and Vanzetti had essentially said for six years. There was only one problem: The press did not take much interest in this latest twist in the seemingly unending case. Although the Medeiros confession was reported in Boston and New York, newspapers elsewhere only covered the story in outline. It was a seemingly sensational development but the news media in the United States did not treat it that way. Bartolomeo Vanzetti was incensed enough with the lack of newspaper coverage of this case's latest episode that he bitterly harangued the "capitalist press." In an essay he titled "Awaiting the Hangman: A Journalistic Conspiracy of Silence," Vanzetti condemned the "Yellow Press" for its indifference to the latest developments in his case. "We say at the time our arrest the press presented ourselves to the public in the worst possible way. Hence the journalistic conspiracy of quietness that follows its former turmoil was imperiously required in the interest of persecution."[39]

It certainly must have seemed that way to someone locked away in a penitentiary. But the press in the United States was totally unlike that of Western Europe. For one, there were fewer radical papers in America and the ones that existed seldom circulated beyond their target audience. That meant, of course, that the radical press in the United States had only, at best, marginal influence. Then there was the more openly political nature of the European press. All of this served to make Vanzetti think that the American mainstream press was intentionally against him. He had at least part of a point: By 1926, the American mainstream press was not going to dig very far, if at all, into the "new evidence" of the Sacco-Vanzetti case. For William Thompson, as well as his now renowned clients, that well might be a blessing in disguise.

For his part, Thompson did not bother to spare the feelings of the U.S. Justice Department. He charged that federal agents wanted Sacco and Vanzetti convicted in order to placate then Attorney General A. Mitchell Palmer.[40] Thompson even went so far as to imply that Palmer needed convictions to bolster his chances to become a presidential candidate. It was an audacious, if not altogether irrational, claim. Palmer knew little or (more likely) nothing of Sacco and Vanzetti until well after their convictions were secured. From the point of view of propaganda, though, it was a shrewd claim, one that could not be refuted publicly. Tying Palmer to the case with a charge of political influence would remind people of the raids of 1919–1920, as well as the Dreyfus case. Not everything, however, went Thompson's way. For example, in the mid-September court session, Dudley P. Ranney, Assistant District Attorney of Norfolk County, introduced an affidavit by Joe Morelli that stated Morelli had never known or met Medeiros. Morelli also denied knowing anything about the South Braintree crime. Moreover, three of Morelli's brothers also signed the affidavit.[41] In a court session several days later, Ranney described the affidavits of Letherman and Weyand as inaccurate and misleading. The young assistant district attorney explained that it was Department of Justice policy not to reveal the contents of its files. He assured the judge that the information in the dossiers of the anarchists was devoid of any evidence of conspiracy.

Historical evidence would largely support Ranney on both counts but that would not be revealed for another fifty years. His answer to Thompson's demand for public revelation of the files might have seemed defensive if not downright evasive to Sacco and Vanzetti supporters. After all, this was an extraordinary circumstance—the lives of two men hung in the balance. It was all well and good for Ranney to say that there was no government plot against Sacco and Vanzetti but how much did he really know about the contents of those files?

The Justice Department had emerged from the latest Sacco-Vanzetti motions looking somewhat disconnected if not inept. The entire episode was nothing less than an unmitigated international public relations disaster. The fact that federal agents had spied on the Sacco-Vanzetti Defense Committee and on Nicola Sacco appeared to validate the conspiracy theory of the case. In a late September 1926 edition of the *Nation,* defense committee writer Thomas O'Connor pointedly noted that although he was no longer Attorney General, "a remnant of Palmer and his gang is still in the department. Who is sitting on the lid?" A week later, the *New Republic* weighed in on the case with its assessment of this latest development. The liberal opinion journal thought that the Boston Bureau of Information initially wanted to deport Sacco and Vanzetti. When agents were not able to get enough evidence to accomplish that goal, they focused on manufacturing evidence to convict them for murder.[42] It was an old theory from Fred Moore's tenure but now, in 1926, the Letherman and Weyand affidavits seemingly lent it a degree of official gravitas. The story behind this aspect of the case would not be known for more than fifty years. Both Letherman and Weyand had been political appointees who were forced out during J. Edgar Hoover's purge of the Bureau in 1924, but neither man was intimately involved in the Sacco-Vanzetti investigation. Their claim that other agents in the Boston office shared their opinion that "professional highwaymen" committed the crime at South Braintree had little, if any, documentary support.[43] By Fall 1926, Hoover knew that Weyand and Letherman were disgruntled former agents bitter at their expulsion from government service.

But for Hoover to leak that information, true though it was, might well invite further disaster. It might seem that the Justice Department was desperate to discredit two of its former agents in a desperate attempt to stifle news of an embarrassing "frame-up." No matter what happened, it was a ticklish situation that favored the defense. The Bureau could not publicly challenge Weyand and Letherman as inept and incorrigible agents without using confidential information from the Sacco-Vanzetti files. Doing that would violate the Justice Department's own policies. All that could be done was to assert that the former agents' affidavits were inaccurate and untrue. It was an image disaster of the first magnitude, perhaps the worst of the entire nightmarish case for the government. The affidavits of Letherman and Weyand strongly reinforced the view that Medeiros had told the truth. Moreover, they appeared to provide support to the charge that Frederick Katzmann had cut a separate deal with the Justice Department in order to frame two innocent radical immigrants.

The Justice Department's role in the case was not clarified and fully explained until the mid-1970s when Francis Russell and other historians obtained declassified Bureau of Information files on the dismissed agents that strongly suggested they lacked credibility.[44] In any event, William Thompson had engineered a neat propaganda victory (evidently sincerely believing both his clients innocent) that Willi Münzenberg could admire for its simplicity, drama, and ostensible relevance. From the pens of two disgruntled agents, he had squeezed the conspiracy theory that Fred Moore asserted but never really coherently developed in any detail.

Several months later, Felix Frankfurter would make the affidavits of Weyand and Letherman part of the cornerstone of his article (eventually expanded into a book) about the case.[45] Meanwhile, the *New York Daily Worker* had stepped up its coverage of Sacco-Vanzetti.[46] In Spring 1926, it gave extensive front-page coverage to the confession of Medeiros and noted that two ex-Justice Department agents had revealed evidence of a "frame-up" against Sacco and Vanzetti. It was stale news, and sometimes farcically inaccurate in detail but at least the case was targeted to the radical community and enjoyed the backing of the increasingly powerful membership of New York City needle unions. Mostly, the *Worker* had labored earnestly after mid-1926 to expose the "frame-up" of Sacco and Vanzetti. Although it was a poor selection to help recruit badly needed middle-class volunteers, it was the perfect vehicle for anti-capitalist propaganda. The problem was that next to no one outside party membership and a handful of the bored or curious read the newspaper. Nevertheless, the *Worker* soldiered on and did its best, though the result, to those outside its tightly circumscribed circle, was often indisputably dreadful. Day after day, beginning in summer, the *Worker* explained and extolled the confession of Medeiros, describing him as "a piercing ray of sunlight into the pitch black dungeon of gloom of Dedham jail."[47] Where the *Worker* had ignored the case for years, it now unleashed a torrent of details of the "shameful conspiracy surrounding the case." According to this view, the Morelli gang had committed the South Braintree crime, which the "U.S. Government and Commonwealth of Massachusetts seized upon as a weapon with which to railroad Sacco and Vanzetti."[48]

The *Daily Worker* now routinely featured its less-than-original theories courtesy of the Sacco-Vanzetti Defense Committee. Unlike William Thompson and Herbert Ehrmann, the *Worker* brashly attributed the conspiracy to a government desire to rid America of radicals. It even went so far as to suggest that the U.S. Secret Service was part of this convoluted plot.[49] It also implicated the U.S. Attorney General in the emerging cover-up. The Justice Department was said to have in its possession secrets "that would prove the innocence of the two Italian workers—victims of New England greed."[50] True to its theoretical framework of class persecution, the *Worker* described the anarchists as "labor martyrs." This confused and confusing message resonated only within radical circles, thus ensuring a marginal reading audience. It hardly mattered, though. As much as Mary Donovan, Gardner Jackson, and Felix Frankfurter hated to admit it, in some ways the communists were effective allies. While in overall numbers they were small, they made up for their lack of proportion in volume, determination, and intensity. Further, they knew how to

get their members and allies into the streets and did not hesitate to stir up
trouble if that's what the Comintern wanted—as it did, indeed. In fact, it
was what Willi Münzenberg had been ordered to do, *tout de suite*. By Fall
1926, the Sacco-Vanzetti case had become in Europe a cause cèlébre very
nearly equal to that of the Dreyfus case. More importantly, that impetus
had come from the United States, which at long last had begun to show
some interest in the case. Münzenberg was determined that he would not
lose any political momentum that had swung his way. He seized the initiative, quickly organizing a publicity juggernaut that would have made
Napoleon or World War I British propaganda chief Lord Northcliffe
proud. Within weeks, the International Red Aid Society unleashed a torrent of press releases, circulars, and posters about the case and then sponsored labor rallies, protests, torch-light rallies, and noisy meetings in town
squares.[51] It was thrilling street-theater at a time when much of Europe
resented the seemingly limitless prosperity of the United States. The case
also received more international publicity in late October. News that
Judge Thayer had denied Sacco and Vanzetti a new trial rippled across
the Atlantic.[52] It was more proof that the American governing class was
caught in a terrible lie. Why else would a judge turn down a request for a
new trial after another man had confessed to committing the crime? Why
would a request for a new trial be declined after two federal officers
swore that they knew Sacco and Vanzetti to be innocent? To those overseas, the facts from America seemingly spoke volumes for themselves. For
Europeans, especially the French, it was infuriating that the cradle of
modern democracy, of opportunity and justice for all, was something less
than advertised. Authors and historians of the Sacco-Vanzetti case frequently depicted Judge Webster Thayer as the stock villain of the case.
His much discussed but sketchily documented off-the-bench behavior has
been noted in many accounts. Still, it is often overlooked that on the
bench, Thayer was usually even-handed in his treatment of the defense.
His refusal to grant a new trial has also been harshly criticized for several
generations. In many other states, another judge would have automati-
cally been assigned an appeal but in Massachusetts, the trial judge heard
the initial petitions for a new trial. In denying the so-called "Medeiros"
motion, Thayer referred to the convicted murderer as a "crook" and a
"liar." He also dismissed the affidavits of Weyand and Letherman as
"unimportant."[53] Whatever else could be said about him, no one could
accuse Thayer of unseemly haste: He had almost a year to consider the
motion. His response was a spirited, eighty-page opinion that obviously
was crafted partly as anti-propaganda. "Although exceedingly painful to
the Court, if it should allow these charges, if untrue, to go unnoticed and
unchallenged, and to be broadcast throughout the state, nation and foreign countries, with their tendency to inflame public opinion against these
two great governments, then this presiding judge shall be branded for all

time to come a judicial coward and unworthy of the high honor conferred upon him by this Commonwealth. Cases cannot be decided upon the ground of public opinion but upon reason, judgment and in accordance with law; for cases cannot be decided upon by mystery, suspicion, or propaganda but upon the actual evidence that is introduced at the trial."[54] Although Thayer did not say so, letters, cards, and telegrams from throughout the world had inundated his office. Some contained threats—several even had death threats. Nevertheless, Thayer's comment about cases not being decided by public opinion was telling. Contrary to popular belief, most trials are not even remotely influenced by public opinion, usually because the public is either uninterested or is unaware of most cases. In order for a cause cèlébre to succeed, public opinion usually must be brought to bear after a trial on the legislative, judicial, or executive branches of government. That can only be accomplished through a large-scale, systematic, and effective propaganda campaign. Willi Münzenberg and James Cannon had done much to set a political trap for Judge Webster Thayer. The elderly jurist was astute enough to detect evidence of an organized propaganda campaign, but likely he did not realize that his adversaries wanted him to dismiss appeals for a new trial. It was a cleverly set snare that a proud, stubborn, but not especially perceptive, judge seemed unable to notice let alone avoid.

The *Daily Worker*'s determined but ultimately fraudulent campaign on behalf of Sacco and Vanzetti was helpful but misdirected and woefully inadequate.[55] The *Worker* simply did not reach enough politically main-stream Americans to make a difference. It admitted as much when it said so after Judge Thayer's holding when it noted that it was "grievously handicapped."[56] What the Sacco-Vanzetti movement needed in the United States was an editorial voice from a capitalist daily that would endorse a plea for a new trial. That seemed surpassingly unlikely until the hand of God seemingly struck again in October 1926 when the *Boston Herald* published an editorial politely requesting a new trial. *Herald* writer F. Lauriston Bullard wrote a lengthy, modulated essay challenging the Commonwealth to avoid catastrophe and resolve the doubts surrounding the case. Judge Thayer's latest holding had pricked the conscience of at least one newspaper that now walked where others had feared to tread. Closely read, though, Bullard's editorial was hardly a ringing endorsement of the conspiracy theory first espoused in 1920 by Fred Moore, then fleshed out several years later courtesy of Herbert Ehrmann. "In our opinion Nicola Sacco and Bartolomeo Vanzetti ought not to be executed . . . We do not know whether these men are guilty or not. We have no sympathy with the half-baked ideas which they profess. But as months have merged into years and the great debate over this case has continued, our doubts have solidified slowly into convictions and reluctantly we have found ourselves compelled to reverse our original judgment."[57]

Ironically, Bullard's editorial would win a Pulitzer Prize only months before the executions took place. Again, fate had intervened on behalf of the imprisoned Italian anarchists. Fred Moore's "radical" thesis—that Sacco and Vanzetti had been convicted under less than just circumstances—had penetrated editorially to a mainstream newspaper audience. If an editorial is a formulaic, subtly disguised type of propaganda, then Bullard's piece was the most effective message of the case. The *Herald* was then the morning newspaper of establishment Boston. Within hours of the editorial's publication, Boston buzzed with discussion about the case. Were the Reds the driving force behind it all? Would there be a new trial? Would Governor Fuller intervene? Fuller ducked that question by taking a much-publicized vacation to France. To say the least, the timing of his sojourn was another in a long list of ironies surrounding the case. While Fuller toured the French countryside and Parisian suburbs, major cities in France swelled with restive Sacco-Vanzetti partisans.[58] (Ironically, Fuller had long dreamed of being the American ambassador to France.) The *Boston Globe* dispatched a reporter to France to gauge French hostility for the United States. The experience left the correspondent with the feeling that he was witnessing a revolt against France's traditional ally: "American justice, besides being held up to scorn before hundreds of thousands of workers in various parts of France today, is pilloried in the newspapers. All the papers publish the protests sent by radical and socialist deputies to President Coolidge, calling to the attention of the United States the impression the executions would make abroad. The liberal newspapers openly attack the American court."[59] Of course, both the French and the *Globe* reporter were mistaken. Sacco and Vanzetti had not been sentenced to the electric chair—that would happen another six months. For his part, Governor Fuller seemed almost theatrically oblivious to the uproar around him in Paris. An Associated Press reporter described the Massachusetts governor's reaction to his sudden and not entirely unpleasant celebrity with a whimsical nonchalance that suggested a character from *Alice in Wonderland.* "If anyone has been following me about today with a bomb in his hand he must have been pretty busy because my family and I have been all over the city and the suburbs."[60] What Fuller pretended not to know was that a praetorian guard provided by the French secret service had literally enveloped his family in a security cocoon. For good reason, too: Fuller had received many threats in France. For example, the French communist newspaper *L'Humanité* warned the visiting American dignitary of "consequences" that might befall him if Sacco and Vanzetti should become martyrs. It went on to speak of its "unshakable determination to wrest these two anarchist workmen from the electric chair . . ."[61] Back in New York, the *Daily Worker* lamented that American laborers lagged behind Europe's blue-collar workers in support of the two Italian labor heroes. "Sacco and Vanzetti will be the victims of this class war if American labor does not use its class power to shield them. European labor, through its ceaseless fight for Sacco and Vanzetti, should inspire the workers in the

United States to enlist . . . in this war against their historic enemy."[62] And yet, not all was hopeless in America. The *New York Times* reported that just before Thanksgiving, 10,000 trade unionists met in Madison Square Garden for a Sacco-Vanzetti rally. The U.S. Communist Party, headed by the dour-faced William Z. Foster, had decided to display an uncharacteristically rare show of solidarity. Norman Thomas, head of the American Socialist Party, spoke at the event as did *Nation* editor (and ACLU director) Arthur Garfield Hays.[63] The highlight of the evening was a resolution demanding that Congress investigate the Department of Justice role in the Sacco-Vanzetti case. It was an impressive moment, one that no doubt made Mary Donovan and the defense committee leadership jittery.

The Communist Party had a reputation for trying to usurp movements from its original hosts only to appropriate them for its own purposes. The Sacco-Vanzetti Emergency Committee sponsored the rally at the Garden: It was only one of several committees the party had assembled to compete with the non-communist Sacco-Vanzetti Defense Committee. Put mildly, some among the politically and ideologically uninitiated now found entry to the movement somewhat confusing. Moreover, by Christmas 1926, the Sacco-Vanzetti movement still lacked the supporting voice of a major literary figure. *Belles lettre* novelists and writers such as F. Scott Fitzgerald, Sinclair Lewis, and Edith Wharton politely steered clear of the case. H. L. Mencken spoke in favor of a new trial but privately confided he thought that both men were guilty.[64] Eventually, such literary lights as Dorothy Parker, Katherine Anne Porter, Edna St. Vincent Millay, John Howard Lawson, and Grace Lumpkin would write and demonstrate on behalf of Sacco and Vanzetti.[65] But as late as New Year's Day 1927, only John Dos Passos represented the first-tier of *literati* actively attached to the cause. Dos Passos had not yet attained the status he would achieve in the 1930s, but he was already well-known and well-received among critics and intellectuals. Moreover, his credentials as a radical were impeccable: a fellow traveler, just a whisper's remove from card-carrying party membership. Handsome, prematurely balding, and charismatic, Dos Passos was liked and trusted by a wide range of very different people in the movement.

His introduction to the case was an assignment from *New Masses* editor Egmont Aronds. Dos Passos's research prompted him to interview Nicola Sacco at Dedham jail and Bartolomeo Vanzetti at Charlestown State Prison.[66] The interviews convinced Dos Passos that Vanzetti had had two unfair trials and Sacco one less than his comrade. His political conscience twitching madly, Dos Passos soon began commuting from New York to Boston to work voluntarily for Sacco and Vanzetti. Although Dos Passos was a confirmed fellow-traveler during this time, he seems to have accepted a role as *ex officio* recruiter for writers, journalists, and other artists. The Communist Party was only too happy to have him roam as he pleased, hobnobbing with the likes of Parker, Porter, and Felix Frankfurter. The American branch of the party, sometimes dense in the ways of

propaganda and publicity, wisely let him bring authors and other celebrities of real and imagined radical political status to the movement. That
was not done easily—or overnight for that matter. Gathering intellectuals
into one coherent flock for the sole purpose of saving two obscure immigrant anarchists was challenging. Dos Passos, of course, became famous
writing about the case, but he accomplished just as much speaking about it
individually to people. His calm, at-peace-with-the-world manner convinced them the cause was just, as well as *de rigeur*. Not long after joining
the case, Dos Passos wrote a series of articles on the case for the *New
Masses* and the *Daily Worker*. More than anything else written about
Sacco and Vanzetti, these stories explained the movement from the experiences of the Galleanisti. Perhaps his most acclaimed essay, published as an
article in the *New Masses*, eventually was expanded into a lengthy
pamphlet for the Sacco-Vanzetti Defense Committee: "Facing the Chair:
the Story of the Americanization of Two Foreignborn Workmen."

Many Italians planted the perfect city of their imagination in America. When they
came to this country they either killed the perfect city in their breasts and submitted to the system of dawg-eat-dawg or else they found themselves anarchists. There
have been terrorists among them, as in any other oppressed and despised sect since
the world began. Good people generally have contended that anarchism and terrorism were the same thing, a silly and usually malicious error, much fostered by
private detectives and the bomb squad. An anarchist workman who works for the
organization of his fellow workmen is a man who costs the factory owner money:
Thereby he is a bomb-thrower and possible murderer in the minds of American
employers . . . The people of Massachusetts centuries ago suffered and hoped terribly for the city of God. This little white courthouse town of Dedham, neat and
exquisite under its elms, is the symbol of a withered hope, mortgaged at six percent
to the Kingdoms of this World. It is natural that New Englanders, who feel in
themselves a lingering of passionate barbed desire of perfection of their ancestors,
should hate with a particular bitterness anarchists, votaries of the Perfect
Commune on Earth. The irrational features of this case of attempted communal
murder can only be experienced by a bitterness so deep that it has been forgotten
by the very people it moved most frequently."[67]

In middle age, Dos Passos converted to political conservatism, thus
philosophically repudiating his radical youth. Reading his account of the
case now, it's difficult to tell whether he really believed all of what he
wrote about the Galleanisti in 1927. In a 1966 memoir, Dos Passos hinted
that he realized even then that reality was more complex than his stirring
but one-dimensional rhetoric indicated.[68] His was great propaganda, a
lyrical argument explaining out-of-control law enforcement fueled by
xenophobia used in the service of political persecution. Dos Passos came to
the case rather late but his timing was nearly perfect. With Gardner
Jackson and Felix Frankfurter connecting with more traditional liberal

constituencies, Dos Passos appealed to those who did not fit into any particular party or sect. An intellectual and a gifted writer, Dos Passos was able to relate to the successful and the aspiring, the unpublished novelist and composer, the neophyte sculptor, the struggling musician. By then, though, they were arguably just as important as the more wealthy Boston patrons from Beacon Hill and Back Bay. Each voice was needed, each pair of hands and feet desperately required for volunteer duty. Dos Passos was another in a series of seemingly divine interventions that the Sacco-Vanzetti movement reaped, beginning with William Thompson's hiring. The Sacco-Vanzetti case is often described and analyzed in terms of what went wrong. This overlooks the fact that much went right and that the case's propaganda efforts from 1926 on became a model of "how to" develop and expand causes against seemingly impossible odds.

There was bound to be competition among the Sacco-Vanzetti groups and it was guaranteed to intensify. The competition for donors, dollars, and volunteers would turn nasty—but nothing could stop the forward momentum of an international campaign whose time had come. It was an irony rich in the dynamism of political infighting and fundraising. Only six months earlier, the original committee was still worried about a cause cèlébre's worst enemy: apathy. Now there was plenty of interest coming from several different directions, not all of it necessarily welcome. Nevertheless, Celestino Medeiros received a third reprieve from execution in late January 1927.[69] Each time Medeiros's name appeared in the newspaper, more readers learned of his confession and claim that Sacco and Vanzetti had not committed the South Braintree crime. A week after Medeiros received his third postponement of execution from Governor Fuller, Thompson and Ehrmann argued for a new trial before the full bench of the Massachusetts Supreme Judicial Court. Again, the appeal was based on an argument of newly discovered evidence.[70] Thompson referred repeatedly to the motion's sixty-three affidavits, particularly to the statements of former agents Weyand and Letherman. He pointedly noted that the district attorney of Norfolk County had refused to have the case reinvestigated despite the interest of "millions of people all over the world . . ."[71]

Whether or not Thompson would obtain a new trial for his clients was an open question. There was little doubt, however, that with each new court appearance more publicity (and donations) would redound to their benefit. In Europe, interest in the case remained most intense in France. In late February, socialists and communists picketed the American Embassy in Paris. Police said the demonstration was an attempt to pressure American Ambassador Herrick into convincing President Coolidge to intervene on behalf of Sacco and Vanzetti.[72] Leon Blum, head of the French Socialist Party, was reported to have taken special charge of the effort. Blum had already contacted Herrick's office and urged him to meet with a joint delegation of socialists and communists. The ambassador informed an

unimpressed Blum that he had no jurisdiction in the case and concluded it
was a matter for the Massachusetts state courts. Herrick's explanation
notwithstanding, Blum threatened to show up uninvited with his delegation. Panicky American Embassy officials set up an alternate meeting but,
in the end, Blum and his delegation stayed away. The campaign in Europe
on behalf of Sacco and Vanzetti had succeeded in shaking up the American
expatriate and diplomatic community. The *New York Times* reported that
the case had "been a constant source of worry and anxiety to the ambassador since the men were sentenced."[73] Moreover, Herrick was reported to
have received death threats linked to the outcome of the case. In Massachusetts, Judge Thayer had also received additional death threats.

In Dedham and Paris, detectives and private security kept an anxious
eye on incoming packages and parcels. Bartolomeo Vanzetti and Nicola
Sacco were not the philosophical anarchists that John Dos Passos
described in his impassioned articles. They were determined members of
the most militant anarchist sect in North America, disciples of the brilliant
and charismatic Luigi Galleani. Still, the "good fisherman and humble
shoemaker" phase of the case was well underway. Both men, however,
clearly expected to die in the electric chair. Neither wanted political compromise; for them it was, in Vanzetti's words, "freedom or death."[74]

Somewhat embarrassingly for the Sacco-Vanzetti Defense Committee,
both men made plain their desire for revenge. In a 1924 letter to Alice Stone
Blackwell, Vanzetti (Sacco rarely wrote letters for publication) expressed a
desire for retribution that approached bloodlust: "I will ask for revenge. I
will tell you that I will die gladly by the hands of the hanger after having
known to have been vindicated. I mean eye-for-an-eye, ear-for-an-ear and
even more since to win it is necessary that 100 enemies fall to each of us."[75]
More than a year later, he made the same call-to-arms, writing that it would
be desirable to "bring with us some enemies, some blackguards."[76]

Few outside of the defense committee found out about this darker side
of the imprisoned men until publication of their prison letters in 1928. It
was a quite intentional policy decision. The committee carefully screened
visitors to Sacco and Vanzetti and made sure that most reporters came
from friendly or reasonably congenial publications such as the *Daily
Worker,* the *New Masses,* the *New Republic* and the *Nation.* It was a pru-
dent strategy, even though the violent tactics of the Galleanisti had mostly
ceased. Nevertheless, as the following weeks would show, they still had
some umbrage left in their political lifeblood.

By New Year's Day 1927, the ILD was aggressively soliciting funds for
Sacco and Vanzetti. In the next eight months, it and the Red Aid Society in
Europe would collect a great deal of money on behalf of the cause.
Authors and historians invariably note that only about $6,000 was ulti-
mately turned over to the Sacco-Vanzetti Defense Committee in the United
States.[77] In a strict accounting-ledger sense, this sum is beyond dispute.

Still, it overlooks the tremendous organizational and promotional expenses that Willi Münzenberg had Red Aid incur in publicizing the case throughout the world. In Boston, though, Gardner Jackson, Aldino Felicani, and Mary Donovan hardly appreciated the effort. They had labored long and hard to develop a link to well-to-do and wealthy donors and now the ILD was encouraging defections to its upstart Sacco-Vanzetti Emergency Committee. The Sacco-Vanzetti Defense Committee had attempted, without success, to obtain reports of ILD collections and disbursements.[78] The older committee feared, not without substantial justification, that ILD collections would not be channeled into activities on behalf of Sacco and Vanzetti. It was the initial skirmish in what would become open political warfare between the rival committees. Shortly after news of this dispute appeared, three Massachusetts men, described in the press as the "car barn" bandits, were executed at Charlestown State Prison.

In October 1926, one of the bandits killed an elderly night watchman during a robbery attempt at a streetcar barn in Waltham.[79] All three of the men were convicted of murder and sentenced to die in the electric chair. Defense attorneys claimed that at least one of the defendants was mentally ill. In the months before the executions, public sentiment in Massachusetts increased for commuting the sentences to life in prison. Governor Fuller, however, declined to commute the sentences and explained his position in detail in an article published in a nationally distributed magazine. His decision to not pardon any of the defendants raised some eyebrows and also angered opponents of capital punishment. Sacco-Vanzetti partisans could not help but notice that the governor was unmoved by numerous requests for commutation from throughout the world. By this point, though, it was a foregone conclusion that Judge Thayer would sentence to death Sacco and Vanzetti. The question of how sympathetic the governor would be to a plea for executive clemency on behalf of the Italian anarchists did not exactly inspire widespread confidence. Governor Fuller had made it clear that he unreservedly supported the death penalty. The Sacco-Vanzetti Defense Committee now had to tread water even faster. Its enterprising fund-raising volunteers had to solicit that much more money to help underwrite the expense of appeals. It was in the state courts that their best chances lay—a new trial would circumvent the need for requesting executive clemency. By this time, though, James Cannon knew two things for sure: (1) The Sacco-Vanzetti case would not soon again fade and (2) Judge Thayer and Governor Fuller could be counted on to cling to their positions. The only major obstacle for the communists remained the Massachusetts Supreme Judicial Court. Could it be counted on to uphold Judge Thayer's ruling? Executions well might translate to a resounding propaganda victory that would echo across several generations. An unexpected ruling allowing a new trial for Sacco and Vanzetti might delay or even short-circuit the entire international campaign. It was clear only one of two positive things could realistically happen: a new trial or executive clemency. Both were unlikely options. Still, the case was gradually making its way from the back to the front burner of the news agenda. A resolution calling for an investigation of the Justice Department's role in the Sacco-Vanzetti case had recently been introduced in Congress. The *New York Daily Worker* acerbically observed that the bill "slumbers in the archives of Congress, like thousands of 'scraps of paper.'"[80] Still, the *Worker* urged an intensive push by labor to politically pressure the Supreme Judicial Court to grant a new trial. In this view, federal investigation would trigger enough popular support that the State Supreme Court would be pressured to overrule Judge Thayer. It was either hopelessly naïve or disingenuously cynical, depending on one's political point of view. In any event, the Massachusetts State Supreme Court apparently was not listening. On April 4, 1927, the court upheld Judge Webster Thayer's decision not to grant a new trial. The Associated Press noted their sentences would soon be passed and that, in all likelihood it would be death in the electric chair.[81]

A month before the court's decision, Felix Frankfurter's article on the case appeared in the *Atlantic Monthly*. The result of the publication of this twenty-three-page essay worldwide was nothing less than extraordinary. In the United States, thousands of law school faculty and students rushed to join or establish local Sacco-Vanzetti defense committees. In Berlin, Willi Münzenberg had Frankfurter's essay reprinted and distributed *en masse* throughout major European cities. For Münzenberg, the publication of the *Atlantic Monthly* article could hardly have been better timed. Sentiment in favor of Sacco and Vanzetti in most countries in Europe had only recently swelled to a sustained level. Now there was a lengthy essay by a ranking faculty member of America's most respected law school rebutting the prosecution's case on a point-by-point basis. Overseas, American diplomats and government officials were flabbergasted. Few U.S. citizens living abroad knew who Sacco and Vanzetti were or of what crime they had been convicted, let alone the intricacies of their case. For American embassies and consulates it was a nightmare—the State Department had distributed a circular-telegram on the case, but that was back in 1921.[82] By 1927, the Sacco-Vanzetti case was all but forgotten to the diplomatic and foreign service community. Felix Frankfurter's article was rapidly changing all that. In London, H.G. Wells, inspired by Frankfurter's bristling analysis, took up the cudgel in behalf of the cause in his syndicated newspaper column, denouncing American officials in distinctly unflattering terms.

It truly was an extraordinary phenomenon. Eventually Frankfurter's article on the case was accepted worldwide as holy-writ. It would be cited by two generations of college and law students, historians, and case buffs as damning if incomplete proof of a government conspiracy against the anarchists.[83] By the late 1950s, authors Robert Montgomery and Francis Russell had checked the retired U.S. Supreme Court justice's claims against the trial record and found some of them quite suspect, with surprisingly little evidence to support them. In reality, Frankfurter's article was far from the airtight legal brief many assumed it was in 1927 and for years thereafter: well-written and compelling to be sure, but one lacking in serious supporting documentary evidence. While Frankfurter alleged a charge of frame-up, he failed to provide documentary support for his position beyond a dramatic assertion of falsification of evidence. Frankfurter denounced Judge Thayer, including the judge's on-bench behavior, without citing specific instances of the alleged misconduct. Perhaps most misleading of all was his kid-glove treatment of Celestino Medeiros's confession. Medeiros may have been telling the truth, but as a convicted murderer under sentence of death, his account would raise suspicion in a first-semester law student. Frankfurter wrote that the fact that Medeiros had confessed to a capital crime was confirmation of his confession's veracity.[84] What he did not say, however, was that Medeiros had not submitted this confession until his own murder conviction was undergoing appeal. As one of the most penetrating legal minds of the twentieth century, Frankfurter had to know very well that if Medeiros was acquitted in a second trial, he would almost certainly not face charges for the South Braintree crimes. *If* that happened, Medeiros could easily recant the South Braintree confession and walk out of prison a free man. Such was not to happen, though, and the convict's gamble failed. Interestingly, Medeiros was convicted in a second trial in 1926—and again sentenced to death. Felix Frankfurter was not acting as an outraged impartial observer when he wrote his article; he was an advocate fighting for the clients of a friend and a cause cèlébre his wife passionately supported. As such, he used the most powerful weapon possible at his disposal: international propaganda. Still, no one in the United States bothered to verify the accuracy of Frankfurter's claims until thirty years after the executions. It was an almost perfect example of how a dramatic, powerful, and articulate propaganda statement can manage to escape the scrutiny of rigorous examination. Nevertheless, Frankfurter's essay was truly a shot heard around the world. Perhaps no article, other than Zola's "J'Accuse," is so identified with a cause cèlébre. Frankfurter's essay caused a terrific sensation and reinforced what many in Europe had long suspected: that America had been unjustly punishing its political enemies. Reaction to the article's publication in the United States was almost immediate: Sacco and Vanzetti defense committees sprang up seemingly overnight in cities nationwide. Organized labor, especially the American Federation of Labor, was forced into a more aggressive patron role in supporting the case. University and college students began to take a sharp interest in the case. This diverse, odd-bedfellows juggernaut received added thrust when news flashed across the country that Judge Thayer had sentenced Sacco and Vanzetti to death in the electric chair.

The Long Good-bye

Independently of the official Sacco-Vanzetti Defense Committee the Party carried on a campaign of its own, agitating and collecting funds through the International Labor Defense. Hundreds of meetings were held, gigantic demonstrations organized, the Party contributing greatly toward the extension of the movement to Europe. Yet the Sacco-Vanzetti Committee had the temerity to complain that the funds we collected for the Sacco-Vanzetti cause were never turned over to it. The complaint was true, of course, and could be easily substantiated. Some of the money went to the *Daily Worker,* which financially has always been a bottomless pit, and the rest was spent on campaigning to enhance the prestige of the Party.[1]

—*Benjamin Gitlow, Communist Party candidate for*
Vice President of the United States in 1924 and 1928

Once again, the quaint, elm-shaded, sun-dappled square of Dedham was swamped with children, newspaper reporters, photographers, state troopers, spectators, and a collection of the morbidly curious. This time, unlike in 1921, a new species of news media communicators—newsreel photographers— joined the lengthening queue. Nevertheless, reporters noticed that Judge Thayer had visibly aged. Appearing frail, his jaundiced face jutted sharply above a starched white collar and black judicial robe. Filing into court, Sacco and Vanzetti also had the chalky pallor of men who had spent many years deprived of sunlight.

Both defendants accepted the opportunity to address the court. In "absolute silence" Nicola Sacco began, noting that he had "never heard, even read in history anything so cruel as this court."[2] Sacco, with a tacit nod toward the assistance of the Communist Party, said that the sentence was the result of a collision between the "oppressed class and the rich class." He then accused the judge of persecuting him and his family. Sacco was politic enough in his remarks to note "all the population that has been with us for seven years to sympathize and give us all their energy." The anarchist concluded his speech by saying that Judge Thayer knew that "he had never been guilty." Since his 1921 trial, Nicola Sacco's command of English had only improved marginally. Bartolomeo Vanzetti, however, had become quite fluent in English and put his skill to good use. His speech to the court was gripping and impressive, a well-thought-out and rehearsed oration that consumed an astounding forty-two minutes. Vanzetti began claiming innocence of participation in the Bridgewater and South Braintree crimes and brashly asserting that there had never been a more prejudiced and cruel judge as Thayer. "Now, I should say that I am not only innocent of all these things, not only have I never committed a real crime in my life— though some sins but not crimes—not only have I struggled all my life to eliminate crimes, the crimes that the official law condemns, but also the crime that the official law sanctions and sanctifies—the exploitation and the oppression of the man by the man, and if there is a reason why I am here as a guilty man, if there is a reason why you in a few minutes can doom me, it is this reason and none else."[3]

Vanzetti's eloquence was deeply affecting but, as noted, far from spontaneous. His fluency was now remarkable but he nevertheless pressed his luck too hard when he paraphrased socialist leader Eugene Debs, lost his train of thought, and said: "Not even a dog that kill the chickens would have been found guilty by American jury with the evidence that the Commonwealth have produced against us. I say that not even a leprous dog would have his appeal refused two times by the Supreme Court of Massachusetts, not even a leprous dog."[4]

As Thayer was about to pronounce sentence, Vanzetti interrupted him, leapt to his feet, and said that he wanted to confer with his lawyer. Thayer ignored Vanzetti and continued speaking; then Sacco leapt to his feet and shouted, "You know I am innocent." Sheriff's deputies moved toward him as he sank into his chair, silent.[5] While Judge Thayer had cause for some discomfort, what he heard next must have cut through him like an ice-pick. Vanzetti continued speaking, condemning the judge for his tendency to discuss in public the propaganda efforts on behalf of Sacco and Vanzetti, then mentioned incidents involving comments the judge reportedly made about the case at the University Club of Boston and at the Golf Club of Worcester.[6] Bitter remarks by defendants are not unusual but the combination of the extraordinary circumstances and the tension of the moment enveloped the courtroom in a pocket of electricity. When things settled down, Thayer then sentenced the defendants to death in the electric chair, intoning the ritualistic legal phrases familiar to lawyers, judges, and reporters. After Judge Thayer pronounced the sentences, a woman from the Sacco-Vanzetti Defense Committee wept openly, momentarily consumed by anguish and fear.

Despite being condemned to death, Vanzetti had managed to hit a tender nerve. In fact, Judge Thayer had been so rattled by the success of the Sacco-Vanzetti movement that he occasionally vented about the case in public. While he did not make on-the-record statements to reporters, Thayer complained to anyone who would listen or looked vaguely sympathetic (including strangers) about the terrible propaganda campaign he had endured. The result was that even before he pronounced sentence, it was more or less an open secret that Thayer would "teach the anarchist bastards a lesson." The judge was widely rumored to have made such a remark to friends—or something similar to it. There was nothing the defense could do for the time being, though. Everything that was known about Thayer's remarks had arrived at least second- or third-hand. Without (and perhaps even with) supporting affidavits, it was literally no more than country-club gossip.

Still, whether it was true or not was entirely beside the point. Now that Judge Thayer had at last sentenced the men to death, the final phase of the propaganda campaign could begin. Sacco and Vanzetti were scheduled to be executed at Charlestown prison in July. No time could be lost in trying to promote the fight to save their lives. The key difference between the Sacco-Vanzetti Defense Committee and the Sacco-Vanzetti Emergency Committee was that the former organization sincerely was committed to saving the two Galleanisti. Now that William Thompson had exhausted his fight in the Massachusetts state court system, he could divide his attention between Governor Fuller and the federal courts. It would not be easy. Both men understood that their chances of continued survival for more than a few months were slim. For this reason, they seemed to identify with the communists, perhaps already knowing that the radical-anarchist point of view could not achieve political climax without executions serving as a triggering mechanism.

Bartolomeo Vanzetti remained convinced that he had been convicted largely because of "wartime hysteria."[7] It was a pointed reminder of just how long the case had lasted. The Red Scare of 1919–1920 was now a distant and disproportionately ugly memory. Americans had mostly forgotten this marriage of post-war xenophobia and anti-radicalism. But now it seemed almost every other major nation in the world remembered it only too well. The United Press reported that Governor Fuller's office had been deluged with letters, cables, and telegrams requesting executive intercession.[8] The article noted that the editor of the Italian labor newspaper, *Il Nuovo Mondo,* had called for a nationwide strike in Italy. The article said that Sacco and Vanzetti had undergone "two years of terrorization" in a specially padded cell.[9] In Berlin, the communist and socialist press was said to be "much disturbed" by the sentences.[10] *Die Rothe Fahne* urged its readers to "demonstrate without a moment's notice" and to write to the American government in Washington and the American embassy in Berlin. The socialist newspaper *Vorwearts* proclaimed that if the executions were carried out it would represent "judicial murder in the fullest sense."[11]

In Paris, socialists and communists, in rare solidarity, announced a concerted effort to obtain a pardon for Sacco and Vanzetti.[12] Albert Einstein, joining authors Henrí Barbusse and Romain Rolland, sent a cable urging President Coolidge to extend presidential clemency. In Buenos Aires, several labor organizations announced the end of various strike actions held in protest of the death sentences. Meanwhile, in Washington, D.C., Secretary of State Frank B. Kellogg was assigned a guard as a precaution against possible violence. The Communist Party announced a massive demonstration on behalf of Sacco and Vanzetti in New York City at Union Square.[13] Robert Dunn, Treasurer of the Sacco-Vanzetti Emergency Committee, said that the demonstration would be a preliminary to "a national conference of liberal sympathizers" supporting the Sacco-Vanzetti movement. Dunn noted that a million signatures would be collected on behalf of the anarchists and also made it clear that the emergency committee would no longer play second fiddle to the original Sacco-Vanzetti Defense Committee. "The sentencing of the men will only intensify the work of their sympathizers. There is no doubt in our mind that they are . . . innocent and should be set free. There will be plenty of agitation in their behalf between now and the date set for their execution."[14] Dunn assured that he had the support and beneficence of labor leaders, civil liberties groups, and a variety of unnamed fraternal organizations.

Judge Thayer's icy demeanor in the courtroom carried over into a quixotic and highly personal anti-propaganda campaign. At an impromptu news conference, he noted: "I have nothing and nobody to fear. I had my duty to perform according to the statutes of the Commonwealth and my oath to uphold the constitution and the laws. I have performed that duty according to my oath and conscience."[15] In this statement to the press, Thayer also noted (in a possibly intentional malapropism) that "Professor Frankenstein's" article in a recent *Atlantic Monthly* would be refuted by "one of the best authorities in the United States at the proper time." As a parting shot he noted, quite accurately as it turned out, that the newly discovered evidence in the case "was not completely favorable to the defense."[16] The sentencing stirred emotions everywhere in a variety of ways and for different reasons. A congregational minister and member of the Massachusetts state legislature introduced a resolution requesting the appointment of a commission to study the facts of the case and to report its findings along with a recommendation.[17] The minister's voice was not a lone cry echoing in the wilderness of regional back-bench politics. The call for a panel of distinguished citizens to evaluate the justness of the convictions and sentences would swell to a rolling crescendo in the coming weeks. Surprisingly, though, there was not much in the way of mainstream editorial comment on any aspect of the case.

Several major dailies, most notably the Pulitzer-owned *St. Louis Post-Dispatch* and *New York World,* began advocating a new trial in late Spring 1927. But in the days following the sentencing, few major newspapers took an editorial position on the death sentences. Bartolomeo Vanzetti immediately ascribed this indifference to the press's xenophobic hatred of radicals. A more likely explanation is that most American editors were unfamiliar with the details of the case and regarded it as a regional cause. The *Milwaukee Journal,* however, was a notable exception. That Midwestern newspaper felt well informed enough to publish an editorial on the case several days after Judge Thayer's rather theatrical statement appeared in the press. "Every re-examination of the case offers more convincing evidence that in sentencing Nicola Sacco and Bartolomeo Vanzetti for the murder of Parmenter and Berardelli at South Braintree seven years ago, a court of Massachusetts was committing a judicial wrong."[18] The editorial asserted that the refusal of the trial judge to allow a new trial in the face of "a mass of new evidence" was difficult to understand. The *Journal* made generous reference to a now much-quoted editorial by the *Springfield* (Massachusetts) *Republican.* "To many the most distressing aspect of the decision was the Supreme Court's affirmation of its own powerlessness. It is not imperative that a new trial be granted even though the evidence is newly discovered, and if presented to a jury would justify a different verdict . . . we are now forced to declare that a dog ought not to be shot on the weight of the evidence brought out in the Dedham trial of Sacco and Vanzetti."[19]

The *Hartford Times* made a salient point that struck to the very heart of the propaganda battle Judge Thayer had joined. "The Judiciary of Massachusetts seems to be obsessed with the curious notion that if these two men are executed—whatever the facts of their guilt may be—the Reds will have won a victory over the state and law and order."[20] Several smaller regional dailies also spoke out on the issue during the week after the trial. The *Duluth Herald* and *Macon Telegraph* both unequivocally advocated a second trial. The *Herald* said that while it did not know whether the anarchists were guilty, it believed them not guilty ". . . if they had been Smith and Brown, Democrats and Republicans and supporters of the war, the jury would have taken two minutes to acquit them on the evidence presented against them. And it knows that no greater harm could happen to the fabric of the law in this land than to have men executed for murder merely because they are foreigners, radicals and pacifists."[21] The *Telegraph* was even stronger in its language—as well as its convictions. "This rotten business in Massachusetts about Sacco and Vanzetti is now too old by far for temporizing. The time has come for all who love justice to get just as excited as possible and to make a noise about it. Joshua had the right idea. He did not bring Jericho down with any well-considered argument . . . The walls came down because he dared to make a din. Why should any of us consent now to be polite about Judge Webster Thayer and the dirty work in Dedham?"[22] That was the extent of notable editorial comment in the mainstream press in the United States.

The *Daily Worker* was anxious to stake out a place in the radical journalistic firmament as the bright star that would guide wayfaring liberal and confirmed radical alike toward Willi Münzenberg's sought-after tragedy: a Marxist *ecce homo* wed to the plot of a blockbuster political soap opera. Under the deck-headline "Thou Shall Not Die!" the *Worker* roused itself to torturously overwrought prose so absurd it well may have left even Sacco and Vanzetti flabbergasted. "Weak in body but with minds like fire flashing through crystal, into phalanxes of workers' battalions forming for struggle, gave blow for blow though their hands were manacled to the Massachusetts murderers, to American capitalism and all its agents. Sacco and Vanzetti spoke quietly and calmly but the whole world heard. Through the windows of the courtroom, over the heads of the hangman assembled there, past the mercenaries who guarded its portals, the words of Sacco and Vanzetti, magnified a billion times by the gigantic microphone of the class-struggle were transmitted to the hundreds and millions of workers and farmers of all lands."[23] Few in the United States seriously believed this interpretation of events. Still, the *Worker* did have a point: The death sentences would impel many to act. A debate would slowly build, abetted by an ever-closer execution date. Where would all these newcomers to the cause go? The question lingered at the back of many minds as William Thompson and Herbert Ehrmann prepared for the final legal battle.

The *Times* of London raised an arched eyebrow, reporting that "a flood of protests from all parts of the United States and many other countries against the way in which the case against Sacco and Vanzetti was conducted is pouring in on Mr. Fuller. . . ."[24] The *Times*' ultra-low-key report, buried on page thirteen, failed to describe the unusual circumstances that the governor of Massachusetts faced. With the death sentences a *fait accompli,* the storm clouds surrounding Sacco and Vanzetti rumbled even louder. Fuller was moving ever closer to the eye of the storm when William Allen White, editor of the *Emporia Gazette,* wrote to him about a recent trip he had made through New England. One of the most admired populist press commentators of 1920s America, White was unsparing in his remarks about what he had encountered on his trip.

"I have just returned and I was surprised beyond words to find the bitterness and hate which had sprung up in New England, particularly in Massachusetts, among those who hear that Sacco and Vanzetti will not be executed. Until I went into Massachusetts . . . I had no idea that one could let their passions so completely sweep their judgment into fears and hatreds, so deeply confuse their sanity."[25]

White might not have known it, but his letter told Fuller nothing the governor did not already know. This extraordinary case had re-ignited passions, many of them obviously anti-immigrant, that had lain dormant for years. An atmosphere that sometimes resembled a lynch-mob intermittently surfaced in smaller towns and suburbs surrounding Boston. The subject of Sacco and Vanzetti had provoked countless dinner-table arguments, speak-easy fist fights, fraternity bull-sessions, town hall meetings, and the uneasy sensation that no possible compromise existed. Religious leaders faced great pressure to advocate citizen review of the case. Massachusetts's Cardinal O'Connell urged the governor to seek advice "so that no human life will be taken while there is a reasonable doubt as to the perpetration of the crime."[26] In New York, the Union Theological Seminary's William Sloane Coffin warned that executing the anarchists would result in a "blot" upon American institutions.[27] On behalf of American organized Jewry, Rabbi Stephen S. Wise also spoke out in favor of extra-judicial review. Most significant, though, was the public recommendation of the Episcopal Bishop of Massachusetts, William Lawrence, that Governor Fuller appoint a committee to evaluate the prosecution's and trial judge's behavior in the case. A *Boston Herald* editorial on April 19, 1927, urged the governor to take the advice of Bishop Lawrence. The *Herald* pointed out that Great Britain in "similar conditions" had investigated convictions resulting from particularly controversial trials.[28]

The *Herald,* though, was quick to distinguish itself from most Sacco-Vanzetti sympathizers. It asserted that should a committee find that the trial and appeals process had been fair, "then we should all be satisfied to see the sentence carried out."[29] The combination of religious and journalistic sentiment for executive-appointed review was quite potent. The political fallout was now too significant for Governor Fuller to ignore much longer. Felix Frankfurter's article had changed all that, helping transform an obscure case from suburban Boston into "topic-A" conversations from Portland, Maine, to Puget Sound, Washington. With each passing day it seemed that yet another newspaper inveighed against the death penalty. The *Hartford Courant* analyzed the case in terms that would surely have pleased Münzenberg. "If the penalty of electrocution is carried out, millions of workers throughout the world will believe that justice has been murdered in a class-war."[30] The *Brooklyn Eagle* agreed, was like-minded, noting in an editorial that "half the thinking world will believe they die(d) as the victims of judicial murder." The *New Haven Journal* questioned the "anti-social" attitudes of Sacco and Vanzetti but declared that it had "not yet become the American policy to hang people for their views."[31] The *Cleveland Press* asserted that it would be "a bad thing for an organized society if these men are executed."[32] The *New York Times* did not offer an editorial opinion on the case. It did, however, assign Louis Stark to write a lengthy review of it for its Sunday weekly review section. Stark's article, "The Facts in the Sacco-Vanzetti Case," was nonetheless rendered in tones suggesting some sympathy for the defense. For example, Stark predicted that the sealed Department of Justice files on the case were of "supreme importance" to Thompson's and Ehrmann's efforts for a new trial.[33] Stark's analysis was tellingly prescient: The issue would arise again with dramatic impact in the near future.

The *New Republic,* however, saw the matter in a somewhat larger context than did Louis Stark. The opinion journal cited a "cult of judicial infallibility" for the predicament confronting Massachusetts. "An issue is being joined in Massachusetts, which is going to the very souls of men and has not had its like for decades . . . Behind the fight for these two human lives lies the deeper challenge to the arrogant claim that courts are infallible, and that to subject them to scrutiny is to weaken the bonds of society."[34] On the same day, the *Nation's* George Kirchwey advanced a somewhat different perspective, claiming that Sacco and Vanzetti were cast out of the "futile propaganda" of anarchism and into the more noble propaganda of "making justice just."[35] Kirchwey might well be accused of being somewhat naïve in his description of the campaign. Sacco and Vanzetti did seek justice but it was not the benign agrarian, village-square egalitarianism of Jefferson and Madison. Rather, it was a post-world-war, revolutionary form of protest that sought to annihilate oppression, dissolve class distinctions, and unite working people against their plutocratic tormentors. That much the two Galleanisti could bring themselves to endorse in the international Marxist campaign written in their names. Nevertheless, Nicola Sacco refused to sign the petition addressed to Governor Fuller. He explained that an anarchist would only sign a communication addressed "directly to the people."[36] Governor Fuller received a petition requesting executive clemency on behalf of Sacco and Vanzetti in mid-April 1927. The document formally requested an impartial executive and extra-judicial investigation of the case. The Sacco-Vanzetti Defense Committee had publicly suggested that five "respected" citizens would constitute a satisfactory panel.[37]

Meanwhile, bag after bulging mailbag of letters, telegrams, and cablegrams about the case continued to pour into the state house mailroom in Boston. Administratively, Governor Fuller was now less the governor of a state than the caretaker of a suddenly infamous political cause. Since the sentencing, his meetings, conferences, and head-huddles were consumed by discussion of what to do about the Sacco-Vanzetti affair. Nearly everyone in the Massachusetts legislature wanted it to go away but, still, it hung around

Fuller's neck week after week, an implacable political albatross that seemed to grow larger with each passing day. By late April, it was apparent that the public would not trust Fuller alone to review the cause. When a diplomatically worded petition signed by Harvard Law School's Roscoe Pound reached his desk in late April, the governor was running out of options.[38] Various law school faculties throughout the nation now daily called for an independent investigation of the case. Arthur Garfield Hays, national president of the ACLU, insistently urged Judge Thayer's impeachment.[39]

From the third of April through the second week of May, Felix Frankfurter answered a series of poison-pen letters from Northwestern University Law School Dean John Wigmore. The letters appeared in the *Boston Evening Transcript,* commanding much attention as well as prompting intense discussion of the case. The publicity the exchange generated surely aided the always cash-starved Sacco-Vanzetti movement. The mainstream press in the United States had either muted its editorial criticism of the governor and Judge Thayer or refrained from comment at all. Oddly, though, for the first time in American history, a case had become a major international cause without extensive nationwide journalistic coverage and comment. Moreover, the growing and increasingly powerful labor movement had helped fill in the information gap. The Sacco-Vanzetti Defense Committee, with assistance from Felix Frankfurter's article, also helped compensate for the lack of reportage.

One person in the case whom reporters did not hesitate to interview and write about was Governor Fuller, the type of self-made, up-by-the-bootstraps, multi-millionaire that correspondents of that era delighted in interviewing. Fuller was easy to profile and a congenial interview subject. He is remembered today as the governor who sent Sacco and Vanzetti to the electric chair. Before 1927, though, he was widely known throughout New England as a fabulously rich, executive-turned-politician who prided himself on a prickly but principled New England independence. A real-life Horatio Alger success story, Fuller had amassed vast wealth in the early 1900s from the infant auto sales industry in New England. Though his estate was estimated at $40 million, and he owned an internationally respected art collection, Fuller wore the gray flannel suits, button-up shoes, and celluloid collars of a small-town bank president. Like some wealthy men who make their fortunes early in life, he viewed elective office as requisite public service for having achieved such fabulous private wealth. Fuller was elected to Congress and served two largely uneventful terms in Washington. He found the routine of Capitol Hill dull; the tedium of committee meetings, votes, quorum calls, and endless rounds of debate bored and irritated him. After leaving Congress, he was elected lieutenant governor and served under then Governor Calvin Coolidge. But it was as governor that Fuller located his political niche. Quite popular with voters, he exuded a high-level corporate executive's disdain of political infighting

and haggling that provided something of a benchmark for future generations of wealthy Bay State politicians.

Still, nothing existed in Fuller's background as either a businessman
or a politician to prepare him for the Sacco-Vanzetti case. Indeed, until
late 1926, Fuller appears not to have given much thought to the unusual
affair. After the Massachusetts Supreme Judicial Court turned down
Thompson's appeal, Fuller suddenly was thrust into the unflattering glare
of the international limelight beside Judge Thayer. Fate, in fact, had placed
Fuller in an extremely tenuous situation. Sacco and Vanzetti did not want
their sentences commuted; they demanded a new trial to clear their names.
Further, public opinion in the Commonwealth was now overwhelmingly
against commutations. In early June, Fuller privately admitted the futility
of the situation to *Boston Herald* publisher Robert Lincoln O'Brien. The
governor knew by now that the convictions were based, at least partly, on
dubious eyewitness testimony and some decidedly questionable prosecution tactics.[40] Although he was not a lawyer, Fuller was also aware of
Judge Thayer's outrageous *ex parte* comments about Sacco and Vanzetti
made both during and after the trial.

Privately, Fuller believed both men guilty but he also realized that an
appeal for a new trial, Judge Thayer's statement to the contrary, was not
lacking in substantive legal merit. This left him with several alternatives:
(1) do nothing; (2) investigate the trial himself and reach a decision; or
(3) appoint a blue-ribbon commission to evaluate the fairness of the trial and
let it make a recommendation. Fuller's inclination was to assume the chore
himself and then make a decision: commutation of sentence; order a new
trial; or let the sentence be carried out. This was his intended course of
action until the Sacco-Vanzetti Defense Committee, and its growing number
of allies, demanded that he appoint a fact-finding "advisory committee."
Eventually, Fuller was pressured sufficiently enough by Boston's political and
religious community into appointing a panel of three distinguished citizens.

Alvan Fuller did not really want to decide the fate of Bartolomeo
Vanzetti and Nicola Sacco. It was an impossible situation, especially for
someone rumored to be a presidential candidate. Once Fuller was thrust
into the role of executive referee, however, he did not hesitate to assume
full responsibility for the case. This position would soon create a public
relations dilemma of proportions the governor surely had not anticipated.
Fuller had witnessed first-hand the scope and intensity of the Sacco-
Vanzetti movement in France but he had assumed it would never come
anywhere near reaching that same level at home. It was perhaps his most
serious miscalculation of the entire affair. Then again, Fuller was privately
determined that Sacco and Vanzetti would pay for their crimes. Only a
recommendation for a second trial from the advisory committee would

force him to find otherwise. A more conventional politician would have searched for a possible compromise (i.e., a commuted sentence in exchange for an end to the propaganda campaign). That, however, was not in the governor's nature and limits of tolerance.

Unquestionably, Fuller was stubborn but there is nothing in the record to indicate that he had acted out of anything but a clear conscience and good intentions. Even many of his harshest critics would privately admit as much. But there was nothing in his experience that could help Fuller respond to an intelligently conceived and well-organized international cause cèlébre. Although it would be more than two months before the melodrama would reach its peak, it was obvious that the immovable object of provincial hubris was about to collide with the irresistible force of an international political movement.

Suddenly, the rest of the country wanted to know more about this middle-aged tycoon-cum-politician with a face that looked simultaneously cherubic and grimly middle-aged. Newspapers from coast to coast ran wire-service features that invariably mentioned that: (1) Fuller was a possible presidential candidate and (2) he would act according to his conscience.[41]

The *New York World* said that although Fuller would make a decision based on principle, the governor was not a lawyer and was largely unfamiliar with jurisprudence and judicial institutions. In the words of the *World* reporter, "the thought-habits of a lifetime are not easily overthrown, even by a strong conscious effort."[42] Governor Fuller *would* act as he saw fit. From here on in, though, the terms of the process would be at least partially out of his hands. Then there was the tremendous worldwide pressure to either commute the death sentences to life in prison or to order a new trial. The torrent of mail Fuller received from outside the Commonwealth was reported to favor any option but executions.[43] The governor's independent investigation continued, but the tide of publicity increased even though the inquiry was closed to the public. In mid-May, Michael Musmanno, a Pittsburgh attorney, pleaded personally to Fuller for a pardon on behalf of the 500,000-member Sons of Italy, a fraternal organization.[44] On the heels of Musmanno's meeting with Fuller was a statement by Thompson to the press that was aimed directly at any adult with an ounce of liberal angst or a troubled social conscience. "I went into this case as a Harvard man, a man of an old American tradition to help two poor aliens who had, I thought, been unjustly treated . . . I have arrived at a humbler attitude. Not since the martyrdom of the sixteenth century has such steadfastness to a faith, such self-abnegation as that of these two poor Italians, been seen on this earth."[45] Each passing day brought renewed pleas on behalf of the anarchists from a major political or public figure. In the midst of a steadily accelerating campaign, the Sacco-Vanzetti movement received its most memorable publicity boost ever. In early May, reporter Philip D.

Strong interviewed both Sacco and Vanzetti in prison. Although his report would appear initially in the *New York World,* Strong wrote the article for the North American Newspaper Alliance.[46] The *World* had already editori- alized its desire that Governor Fuller appoint a commission to evaluate the trial. Gambling that Strong would write a reasonably sympathetic profile of both men, the Sacco-Vanzetti Defense Committee granted permission for the interview. Except for one striking passage in the article, it was a mostly unremarkable story. Nevertheless, Strong's description of the men could have fitted hundreds of condemned prisoners at state prisons on morning break. "A gate swings open from an elevated tier, Sacco and Vanzetti lounge out of their cells, smiling and walk toward the central enclosure briskly. Both men expect to die. They say so and grave, severe characters are written with conviction on the face of Bartolomeo Vanzetti. Tears touch the face and the eyes of the young man 'Nick' for a moment but his voice is steady." Strong introduced many of his readers to their first and only behind-the-scenes view of the two men now elevated to iconic status in a strange, ideological tug-of-war. He noted that Vanzetti was overwhelmed by thousands of letters a week. A recently ended hunger strike had left Sacco pale and thin. Strong found himself bubbling over with questions after he was struck by the realization that "these men are to die in a straight wooden chair just as the world goes on its summer holidays."[47]

His article should have dissolved into the ebb and flow of prison-yard newspaper boilerplate. Later, though, in a private interview with Vanzetti in his cell, Strong asked the prisoner for a parting statement. It appeared the next day in the *World* and had an immediate, salutary, and electrifying impact. "If it had not been for these things, I might have lived out my life, talking at street corners to scorning men. I might have died, unmarked, unknown, a failure. Now we are not a failure. This is our career and our triumph. Never in our life can we hope to do such work for tolerance, for joostice (sic), for man's understanding of man, as now we do by accident. Our words . . . our lives, our pains—nothing! The taking of our lives— lives of a good shoemaker and a poor fish peddler—all! The moment you think of belongs to us—that agony is our triumph!"[48] This searing quote has since inspired much controversy and extensive literary speculation. Some accused Strong, an aspiring novelist, of fabricating it out of whole cloth.[49] In 1929, he said that he was not a good enough writer to create the galvanizing words that ran in the May 13, 1927, *New York World* and newspapers nationwide. In any event, some said those stirring, elegiac words became to Sacco-Vanzetti supporters in 1927 what Lincoln's Get- tysburg address represented in 1864 to abolitionists. Vanzetti's memorable quotation could not have been much better timed, either. Appearing in newspapers throughout the nation just weeks before the spring semester ended, it held great appeal for politically liberal-minded college students and faculty. In fact, many would give up their summer vacations and jobs to travel to Boston and volunteer their services to the swelling ranks of the Sacco-Vanzetti movement.

Once Governor Fuller's investigation began, he routinely worked fourteen hours a day interviewing witnesses, reviewing case documents, and sifting through trial testimony.[50] Assisted only by his secretary, Herman McDonald, and his personal attorney, Joseph Wiggin, Fuller was soon out of his depth. The *New York Times*'s Albert Gordon depicted Fuller in near-valiant tones but Gordon was also astute enough to recognize that the case had long ago been "thoroughly" politicized. He described the Sacco-Vanzetti affair as the most international political cause cèlébre since the Dreyfus case. For Fuller, who had dropped out of high school at age sixteen to support his family, it was a challenge he both dreaded and relished: feared because he knew it was a political booby-trap, savored because he could not resist the call to duty. Indeed, pressure mounted steadily on the besieged governor from several directions. Boston postal authorities intercepted a parcel packed with dynamite addressed to him. A note accompanying the explosives ominously said the sender had a quarter ton more of dynamite; it was signed by a "citizen of the world."[51]

By late May, Fuller was forced to add six additional stenographers to his staff. The new employees did nothing else but answer the thousands of letters and cards about the Sacco-Vanzetti case that continued to pour into the Massachusetts state capitol mailroom.[52] Despite the overwhelming pressure for a special commission, Fuller informed the Sacco-Vanzetti Defense Committee that he alone would investigate the circumstances and evidence surrounding the case. The statement was odd, as well as ill-timed, for it was now apparent that Fuller alone could not reach a decision that would be accepted outside of Massachusetts. After Bishop Lawrence "suggested" that Fuller appoint a blue-ribbon panel to study the case, the governor's hand was forced. On June 1, 1927, the governor announced the appointment of a three-person advisory committee. The names of the men appointed to the panel likely meant little outside of Massachusetts— even at that only one, Harvard University President Abbott L. Lowell, was an easily identifiable name within the state. Retired Judge Robert A. Grant and Massachusetts Institute of Technology President Samuel W. Stratton were respected local establishment figures who could not be accused of harboring liberal political connections.

It took strenuous effort for Fuller to swallow his not inconsiderable sense of pride and appoint an advisory committee he clearly opposed as a potentially meddlesome nuisance. Nevertheless, once he made the official announcement that he would be assisted in his efforts by a panel composed mostly of respected establishment figures, Bostonians heaved a collective sigh of relief. Now the matter could be decided out of the glare of worldwide scrutiny (i.e., nosy newspaper reporters, blabbermouth syndicated columnists, and intrusive photographers). Or would it? No, it would not and could not. Yet, the governor struggled to keep the operation of the committee behind closed doors. To an even greater extent, Fuller also conducted his own inquiry almost exclusively in private. In retrospect, this effort at preserving confidentiality appears to have been a well-intentioned attempt by a somewhat politically naïve man. As soon as it was known that both investigations would be largely closed to press and public, Fuller was criticized for conducting important public hearings in secret.[53] The governor was not without just cause—he lacked subpoena power. Because witnesses would only appear voluntarily, he did not want them to feel pressured or unduly intimidated by the glare of publicity. Still, the resulting controversy became yet another public relations fiasco for the Commonwealth. Matters did not improve any when an editorial in the *Boston Evening Transcript* criticized the governor for capitulating to his adversaries. It upbraided Fuller for being "stampeded into scrapping the ways that have stood the test of time and experience."[54] The *Transcript* could not have been more wrong. It was precisely because the state of Massachusetts had failed to assure the public that Sacco and Vanzetti were tried and convicted fairly that the governor was forced to create two separate committees to investigate the lengthy record of the case. And it was an extraordinary phenomenon. Although there had been other causes cèlébres, nothing quite on this grand scale had ever happened before in American history. There simply was no modern established precedent, procedure, or protocol for resolving a political case such as this unusual episode in New England history.

Because the advisory committee (soon to be known in the press as the Lowell Committee) was hastily created and assembled, no one seemed sure of how it would operate or even what its designated mission was. Newspaper reports said stenographers would keep documentation of the proceedings but it would not be an official court record. Not surprisingly, all of this unprecedented activity proved somewhat confusing all around. There were many questions from different quarters about the exact role of the panel. It took a delay of several rather embarrassing days before the governor was able to tell the press that the committee would deliberate the fairness of the trial and also evaluate whether or not the defendants had been convicted beyond a reasonable doubt. In other words, the committee could recommend a second trial and most likely if it did, Fuller would be straight-jacketed into that option.

Nevertheless, William Thompson and the Sacco-Vanzetti Defense Committee were outraged. Despite all his talk about new evidence, Thompson knew that the real strength of his appeals lay in the weakness of the prosecution's eyewitness identifications and Frederick Katzmann's blunderbuss courtroom tactics during the trial. When the governor noted that the defense would not be permitted to question prosecution eyewitnesses, it seemed to imply that the Commonwealth had much to conceal and little

to gain by a frank and full disclosure. That was not true, but by now outward appearance had approximated reality. Moreover, there was the issue
of the execution dates. If Sacco and Vanzetti were to be executed the week
of July 10, the governor and the Lowell Committee would have to work
fast. Alvan Fuller had extended the advisory committee an extraordinary
degree of independence. Yet, because he arranged to keep its deliberations
and investigation out of public view, some took the panel to be nothing
more than a rubber stamp. There was just enough truth in that claim to
make it seem a reasonably plausible charge. While Fuller had selected the
commission with an eye toward upholding justice in Massachusetts, along
with the status quo, there is no extent evidence that suggests that he tried
to either overtly or covertly influence its members.

The governor's investigation continued at a brisk pace. Fuller's policy of
conducting his inquiry behind closed doors had predictable results: News
leaks popped up on an almost daily basis in the Boston newspapers. Sometimes the information was disturbingly accurate; other times it was distorted, sometimes comically so. Certain unidentified witnesses would
speak "off the record" with reporters. Others would leave by back and
side doors and avoid the crush of tourists, partisans, and hangers-on.
Whether or not what was reported happened to be accurate, Fuller's intent
had been to prove to the world that he cared about justice. Now, at least
to some, it appeared that he was concealing what he had learned in his
investigation. The *Daily Worker* referred to the proceedings of the governor and the Lowell Committee as a "star-chamber" affair.[55] People of far
less radical political outlook than that of the Communist Party made the
same charge. Across the Atlantic, the playwright George Bernard Shaw
commented that it was "impossible for us on this side to feel that the executions would have been so long deferred if the case were clear enough to
justify its infliction."[56]

Although Shaw confided to his friends privately that he thought both
men guilty, his point was well made. Because there were many appeals for
the court to process, it certainly appeared peculiar to the outside world,
particularly to Europeans, that it would take seven years to execute the
convicted. Alvan Fuller was forced to practice what a later generation of
political consultants would describe as "damage control." His decision
backfired, though, and he inadvertently stoked the flames of worldwide
Sacco-Vanzetti indignation. Politically, Fuller was now trumped into seeing his arrangements through to the end, no matter where that might lead.
Behind the scenes, the American Communist Party (represented by the ILD
and its sister organization the Sacco-Vanzetti Emergency Committee) and
the Sacco-Vanzetti Defense Committee battled for the services of the latest
influx of volunteers. One of them was the future Pulitzer Prize-winning
author Katherine Anne Porter. Arriving in Boston in early summer, she

decided to cast her lot with the ILD. Porter joined the communists because she thought they could accomplish more in the brief time remaining. She soon learned, however, that the ILD had not the slightest notion of forcing a second trial. "They were well organized to promote disorder and to prevent any question ever being settled—but I had not then discovered this. I remarked to a communist leader that even then, at that late time, I still hoped the lives of Sacco and Vanzetti might be saved and that they would be granted another trial. 'Saved,' she said, ringing a change on her favorite answer to political illiteracy. 'Who wants them saved? What earthly good would they do us alive?' "[57] The incident cogently summarized the operational paradox of the case—world-weary cynics following a separate agenda leading the naïve down the dialectical version of the primrose path.

James Cannon and the ILD had put their backs foursquare behind the Sacco-Vanzetti movement. The time had come for the communists to make their move. From now on they would do everything possible to attract as many volunteers into their camp, the intentionally but ambiguously named Sacco-Vanzetti Emergency Committee. To bolster its effectiveness party officials replaced *Daily Worker* editor J. Louis Engdahl, a functionary with few journalistic skills, with a professional writer, Robert Minor. Then the left-radical journalist Isaac Don Levine was sent to Boston to help cover the Sacco-Vanzetti story. Meanwhile, in its columns, the *Worker* fired a shot across the bow of the Sacco-Vanzetti Defense Committee. "In the meantime militant labor has found countless obstacles placed in its way by the defense committee, composed for the most part of personal friends of Sacco and Vanzetti, earnest people who have little conception of nationwide agitation and organized propaganda because of their anarchist principles."[58] Whatever the accuracy of its past assertions, the *Worker* was on target with that point. John Dos Passos and Gardner Jackson had done much to boost the publicity and recruiting potential of the original defense committee but they still had to answer to Aldino Felicani and "the Italians." Anarchists, the Galleanisti considered themselves militant revolutionaries, not cliché-spouting ideologues and effete café intellectuals. They made their decisions in private—in semi-communal fashion—and carried out orders with commando-like efficiency. They were seldom caught in the act, only sporadically arrested, and infrequently convicted. Nevertheless, the Sacco-Vanzetti Defense Committee was taking on more Americans each week, many of them wholly ignorant of anarchist thought and principles. Some of them were recognizably famous writers, poets, and actors— Dorothy Parker, Bruce Bliven, Edna St. Vincent Millay, Paxton Hibben, James Rorty, Ida Tarbell, Oswald Garrison Villard, and John Dewey. Some joined the emergency committee instead of the original defense committee; others shuttled between the two groups, not unlike college pledges selecting a fraternity during rush week. Considering the competition for money and members, a unified front between the two groups would have been impossible. ILD chief James Cannon attempted to merge the two very different organizations in mid-1926 (with an eye toward moving them to Chicago) but defense committee organizer Felicani, suspicious of ulterior motives, put a stop to this effort. The communist-backed labor defender then condemned the committee for its decision, which it predicted would hasten the demise of the anarchists.[59]

Cannon now had party approval to invest a good deal of money, time, and people into the case as he saw fit. The results, at least on the surface, sometimes approached the spectacular: Large rallies and meetings took place in cities across the country. Sacco-Vanzetti buttons, posters, placards, and armbands sprouted suddenly and ubiquitously during Spring 1927, seemingly as numerous as dandelions on so many suburban front lawns. ILD fund-raising was also intense, though little of the money reached the coffers of the nominally capitalistic Sacco-Vanzetti Defense Committee. Still, the communists expected more than just money and people to flow into the movement—they yearned for a future stake in the American polity. They expected the Sacco-Vanzetti case to catapult them into a much sought-after popular working-class movement in the United States. Willi Münzenberg hoped that Sacco-Vanzetti would elevate the Communist Party in America on a level with those units of western Europe.[60] That was decidedly wishful thinking, but the huge, slumbering labor movement in the United States made many hearts in Germany beat faster. As June wound down, the question most asked was if the governor and the Lowell Committee would have enough time to reach a decision. With the executions looming it did not appear there would be sufficient time. F. Lauriston Bullard, whose *Boston Herald* editorial on Sacco-Vanzetti had won a Pulitzer Prize in 1926, reported in late June 1927 that the number of people inclined to think Sacco and Vanzetti "probably innocent" was growing steadily.[61] Several days after Bullard's article appeared, Governor Fuller's office announced a reprieve for Sacco, Vanzetti, and Medeiros. It could not have come a moment sooner, either. Both the governor and the committee worked feverishly to hear as many witnesses as possible. Fuller even went to Dedham jail and personally interviewed Sacco and Vanzetti. The cordiality and sincerity of their stocky, distinguished visitor impressed both prisoners. It seemed to make little difference otherwise, though. Both men had embarked on a hunger strike, partly to raise awareness of their plight and partly to protest the closed-door policies of Governor Fuller's investigation.

While Sacco and Vanzetti refused to take nourishment, others had decided to take up political cudgels in their defense. It was truly an amazing phenomenon. Only a year earlier, the Sacco-Vanzetti case was still largely a regional cause cèlébre that had long ago enjoyed brief international exposure. Now it was the greatest ever political movement in American history and arguably as well known as the Dreyfus case. Rich, famous, and well-connected supporters tripped over each trying to arrange visits to the anarchists at Dedham jail. Bruce Bliven of the *New Republic* represented this wing of the movement. Although a correspondent for the *Republic,* Bliven was wealthy enough to be driven to Dedham by a chauffeur. Incredibly, he likened the experience of interviewing the doomed anarchists to meeting two out-of-town conventioneers in a hotel lobby.[62] Although he spoke of "foul judicial murder" and "haphazard victims of a blind hostility," Bliven's article was written with an eye toward the troubled conscience of the upper-middle-class liberal. Many such people were coming from all over the country to Boston that summer and the money and spare time they brought with them would be invaluable. The Fourth of July passed uneventfully in Boston. With the summer heat descending, the number of protesters camped out at the state house steadily increased. Both the governor and the advisory committee quietly continued to take testimony. Some considered the committee's work to be a kind of "second trial." Others said that the fact that its entire inquiry was closed to the public was evidence of a bias in favor of Judge Thayer and Frederick Katzmann. (Both men also made appearances before the panel in July as well as meeting privately with the governor.)

Meanwhile, reporters nibbled on any morsel of information they could pry loose and speculated about possible scenarios and outcomes when none was available. The result sometimes led to notably farfetched incidents. For example, Robert Benchley, drama editor of *Life* magazine, made a brief, if rather sensational, appearance before the committee. Benchley told the members of the committee that while a guest at the Golf Club in Worcester in 1921, he heard another club member say that he overheard Judge Thayer make disparaging remarks about Sacco and Vanzetti.[63] Benchley's secondhand recollection would have been laughed out of any well-run American courtroom as hearsay in more ordinary times. But, in 1927, it made headlines in what was, in effect, a closet trial that was created to reassure the public within and beyond the borders of Massachusetts that justice had been fairly served.

By late July, the advisory committee struggled to finish its work on deadline. Boston's noisy parade for triumphant aviator Charles Lindbergh complicated the panel's final days of deliberation. It seemed to make little difference. The committee ignored the hoopla, seemingly relieved for the respite from prying reporters and shrill, demanding Sacco-Vanzetti partisans. Before they concluded business, panel members heard arguments from various defense lawyers in sessions closed to the public. (Curiously, Fred Moore never appeared before either the committee or Governor Fuller.) Meanwhile, Boston swelled with eager young people anxious to leave their mark on the case and burn the candle at both ends late into the night. The new influx of volunteers helped to give the case added political thrust. Whether it was having any effect locally was another question. For his part, Governor Fuller steadily shielded himself from the outside world in the state house, letting in just enough constituents to transact daily business. This time, though, most people realized that Fuller had in his hands the fate of the two Italian "Reds." It was both impressively melodramatic and improbably true. Moreover, by now people everywhere seemed to anticipate the governor's impending decision. Rumors flew about Boston like so many starlings at sunrise: The variations on a theme were numerous as well as unsubstantiated. Fuller was going to pardon both men. It was rumored that he would commute their sentences to life in prison rather than order a second trial. Others said he would allow a second trial and then pardon both men. Some speculated that the Pope had arranged for a pardon from the comfort of his Vatican office. Another rumor noted Premier Mussolini had reputedly implored the American ambassador to Italy for a second trial for the anarchists, partly as a way of defusing the international campaign on behalf of the anarchists.[64] Yet another reported a Fuller-approved, Solomon-like deal would spare Vanzetti the death march but would allow Sacco to be electrocuted. Others speculated that because the governor was, relatively speaking, an *arriviste* lacking full-fledged Brahmin status, he could seize the opportunity to elevate his caste among bleeding-heart liberals by an act of politically calculated compassion.

Some thought that executing the two anarchists would subvert Fuller's national political chances for 1928. There was just as much rumor mongering on the other side of the issue. Many believed the governor would not grant clemency or order a new trial or grant sentence reductions because he believed that both men had been fairly tried and justly convicted. Further, Robert Benchley's account to the contrary, Fuller thought that Judge Thayer had been reasonably impartial and the jury open-minded and fair. The more cynical thought Fuller would not pass up an opportunity to use the case as a means to exercise his well-documented support of capital punishment. Some figured that the international propaganda campaign had gone too far and that Fuller would appear timorous if he granted clemency or a pardon. Still others were convinced that the governor would never cross the notoriously status-conscious and thin-skinned Massachusetts' judiciary. Then, to bring the rumors full circle, there were those who argued that he would not risk his political future in the Commonwealth with Bay state voters.

It was a dilemma rich in mythological paradox, one that seemed, in a variety of quirky ways, to parody the tragedies of Aeshcylus, Shakespeare, Chekov, Ibsen, and Shaw. However it had begun, the Sacco-Vanzetti case now was a political crucible, a high-stakes drama no longer amenable to compromise or modification. Oddly enough, while hope built elsewhere, neither Sacco nor Vanzetti, or most of the people who worked on their behalf in Boston, really expected the movement to succeed.[65] After Governor

Fuller had appointed the advisory committee, optimism momentarily soared, at least in some quarters. Now six weeks later, it appeared dashed against the rocks of judicial and political reality. After all, the governor had appointed a rather politically conservative commission. Newspapers lauded the committee for its long days, hard work, and old-fashioned nineteenth-century disdain of publicity but few really expected that the panel would recommend the defendants have a new trial.

The Lowell Committee concluded its investigation in the final days of July. News articles speculated that the committee would reach a decision within several days. Governor Fuller's separate, quixotic, but high-energy investigation continued apace. During one day in this period, he interviewed eight case witnesses in his office. That very day, Fuller made a surprise visit to the crime scene in South Braintree. Accompanied on his field trip by two state troopers and a covey of bored, news-starved reporters and photographers, the governor delighted passersby when he got out of his limousine to investigate. He then proceeded to direct the troopers in taking measurements of the crime scene.[66] It was the governor's only notable publicity stunt of his rather torturous involvement in the entire Sacco-Vanzetti episode.

The day after Governor Fuller's outing, the advisory committee made a scheduled but unannounced visit to his office. Each member of the commission was seen carrying a large manila envelope into the executive office. The visit lasted exactly eighteen minutes. The governor and the three members of the committee refused to comment to the press about the substance of the meeting. The brief time the commission took to reach its decision and the swiftness of the meeting transformed pessimism into despair among Sacco-Vanzetti Defense Committee officials. Many reporters and Sacco-Vanzetti supporters privately concluded that the abbreviated visit could only mean that the three-man panel had decided against the defendants. Advisors guessed a longer session would have been appropriate if a recommendation of clemency had been delivered. Newspaper reports noted that the governor would retreat to his New Hampshire summer home to reach a decision. There, a single guard would keep watch over the governor and his family.[67]

More than an ocean away, retired Colonel Alfred Dreyfus declared his rather bridled support for Sacco and Vanzetti. The frail, old man had refused numerous requests for interviews but stated that he was "heart and soul involved with this case." In fact, Dreyfus had hinted that he might make a trip to the United States to plead on behalf of Sacco and Vanzetti.[68] Nevertheless, he was careful to implore reporters to "please keep me out of politics." His words sounded almost touchingly ingenuous in light of the *Sturm* and *Drang* of the current propaganda campaign, one that by now had eclipsed the one on his behalf many years earlier. The juxtaposition of the elderly Dreyfus with the names Sacco and Vanzetti was, of course, entirely intentional. Dreyfus had only lent his endorsement

to the movement after considerable time and many entreaties. His decidedly tardy appearance into the stage-managed limelight of Willi Münzenberg's propaganda extravaganza should have had a thunderous impact.
For reasons solely related to geographic location and American politics, it
did not. Dreyfus would have had to sail to the United States to have any
measurable influence on public opinion pertaining to the Sacco-Vanzetti
case. Elderly and ill, he could not (or would not) travel and his international publicity value thus was squandered. Staying in France and releasing
intermittent statements was the political version of preaching to the choir,
a diminution of historical irony and deflation of potential dramatic effect.
Arguably, the French needed no further convincing that Sacco and
Vanzetti were innocent. The truth was that even if Dreyfus had been
healthy enough to make the voyage across the Atlantic, his arrival in
America would not have been welcome by all Sacco-Vanzetti partisans.
Dreyfus's mere presence in Boston well might force Governor Fuller to
hedge his bets and order a second trial. If that happened, then the surging
international communist-led movement on behalf of the anarchists might
well deflate as quickly as a half-baked soufflé.

Alfred Dreyfus never sailed to the United States. Whatever might have
come of the visit, the distinguished and frail former prisoner's absence
made precious little difference to Nicola Sacco. The anarchist sensed that
all was lost, despite the growing strength of the movement and the protests
and rallies staged on his behalf throughout the world. A young New York
college student, a member of a communist front-group for students supporting the movement, had tried to boost Sacco's spirits. In a letter to the
prisoner the young man prophesied that Sacco's ordeal would soon "end in
freedom." In a terse, bitter reply, the anarchist harshly dismissed the message as "nonsense" and took his young admirer to task. "As I wrote you
before and I repeat again today, only an international clamor—a protest—
can free us. And yet while we are so near the tomb, your letter amazes me
with its unwarranted optimism . . . How you are deluded! This is not even
common sense coming from you. I would say nothing if such talk came
from a man in the moon, but from you, you who are also in the struggle for
liberty, this is too much. Do you not know the end to which the defenders
of the decrepit old society will go? Under the circumstances it pains me to
see such blind optimism in a comrade. Are you waiting to see them kill us
first so that you can build us a monument?"[69]

Both Sacco and Vanzetti were weak from the effects of a lengthy and ill-
advised hunger strike. Although Vanzetti permitted himself to think that
the genial-appearing Governor Fuller would spare them, Sacco was in no
mood to accept false tidings of hope. As prison officials planned to force-
feed both men, the governor concluded his official inquiry into the state's
most notorious case since the Salem witch trials. Newspapers from around
the world awaited daily word from the state house in Boston. By this time,

the *Daily Worker* was convinced that the Hearst newspaper chain was at least indirectly to blame for Fuller's much anticipated refusal to grant clemency. "Under the pretext of 'fairness' and 'impartiality,' the Hearst newspapers of the country are indulging in the most loathsome apologies for the conspirators against the lives of Sacco and Vanzetti." The *Worker* said that the public demand for the release of the two Galleanisti prisoners was so convincing that the Hearst chain, led by the *New York Daily Mirror*, dare not "come out openly in favor of their deaths . . ."[70] Predicting that the advisory committee would rule against Sacco and Vanzetti, the communist daily urged retaliation through picketing of Hearst publications across the country. The logic of the connection was, at best, tenuous, if a strain upon credulity. Nevertheless, the *Worker* was right about at least one thing: Mainstream newspapers now feared giving excessive coverage to this volatile case. Almost all had decided to refrain from any further editorial comment until Governor Fuller announced his decision. To most editors, the question of whether Sacco and Vanzetti deserved a second trial had become hopelessly entangled with the issue of whether they had been victims of political persecution. Throughout the nation, people debated whether or not radical foreigners should even receive the same protection as American citizens. In light of the fact that immigration had been recently curbed by the government, it was a particularly touchy subject among Italian-Americans. Sensitive to ethnic stereotyping and discrimination, they took special notice of the disturbing charges of political prejudice and xenophobia. With the 1928 elections little more than a year away, politicians and government officials might one day have to account for their positions on the Sacco-Vanzetti case. Alvan Fuller, of course, was at the top of that list. While the governor considered his options, 5,000 demonstrators flooded Boston Common to hear roistering speeches urging clemency.[71] In New York, a crowd of 2,000 marched into City Hall Plaza singing the *Internationale* and demanding the freedom of Sacco and Vanazetti.[72] Meanwhile, the famous defense lawyer Clarence Darrow told reporters that ". . . it would be a terrible mistake not to grant a pardon." Darrow did not mention it, but he had been approached about representing Sacco and Vanzetti after Fred Moore resigned. Darrow, perhaps recalling his disastrous experience representing the McNamara brothers in the bombing of the *Los Angeles Times* building in 1910, politely declined the offer and thereafter kept his distance from the case.[73]

A week after meeting with the advisory committee, Governor Fuller announced that he would not grant clemency to Nicola Sacco and Bartolomeo Vanzetti. Fuller revealed that the committee had concluded that the defendants had unanimously recommended against a new trial.[74] In an official announcement, Fuller made clear that he had independently reached the same conclusion. "This task of review has been a laborious one and I am proud to be associated in this public service with clear-eyed witnesses, unafraid to tell the truth and with jurors who discharged their obligations in accordance with their convictions and their oaths."[75] Fuller never believed that Sacco and Vanzetti had been convicted because of political fallout generated by the Palmer raids. His brief but intense study of the trial record had convinced him that Fred Moore had intentionally injected the issue of prejudice into the case. Like Webster Thayer, Fuller thoroughly disbelieved the confession of Celestino Medeiros.

Despite the fact that Governor Fuller had declined clemency and would not order a new trial, he could still pardon the anarchists or commute their sentences to life in prison. Either option now seemed exceedingly remote. The prisoners were moved to the death-row cells near the electric chair in Charlestown prison. Vanzetti had already ended his hunger strike and anxiously awaited the departure of his sister from Italy. Nicola Sacco, meanwhile, continued his fast. Reporters said his mental state had "buckled" from the unrelenting pressure of waiting and the drain of slow starvation. The day after Fuller announced his decision, Aldino Felicani visited both prisoners. Sacco, he recollected, had been well prepared for the blow. Although Vanzetti still held out hope—Felicani had the sad duty to disabuse him of such a notion. He bluntly told his fellow anarchist that "all was lost." Forty years later, Felicani recalled in a journal article that Vanzetti's eyes grew wide behind the bars of his cell at this statement.[76] The prisoner responded with a rupture of anger, bitterly denouncing Governor Fuller as a "murderer" no different in his view than Judge Thayer or prosecutor Frederick Katzmann. Sacco and Vanzetti immediately sent out a call to Galleanisti for revenge; they urged violence to help drive their movement after their executions. Once back at Sacco-Vanzetti defense headquarters, Felicani leaked to the press Vanzetti's inflammatory comments about Fuller. Nevertheless, in line with Gardner Jackson's and Marion Frankfurter's wishes, all other Vanzetti comments about violence and revenge were withheld from pubic knowledge. Such remarks hardly comported with the defense committee's portrait of Sacco and Vanzetti as philosophical anarchists.

6

A Cardinal Calamity

Politics once again had intruded into the Sacco-Vanzetti case and not with much subtlety, either. This time it was on a truly national scale, with the sort of aftershock that haunts for years. To largely parochial fanfare, Governor Fuller announced his decision late on the night of August 2, 1927. Strangely, it came on the heels of President Coolidge's announcement that he would not seek reelection in 1928.[1] Because Fuller had once served as Coolidge's lieutenant governor, the timing of the announcement was ironic, albeit purely coincidental.

New York Times reporter Louis Stark claimed that Fuller initially had planned to commute the sentences to prison terms. Stark speculated that upon learning of Coolidge's decision, Fuller panicked and reversed himself, thinking that a clemency decision would imperil his chance to serve as the Republican Party's standard bearer for 1928. It was an intriguing hypothesis, one that many believed for a long time. Unfortunately, as author David Felix notes, it also lacks any documentary corroboration.[2] Nevertheless, Fuller's decision was popular only in Massachusetts, which now regarded itself as under international propaganda siege. The governor had miscalculated on yet another sensitive issue when he declined to make public the advisory committee's report. This convinced almost everyone on the Sacco-Vanzetti Defense Committee that Fuller was nervous about the information the advisory committee had uncovered. Moreover, the blue-ribbon panel mentioned in a summary of its findings that, while its members had found nothing improper to report, it did describe as "indiscreet"

Judge Thayer's comments about the case outside of court.[3] The reaction that this statement caused was nothing less than extraordinary, triggering a backlash of support that strengthened the Sacco-Vanzetti movement in the final two weeks of the cause cèlébre.

As noted, the decision announced by Governor Fuller was not unexpected. Many newspapers throughout the country carried news of the decision; about half ventured some type of editorial comment. Newspapers that did publish editorials on the governor's decision mostly expressed an admixture of congratulatory relief and proprietary satisfaction. The *Boston Evening Transcript* put itself solidly in Fuller's corner, apparently forgiving him the investigation it only recently chastised as pointlessly craven. The editorial observed that an attempt to conduct "trial by newspaper and propaganda for trial by jury" was a failure that must not again happen. The *Transcript* now praised the virtues of the inquiry as "a vindication of the judicial agencies of the Commonwealth and a belated but effective answer to the domestic troublemakers and foreign agitators who imagined that Massachusetts could be frightened into abandoning her plain duty as a sovereign state."[4] The *Boston Herald,* which had called for a review of the case in Spring, now proclaimed itself "ready to have the law proceed on its course."

The Boston-based *Christian Science Monitor* also lauded the internationally beleaguered governor and his advisory committee for refusing to be intimidated by "irresponsible critics."[5] The *Philadelphia Inquirer* argued that: "no men, convicted by due process of law ever had greater consideration."[6] The *Philadelphia Public Ledger* felt that whatever the merits of Governor Fuller's decision, that it "ought to be accepted as ending the matter."[7] The *New York Times* felt similarly assured, observing that the advisory committee had "run to earth the charge that the two men were convicted not on the evidence but out of prejudice."[8] The *Birmingham Press* asked rhetorically: "Where before in the history of American jurisprudence have three more disciplined minds given to the condemned murderers the benefit of what, in effect, is a second trial?"[9] The *Chicago Tribune* predicted that Governor Fuller's decision eventually would "be accepted by the American conscience."[10] The *New York Telegram,* though, made a point that others had conveniently overlooked: "Governor Fuller's decision doesn't settle the worldwide controversy as to their guilt or whether they had a fair trial." The *Telegram* thought that Fuller's bifurcated, closed-door approach to the investigation had only whetted the international appetite for a new trial conducted in open court. "Governor Fuller and his commission was a trial in star-chamber and a public statement of a decision based on a secret hearing of evidence."[11] The *New York Evening World* tepidly defended Fuller and the committee. (Walter Lippmann, chief editorial writer at the *World,* unilaterally decided that to criticize the decision would appear ungrateful.)

The *World* recognized that although there was no chance for a new trial, commutation of the death sentences was still possible, if not desirable, as a means to defuse a global cause cèlébre. The editorial staff of the *St. Louis Post-Dispatch* could not have disagreed more: "Sacco and Vanzetti were persecuted partly because they were aliens, partly because they did not conform in their political ideas, and partly because of a flimsy chain of evidence connected with a crime which they, in human probability, did not commit."[12] The *Norfolk Virginia-Pilot* said that the advisory committee's report "very much sustains the conviction that doubt commands a stay of execution in the interest of civilized application of the principles of justice."[13] The *Baltimore Sun, Providence News, Topeka State Journal,* and Denver's *Rocky Mountain News* also argued against the impending executions. Nevertheless, according to a poll conducted by *Literary Digest* magazine, the following newspapers spoke in defense of the governor's decision: The *New York Herald Tribune, New York Sun, Springfield Union, Washington Post, Providence Journal, Richmond Times-Dispatch, New Orleans Picayune, St. Louis Globe-Democrat, Kansas City Star, Indianapolis News, St. Paul Pioneer Press, San Francisco Chronicle, Spokane Spokesman-Review,* and *Tacoma Ledger*.[14] While the editorial voice of newspapers is not necessarily the *vox populi*, it was, arguably in this instance, a rough indication that Americans remained unconvinced of the alleged innocence of two obscure radicals who received more international attention than any issue the League of Nations had discussed that year.

In Europe, though, it was an entirely different matter. Not surprisingly, the French press was nearly unanimous in its condemnation of the governor's decision. A *New York World* reporter in Paris observed that France writhed in a sort of collective national anguish not experienced since the Dreyfus case: "Stupefaction, indignation, anger and sorrow are expressed everywhere."[15] Paris *Soir* acidly asked if the "image of Christ is absent from American courts?" *L'Ouvre* quoted Luigia Vanzetti as saying: "Since I have been in France I have found so much sympathy that I now have hopes that my brother and his comrade will not be executed."[16]

The *London Daily Herald* summed the matter more cogently than the mostly aroused French press: "If Sacco and Vanzetti are sent to the chair after a grossly unfair trial, after six long years of imprisonment, and after another man can show their entire innocence of the crime with which they are charged, their deaths will be an incalculable blot not only on the honor of the state of Massachusetts but on the United States."[17] Oddly, only one Italian newspaper commented on the governor's decision. Rome's *Tribuna*, the official organ of the Fascist Party, declared with undisguised contempt: ". . . the executions of the two condemned men, or even postponement of the executions, would conclude in a shameful fashion one of the darkest judicial episodes in history."[18]

An American citizen vacationing in Switzerland was appalled by the success of the propaganda that had attached itself to the case. In a letter to the *Boston Herald,* he fervently counseled against capital punishment. ". . . millions of earnest and intelligent people all over Europe seriously believe that these men are being railroaded to death on shaky evidence for social and political reasons . . . This is a capital international calamity and whatever its history, I should consider the execution of the men in the presence of such widespread conviction a cardinal calamity."[19]

From his spacious office in Berlin, Willi Münzenberg no doubt knew the executions were set to take place in one week. Governor Fuller, of course, still had the option of commuting the death sentences to prison terms. His statements to the press on the matter, though, made that seem a rather unlikely possibility. There would be appeals to the courts, both state and federal, as well as desperate but hopeless pleas to now lame duck President Coolidge. For now, though, the decision of whether or not to execute the prisoners rested exclusively with Governor Fuller. As things now stood, another delay of execution would only help Münzenberg and Cannon prepare for the final tumultuous spasm of anger, propaganda, and protest. The delay came soon enough but at a steep price: William Thompson had resigned, a victim of a shriveled private practice and unrelenting pressures from several directions. A younger Boston attorney, Arthur Hill, who immediately filed a motion for a new trial, replaced him. It would now take something more than a major miracle to just keep Sacco and Vanzetti alive until Fall, when the U.S. Supreme Court reconvened.

Pilate on the Boston Train

The big fellows here want death and nothing else. It's a point of pride with them.[1]

—*Gardner Jackson to* New York World *columnist Heywood Broun, August 1927*

Mary Donovan was boiling with a fury stoked by overwork, a depleted supply of adrenaline, and the realization that her life's ultimate mission would likely end in failure. For some time, the Sacco-Vanzetti Defense Committee leader had been the undisputed director of the American wing of the movement, but she had also worked hard to earn the respect of the Italian anarchists on the committee. It all seemed to go for naught: In a matter of months, the communists had outmaneuvered the original committee in a way that was especially humiliating.[2] The party had sent Isaac Don Levine to Boston to establish yet another front group: the Citizens' National Committee for Sacco-Vanzetti. Levine set up headquarters in Parlor D of the Hotel Bellevue, located adjacent to the state house, where many Sacco-Vanzetti demonstrations and protests had taken place in August 1927. Its proximity to planned events gave to the radical left an enormous advantage over the Sacco-Vanzetti Defense Committee with its cramped office space in the more distant North End. Some last-minute volunteers simply saved themselves the walk to Hanover Street and headed straight for Parlor D. Aldino Felicani and Gardner Jackson could only gasp at their inability to counter-punch James Cannon and a hardworking cadre of single-minded organizers and agitators.

Nevertheless, defense committee officials hit back in their bulletin in mid-May, denouncing the alleged "dishonest methods" of the ILD in language containing scarcely concealed vituperation. Noting "false statements and insinuations," the sheet called on Cannon to halt such practices and advised the reading public to seek accurate information from its organization.[3] (Less than a year before, Cannon had proposed merging both organizations but was eventually rebuffed.)

Although they were loath to admit it, and then only in private, members of the committee had to admit the communists had given the case a publicity surge that would have been difficult to coax from their well-intentioned, disparate, and mostly politically amateur liberal brethren. All across the country, large rallies and protests, some of them involving many thousands, had put Sacco and Vanzetti on the front pages, in the newsreels, and on the new technological *wunderkind,* radio. The communists had worked very hard, there was no questioning that fact. But it was the Sacco-Vanzetti Defense Committee that would bare the brunt of the blame for failure to save the anarchists from the electric chair. It would have to develop a strategy to convince Governor Fuller to realize that he was heading into a mouse-trap of politically ingenious construction. A strategy had to be found to make him quickly see the political light. Part of the solution involved finding a means to convince the American press to help change Fuller's mind. If the major newspapers of the country could be convinced that the governor was about to make a terrible mistake, then perhaps at least some degree of hope existed.

The day after the *New York World*'s editorial appeared, Felix Frankfurter took a train from Cambridge to New York City. Once there, he headed straight for Walter Lippmann's office at the *World*'s corporate headquarters. Frankfurter strutted into Lippmann's *sanctum sanctorum* brandishing a copy of the Sacco-Vanzetti trial record and then launched into a generous, if theatrical, display of high dudgeon.[4] Lippmann's animated visitor told him that his editorial was patent nonsense. A discomfited and somewhat bemused Lippmann listened as Frankfurter continued to vent his spleen. The Lowell Committee had not even bothered to read the trial record, which, in any case, he said, abounded with numerous instances of judicial and prosecutorial misconduct. At first, Lippmann resisted Frankfurter's arguments but eventually he conceded that he might have been too generous to Judge Thayer and District Attorney Katzmann in his analysis of the case. The editorial page editor decided, in effect, to reverse his reversal. Several days after Frankfurter had barged into Lippmann's office, the *World* chastised Governor Fuller for not publishing the advisory committee's full report. Nevertheless, Lippmann hedged his bets, so to speak: After all, the advisory committee *was* only human. "The possibility of error is not wholly disposed of, particularly in the case of Vanzetti."[5] This was, of course, an unmistakable reference to the committee's now notorious "on the whole" reference about Bartolomeo Vanzetti's probable guilt. For the rest of their lives these three simple words would haunt both the advisory committee members and Governor Fuller. Many people read them and wondered how a prisoner could be executed with such a damning qualification attached to the sentence. It was, in some minds at least, a subtle hint proffered by the committee to spare the life of Vanzetti.

Two days later, on August 10, Lippmann responded with a more emphatically worded editorial titled "Mercy." This time, the *World* asked that the governor commute the death sentences of both prisoners. "Once more we respectfully petition the Governor of Massachusetts to stay the executions out of respect for the opinion and conscience of a large portion of the civilized world. We do not question the sincerity of the Governor's conviction that the sentence is just. We submit merely that men can err, and that this case is one in which certainty cannot be had by the very nature of the evidence, which is circumstantial."[6]

To reinforce the point, the *World* ran a cartoon of Governor Fuller standing at the elbow of a sepulchral figure named "Mercy." Under the sketch appeared the words: "It's Not Too Late." In the next two weeks, the *World* would publish a total of eleven editorials on the case. All of them pleaded for commutation of the death sentences to prison terms. By any measure, the *World*'s contribution to the Sacco-Vanzetti case was simply extraordinary, but perhaps the oddest journalistic sidebar of the entire episode involved the newspaper's then well-known syndicated columnist, Heywood Broun. Then at the height of his popularity, Broun had often written about the case late in 1926 and throughout 1927. A rotund, shambling bear of a man with an engaging personality, boundless compassion, and penetrating wit, Broun was not often given to angry outbursts and siding with radicals, but the Sacco-Vanzetti case had presented him a highly novel set of circumstances. By August 1927, the affair had triggered an outrage in Broun that briefly snatched the limelight from the two principals of the case. Broun's wife, Ruth Hale-Broun, had been working in Boston for the Sacco-Vanzetti Defense Committee for some time.[7] With time running out and publicity desperately needed, Hale-Broun cajoled her husband to write more extensively about the case in his widely read "It Seems to Me" column. Broun made an appointment to talk to Ralph Pulitzer, publisher of the *World,* about his plan to write exclusively about the case until it was one way or another resolved. The columnist left his farm, *Sabine,* and took the train to New York where he met Pulitzer in the publisher's executive office.

Broun's conference took place on a stifling hot day in early August. On his way up in the elevator, the tippling Broun gulped a hit of warm gin from a hip flask. Fortified, he then tried convincing Pulitzer that both men were "on the same side."[8] Pulitzer was already nervous about Broun's commitment to a case that was obviously being stage-managed by liberals and far-left radicals. He tactfully reminded his star columnist about his contractual obligations with the *World*. Simply put, these could be summarized as "writers write and editors edit."[9] Broun had promised his wife would attempt to dissuade Pulitzer with a glare of icy contempt if words failed to convince the publisher. Congenial by nature, Broun smiled and the opportunity was then lost as both men shook hands, parting amicably. The writer, having squandered the effort, departed to catch the afternoon train to Boston. While waiting, he drank freely and was soon in his cups, overcome by a deep fear that he had behaved as Pontius Pilate did: washing his hands of Christ. That rather morbid biblical parable stuck, revolving in his mind all the way to Boston where he disembarked into the stifling evening summer heat.

Gardner Jackson met Broun at the train depot in downtown Boston. Disheveled and somewhat hungover, the columnist pulled himself together as the train chugged into the railroad yard. After he shook hands with the younger man on the platform, Broun asked the harried Jackson how things looked. The publicity director admitted that the overall picture was bleak: The governor had just turned down another request for a reprieve. Furthermore, hope that Fuller might soften so far had proved entirely misplaced. In fact, if anything, the mood against Sacco and Vanzetti in the Commonwealth had deepened since the governor's decision was announced. While the rest of the nation gravitated toward sentence reduction, Massachusetts seemed determined to have double executions. For the Comintern and its propaganda chief, Münzenberg, if it was not yet a reality, it certainly was a once-in-a-generation international propaganda opportunity.

Jackson hustled Broun to the cramped Sacco-Vanzetti headquarters in the North End. Ruth Hale-Broun had already been there for some time. She was well known to those present while, at first, her far more famous husband went unrecognized. Jackson had not exaggerated: The mood of the office revealed panic undercut with a paralyzing undercurrent of despair.[10] Broun sat down at his wife's desk and began pounding out his next column on a portable typewriter. As noted, Broun had written in the past about the Sacco-Vanzetti case. Sitting in the cramped headquarters surrounded by impassioned activists, still somewhat tipsy, further emboldened him. In his latest column, Broun wrote about the anarchists with a much sharper adversarial edge. He introduced a conspiracy angle that no other mainstream American journalist or contemporary major political figure had heretofore dared to suggest. Sounding as if he were Jeremiah in the ideological desert, Broun referred to Sacco and Vanzetti as "shining spirits" caught in a maelstrom. He seemed to predict an impending apocalypse, one that would haunt the nation's conscience for many years.[11] "They are too bright, we shield our eyes and kill them. We are the dead, and in us there is no feeling nor imagination nor the terrible lust for justice." Broun's haunted voice ascended from its melancholy timbre to urge a cry from "a million voices." It was a sincere vision from a man tortured by his inability to bend the popular will to the heartbeat of his conscience. He did not think that passionate, well-educated, and nicely mannered people would be strong enough to reverse what he saw as a terrible desire to crush something he believed was terribly misunderstood. Noting that Judge Thayer and Frederick Katzmann were not evil, Broun said that if an injustice had been committed in the Sacco-Vanzetti case, it was one of "thousands" that happened every year in the United States. "Our judicial processes are so arranged that it is to the advantage of district attorneys to secure convictions rather than to ascertain justice, and if it would profit his case, there is not one who would not stoop to confuse the issue in the minds of the jury . . . This is a thing done cold-bloodedly and with deliberation."[12]

In his column the next day, Broun conceded that "the majority of the voters" in Massachusetts wished to see the anarchists executed. He professed consternation and anger with the assumed reasons for this obvious public sentiment. "Mostly the feeling rests upon the fact that Sacco and Vanzetti are radicals and that they are foreigners. Also the backbone of Massachusetts, such as it is, happened to be up because of criticism beyond the borders of the State. 'This is only our business,' say the citizens of the Commonwealth, and they are very weary . . . From now on I want to know will the institution of learning in Cambridge, which once we called Harvard, be known as Hangman's House?"[13]

Broun's acid comment about Harvard, obviously aimed at A. Lawrence Lowell, instantly chagrined the *World*'s Ralph Pulitzer. The publisher ordered Broun *not* to write about the case anymore. Pulitzer had anxiously read both of Broun's columns sent from Boston—they made him wince but he let Lippmann run them. By this time, though, Broun's colleagues, including Lippmann, had sided with Pulitzer. Broun had simply gone too far—at least for a mainstream newspaper columnist. For his part, Broun claimed that he had been the victim of internal censorship. On August 12, 1927, an extraordinary statement of denial and explanation appeared in the *World* under Pulitzer's name. He accurately claimed that what had taken place was not censorship but editorial judgment.[14] Broun was not mollified by his boss's explanation—he resigned from the *World*'s staff five days after Pulitzer's statement appeared. (Broun did not officially leave for another ten months—until May 1928.)

The rotund, brooding columnist laid low, professing outrage and hurt, knowing very well that he had trumped his boss in the publicity game. Broun had managed to appear heroic and put-upon in the same historic instant. Pulitzer, it should be said, was not acting purely out of a newspaper publisher's proprietary sense of editorial balance and equanimity. In fact, Broun's columns had caused cancellations and sparked protests from advertisers, some of whom also were Harvard graduates. Furthermore, Broun, normally a writer with populist-liberal sensibilities, was writing about

Sacco and Vanzetti as if his employer was the *Daily Worker* or *Cronaca Sovversiva*. It was all too much for Pulitzer, whose newspaper after all was trying its editorial best to save from execution two insufferable and ungrateful radicals. Nevertheless, Broun had succeeded in getting more publicity by having his wings clipped by his publisher than he possibly could have had he been allowed to write about Sacco and Vanzetti four times a week. It was yet another in a series of delightful ironies to communists— once again, someone important and powerful connected to the case *appeared* to want to conceal the awful truth. That, of course, was not really the case, but by now the Sacco-Vanzetti case was a propaganda *bete noir* for the Commonwealth and its badly overmatched governor and judiciary.

Boston is as lovely a city in Summer as any American traveler or international tourist can find—hot and often crowded but stately, verdant, and lovely with its hilly tree-lined streets. With many venerable and well-preserved historic buildings and houses, visitors have long flocked to the "America's Athens" despite the muggy heat that gradually settles over the city by mid-Summer. By early August 1927, the tourist trade in Boston was booming with more than the usual complement of sightseers and walking tours. The Sacco-Vanzetti story was front-and-center, splashed all over the front pages of newspapers; it was also on the radio and even featured in movie house newsreels. Boston was a boiling cauldron of political factions, tension, animosity, and frantic at-wits-end organizing and activity.

In the city's famous sprawling common, police patience grew noticeably short-tempered. On a warm Sunday afternoon, as many as 10,000 people swirled though the grounds, most affiliated with the communist-dominated Sacco-Vanzetti Emergency Committee. City officials summarily revoked speaking permits. Eccentric and wealthy Edward Holton James, nephew of the late authors William and Henry James, was among those arrested for "loitering and sauntering."[15]

The tension heightened on August 8 when the State Supreme Judicial Court denied a petition for Sacco and Vanzetti for a writ of habeas corpus and for a writ of error. Arthur Hill, new head defense counsel, was something less than magnanimous in defeat: "The Salem witches were tried by the best men of the day in the Commonwealth who had the reputation of being the wisest, yet we know how greatly they erred. Although unconscious of prejudice we are now, happily, largely free from religious prejudice but, to some extent at least, social and economic questions have usurped the place of religion."[16]

There was more bad news for Hill: Webster Thayer was scheduled to hear yet another motion for a new trial. There was left now only the faintest hope that help might come from Washington. Newspapers reported that the Sacco-Vanzetti Defense Committee had sent an appeal directly to President Coolidge, requesting a federal inquiry into the case. That was not such a far-fetched idea given that the Justice Department was rumored to have information in its files on the case that might provide the basis for a new trial. The Pulitzer flagship *St. Louis Post-Dispatch* concurred. In a powerfully worded editorial, the newspaper informed President Coolidge that only he could "save the country from dishonor in the eyes of the world."[17] The *Post-Dispatch* asked the former governor of Massachusetts to help arrange a "reprieve" for Sacco and Vanzetti for one year. Six months earlier that suggestion would have smacked undeniably of compromise. Now it had the strained resonance of desperation, a tacit concession that the international campaign on behalf of Sacco and Vanzetti was successful.

In the midst of an epidemic of hatred, panic, and fear came just what none of the Americans on the defense committee had expected: a wave of strategically planned and execute acts of terrorism. On August 5, 1927, several bombs exploded across the East Coast, in New York, Boston, and Philadelphia, as well as on the West Coast in San Diego.[18] The bombings, referred to in the 1920s press as "outrages," were a fairly strong sign that anarchism, though moribund, still had a gasp or two remaining. No one was ever arrested in connection with the outrages but, not surprisingly, the mantle of suspicion fell heaviest on the Galleanisti.

The Sacco-Vanzetti Defense Committee angrily denied any link to the string of bombings. Edna St. Vincent Millay later wrote that for a variety of reasons, many people could have committed them.[19] Still, from a public relations perspective, the outrages could hardly have come at a less opportune time. Just when it seemed that the rest of the country was developing second thoughts about the specter of "an American Dreyfus case," acts of terrorism rekindled fading memories of the Wall Street bombings and the botched attempt to kill Attorney General Palmer. Only one thing was certain: The communists were not suspects, at least in the eyes of law enforcement. Everyone who knew anything about politics in America knew that communists in the United States worked through infiltration, recruitment, and agitation-propaganda. Nevertheless, American party leaders were not taking any chances. In fact, they wasted little or no time in disavowing the recent outrages. Saccco-Vanzetti Emergency Coordinator Rose Baron condemned the incidents as "the stupid act of an agent-provocateur."[20] The IWW was also quick to deny any link to the bombings. Both groups suggested a "frame-up" by the capitalist class. Nevertheless, fear welled in many cities; it increased exponentially among some police departments. Bomb squads worked around the clock in Boston, New York, Philadelphia, and other major cities. In New York City, police guarded every subway and elevated train station. In Chicago, police fired on a crowd of 4,000 mostly peaceful Sacco-Vanzetti demonstrators led by a high-school girl.[21] A political paranoia of sorts developed in Boston as local officials began to anticipate the impending executions as a pitched Manichean battle between the forces of lightness and righteousness, darkness and evil.

In the Black Hills of South Dakota, a vacationing President Coolidge was assigned extra security. The United States was not prepared for such a major political calamity. It had little or no experience in such matters and there was no readily available safety valve to defuse the tremendous pent-up pressure of an international political movement. By mid-August, Boston had become an armed police camp. Arrests of demonstrators marching in front of the state house had become a daily spectacle. Paddy wagons drove away filled with dozens of the newly arrested; photographers snapped pictures of the latest best-selling author or renowned philosopher to join the trek to the Joy Street station. Although it had begun as something much different in 1920, by August 1927 Sacco-Vanzetti had become America's first hipster cause cèlébre. Broadway actress and well-known writer Dorothy Parker fashioned her brief presence in Boston into a self-serving publicity stunt.[22] She was far from alone in her audacity. Those that joined that elegantly attired figure in the Joy Street holding cell passed their time singing the *Internationale* as they planned that evening's dining and entertainment.

The Sacco and Vanzetti case's imprint would set the tone for future causes, but, in truth, the vast majority of those participating in picketing and other forms of demonstrations were ordinary citizens; most surnames on arrest blotters suggested Jewish or Italian ancestry. Many were from local branches of the Communist or Socialist Party. In New York City, those in the streets were mostly blue-collar workers, from the needle-trades, almost all of them political radicals of one type or another. One hundred and forty thousand workers had left work in one day of organized work stoppages. Upstate in Rochester, 4,000 workers staged a Sacco-Vanzetti sympathy strike. In Tampa, 15,000 cigar makers had also struck. Four thousand miners in Colorado, many members of the IWW, also stopped work in sympathy.[23] Overseas, there were sympathy strikes and demonstrations in Paris, Cherbourg, and Marseilles.

The Sacco-Vanzetti Defense Committee was heartened by the support, unprecedented since the Dreyfus case, but time was running out and the number of mainstream newspapers in the United States suggesting commutation of sentences was still rather modest. Unlike in Europe, though, there had been no brush fires of editorial protest. That was a major setback. Strong editorial support would count for a great deal more than would hastily planned and frantically arranged rallies and demonstrations. Those were staged events, propaganda spectaculars involving smoke and mirrors. But not all hope was vanquished. There was some reason to believe that President Coolidge would soon order a federal inquiry into the case. After all, President Wilson had done something similar in the Mooney-Billings case and, as a result, both convicted men were spared execution. Coolidge, it must be recalled, was an old friend and former boss of Governor Fuller.

But, then again, perhaps expecting a federal probe was wishful thinking. Many in Massachusetts thought the chance that the president would risk humiliating his former lieutenant governor was slim indeed. Nevertheless, Senator William Borah had gone on record stating that Justice Department files on Sacco-Vanzetti should be opened. "The clamor from abroad should not be disregarded by President Coolidge because we should remember this country's protests in the Dreyfus case and in connection with Russian pogroms were heeded."[24] Borah's words were a comfort but he was one of a small handful of nationally recognized American politicians to express an opinion on the case. As always, it commanded greater attention throughout western Europe. In Great Britain, many newspapers referred to the Sacco-Vanzetti movement as a second Dreyfus case and urged clemency.[25] In Torremaggiore, Italy, Michele Sacco petitioned Premier Mussolini to intervene on his son's behalf. The elder Sacco's request located an anxious, if pessimistic, audience. With execution only days away, the Italian public became increasingly agitated, perhaps not nearly as much as the French, but nonetheless upset at the possibility that two of Italy's native sons might have been falsely convicted. Newspapers throughout the country printed "desperate" appeals for clemency. Two days after the *New York Times* carried news of Michele Sacco's telegram to Mussolini, the Sacco family issued a statement to the international press from Torremaggiore: "Even in this extreme moment we trust American justice. During these seven years when execution seemed imminent we have hoped, as we now hope, and our confidence has now been rewarded. Why should we despair today? We are awaiting my brother although we are expecting him to return at any moment."[26]

The U.S. State Department acknowledged that "long ago" a personal letter from Mussolini had been sent in behalf of Sacco and Vanzetti through the Italian embassy in Washington. In Boston, the Sacco-Vanzetti Defense Committee was embarrassed by the badly timed incident. Surely, Nicola Sacco, a militant anarchist ready to die for the cause, would not want a fascist dictator trying to save his life. To add woe to a steadily worsening situation, a ballistics expert, Calvin Goddard, announced that a new advanced type of bullet "finger-printing" test indicated that Nicola Sacco's pistol had fired the bullet that killed Alessandro Berardelli.[27] Goddard's results were ignored by both the advisory committee and Governor Fuller, but the publicity surrounding a new and reputedly more reliable test made a loud splash in newspapers. News from Moscow muddied the waters even more—that is if you were a non-communist. The Communist International, waiting literally until the eleventh hour, issued a statement urging "toilers of the whole world" to help stop the impending executions.[28] The message, while stirring to hundreds of thousands of workers in Europe, aggravated a far more hostile audience in the United States. Mainstream newspapers in America informed their readers that the powerful *Communist International* had urged American workers to rise up and smite the cruel, exploitative hand of the ruling class. The *Daily Worker* was, of course, the Comintern's dialectical megaphone for the case. "The sentence of death against Sacco and Vanzetti is an unheard of provocation against the world proletariat. It heralds a new, cruel oppression not only toward America but also toward the American working class and toward the whole word proletariat. It testifies that the civilized America of all its technical achievements reserves for proletarian revolutionaries only one: the electric chair."[29]

The order from Moscow, skull-cracking agitation-propaganda, had not been kited into a political vacuum—just the opposite was true. It was hardly necessary in Boston and New York, where panicky, truncheon-wielding, horse-mounted police broke up meetings at the first sign of an uplifted voice or raised fist. Again, it was another example of a tactic that worked marvelously well in Europe but almost always seemed to backfire in the United States. Sacco-Vanzetti Defense Committee members could only hold their collective heads in their weary hands. Nevertheless, it was too late to complain. Rose Baron had already told the *Daily Worker* that the Sacco-Vanzetti Defense Committee and her Sacco-Vanzetti Emergency Committee would unite in solidarity outside Charlestown prison the night of the execution.[30] Governor Fuller had granted another reprieve on August 10 and it came none too soon. The prisoners had had their heads shaved and were ready for execution when Fuller granted the respite, delaying the execution until August 22.[31] (Celestino Medeiros was also granted a reprieve.) Oddly, the late-breaking news stunned reporters more than it did the condemned men. Everyone, Sacco and Vanzetti included, had expected that the anarchists would die that night. Millions worldwide clustered around radio receivers and newspaper kiosks. Nicola Sacco, severely weakened by a hunger strike, displayed no outward emotion. Vanzetti said that he was glad: "I want to see my sister before I die." At that moment, Luigia Vanzetti was in Paris, reportedly awaiting the next ship to New York City.[32]

From a propaganda point of view, the timing of the visit was almost perfect. The reprieve was scheduled for twelve days—more than enough time. At least there was enough time to reunite the Vanzetti siblings, separated by several thousand miles, more than fifteen years, and an unbridgeable political gulf. Their reunion would tug the heartstrings of a nation that now was not only paying attention but was enthralled by the spectacle of a death-house melodrama—amply covered by tabloids, of course. Americans had notoriously short attention spans but no one could say they didn't enjoy a good life-or-death struggle. Galvanized by political radicalism with international outrage thrown into the bargain, the case was an irresistible newsmaker.

After a nineteenth-century battle, Napoleon had said that coverage from a single newspaper could be worth more than a division of soldiers. In

Summer 1927, Willi Münzenberg could say that a single, well-planned publicity stunt was worth more than a month's worth of sympathetic Heywood Broun columns. For Münzenberg, the reunion of brother and sister was based on cold calculation: too late for her presence to have any practical effect on Governor Fuller but just in time for the dramatic execution-watch. President Coolidge, it was now painfully obvious to sincere supporters of the anarchists, would not act. Whatever was in those Justice Department files probably would never be publicly revealed.

Shortly after the reprieve was announced, *Boston Evening Transcript* columnist Laurence Cahill mused aloud that throughout its history, the cradle of American civilization had been gently treated by the fates while other cities had been burned, sacked, or even leveled. "What really are the significances at stake? How name this formless, living shape that roars louder every day? It has been called a social crisis. The Dreyfus case has been likened to it. But the issue at Rennes was petty and trivial—if all the signs and symbols are to be compared and a balance struck. Indeed, the War itself was less a task to the arbiters of social discretion—at least it was like an old transgressor who must create havoc every now and then in an old, thoroughly familiar way. But the matter at Charlestown has no precedent. There is no beaten path to follow. There is not a whisper out of the past to suggest the answer. Yet the answer will be tremendous—a torch flung to lighten or scorch the way."[33]

Lighting the way anywhere without setting fire to something seemed hardly possible any longer. With communists and liberals joined in a desperate, improbable coalition, and Boston police armed to the teeth for an invasion of the Red Army, with the political establishment of the Commonwealth committed to have executions at any cost, there was scant hope of anything remotely enlightening happening. It had been reduced to a savage, partisan local fight over two pathetic immigrant-anarchists elevated to international celebrity by a cocaine-addicted lawyer, a bickering strange bed-fellows committee, and a brilliant propagandist half a world away who spoke no English.

The twelve-day reprieve was not so much an opportunity to save Sacco and Vanzetti as it was additional time to publicize their impending doom. Legally, the door was all but completely shut in Washington. President Coolidge plainly had no intention of acting on the anarchists' behalf. No member of the U.S. Supreme Court would lift a finger, either: There was no compelling federal issue. Still, the Sacco-Vanzetti Defense Committee would exhaust every avenue of appeal possible. If there was only a scintilla of hope remaining, it likely resided in the yellowing, sealed-away Justice Department files on Sacco and Vanzetti. Within those accordion folders there might be just enough information to spare their lives for a few more months.

A young Drew Pearson, beginning a career as a syndicated columnist, described wariness by the State Department regarding the latest Sacco-Vanzetti reprieve. American trade was affected by the boycotts and demonstrations in such distant lands as Morocco, Paraguay, and Panama.[34] "Although making no comment, State Department officials are largely concerned over this revulsion of feeling since it may cut deeply into American commercial files and may handicap the cause of conducting foreign relations."[35] Pearson said there was even speculation that the American Legion would not be able to hold its annual convention in Paris later that month. Secretary of State Kellogg feared that the Sacco-Vanzetti movement had spread from a largely working-class phenomenon in Europe into the more influential middle and upper-middle classes. A *New York Times* editorial was sympathetic in a somewhat peevish way about vacationing Yanks on the continent: "Americans abroad this summer have often been called upon to explain the matter to Europeans interested in the case but have not been able to do so. Some of the violent rebukes to the United States by the press of countries abroad which have known their own famous miscarriages well might . . . study their own judicial records."[36]

The *Milwaukee Journal* was more even-handed in its assessment of the politically charged quandary. In an editorial entitled "Let's Keep Our Heads," the *Journal* advised: "We have been rather silly about this Red business. If it has been anything like the danger the fearful ones have said, we certainly have gone about the wrong way to cure it. Now the Reds have been guilty of hysterical and criminal excesses. Have we no deeper, sounder thought than to reply by hysterical attempts at repression?"[37] The *Journal* was not alone among American newspapers making such counsel. But there were only a handful of other newspapers willing to admit that punishing "Reds" was not the solution to the problem of radicalism. By now almost everyone who had recently read a newspaper in America knew that communists allegedly were behind Sacco and Vanzetti. Nevertheless, even after seven years of this case, most Americans did not know the difference between a communist and an anarchist. That included many reporters and columnists who were sometimes willfully indiscriminate in their ignorance. Moreover, many following the seemingly never-ending episode had long since forgotten that it was about murder and robbery, not revolution and subway bombings. On August 10, acting Attorney General A. G. Farnum said that the Department of Justice had nothing in its voluminous files relating to Sacco's and Vanzetti's convictions.[38] Farnum also reminded his audience that the case was not a federal matter. He was, of course, responding to a groundswell of support for release of the Bureau of Information files pertaining to the case. (Senator Borah, especially, endorsed release of the now controversial and much publicized files.) Farnum was accurate, as far as he went—but he did not mention that a spy had been used in Dedham jail to monitor Nicola Sacco's remarks. The informant's existence was well known to the Sacco-Vanzetti Defense Committee. Many committee members were convinced that the information passed along to the Bureau would help vacate the convictions of Sacco and Vanzetti, or at least go a long way toward giving them a new trial. Some likely realized even then that the truth was far more tangled, more complex, and, as some of the communists and anarchists would privately admit, best left alone. Newspaper reporters speculated that Attorney General John G. Sargent, on vacation in Vermont, would not act unless prompted by President Coolidge.[39] To say the least, that possibility seemed highly unlikely.

Nicola Sacco finally gave up his hunger strike on August 15, relenting only when faced with forced feeding. It hardly seemed to matter, though—his execution was now distressingly obvious *fait accompli* even to the most imperceptive outsider.[40] The same day Sacco ended his hunger strike another bomb exploded—in suburban Boston, partially destroying the house of a juror from the Sacco-Vanzetti trial. Remarkably, Lewis McHardy and his family suffered only cuts and bruises but the timing of the incident again suggested that anarchism was not yet quite a dead-letter.[41] The bombing intensely embarrassed the Sacco-Vanzetti Defense Committee, implying that the Americans had lost control of the Galleanisti. That was not true: The committee had never had complete control over anyone. Like many coalitions, the American and Italian members tolerated each other, ignored many differences, and tried to accomplish the politically impossible. It was a subtle distinction few understood. For its part, though, the *Boston Evening Transcript* interspersed photos of the McHardy wreckage with coverage of other Sacco-Vanzetti news, thus strongly implying a link between the committee and the latest outrage. The task continued in the courts as attorneys argued two bills of exceptions before the Supreme Judicial Court. Arthur Hill gave a passionate speech to the full bench of the court. He told the justices that nothing less than the "honor of the Commonwealth" was at stake.[42] To Hill, the case no longer was about Sacco and Vanzetti so much as it was about those who worked for and against them. "It is the bench and bar of Massachusetts. It is our entire system of criminal law."[43] By this point, Hill had absolutely nothing to lose and everything to gain. Since 1921, Webster Thayer had heard and denied eight motions for a new trial; he had also turned down three supplementary motions.[44]

Hill was right about the honor of Massachusetts being at stake possibly in more ways than he could realize. He knew only a miracle, and a major one at that, would save his clients. It was only too painfully obvious that in this case divine intervention was not going to occur in any courtroom, either state or federal. It was not going to come from the Attorney General, either. It would most definitely not come from President Coolidge. The only chance of survival for Sacco and Vanzetti resided within the plump but by now thoroughly tormented breast of Alvan Tufts Fuller.

The *Daily Worker* could breathe easier now. With almost no chance that either man would be saved from execution, it would be easier to agitate without fear of a possible last-minute reversal. *Worker* columnist Mike Gold pointedly mentioned his arrest (along with Dorothy Parker) in mid-August.[45] Communists could now freely rub elbows with fellow travelers, liberals, even socialists without fear of retribution from party higher-ups. The party had helped bait the police and local politicians of Boston into opposing camps that reminded visitors of a society in the initial stage of civil war. Now Gold and others could justifiably wring their hands and point to twenty-four-hour police shifts, machine guns, a deployed state militia, sandbag encampments, and armored cars as proof that Massachusetts was interested only in quelling protest and not in justice.

The *Worker* claimed the "capitalist" press was shoving the embarrassing news of the executions off the front pages. "The capitalist bloodhounds of Massachusetts dread the white light of publicity. They intend to carry out the cold-blooded murder of our comrades . . . within the dark walls of Charlestown jail."[46] In fact, a more inaccurate statement about Sacco's and Vanzetti's final days has yet to be written. Charlestown prison was a macabre death-watch convention—a large assemblage of reporters and columnists awaiting the executions. Special telephone and telegraph lines had been installed just for the occasion. Radio and newsreel technicians also made a token contribution to the proceedings. It was far from a local affair, too: Journalists from all over the world scurried to Boston, hoping to be one of the lucky few who actually made it inside the ugly, monolithic penitentiary. The 1920s provided many "thrilling" events—none were covered by the press more extensively (or sensationally) than executions. At the apex of this gruesome publicity ritual in Summer 1927 was the Sacco-Vanzetti case. On August 18, the Supreme Judicial Court of Massachusetts turned down Arthur Hill's petition for a new trial. Hill immediately asserted that he would appeal to the United States Supreme Court. When newsmen asked on what grounds he would appeal, Hill replied the Fourteenth Amendment to the constitution: the famous and sometime-misunderstood due-process clause. It was the legal version of whistling past the graveyard and Hill knew very well that the reporters (and many others) realized that he had simply run out of last chances.[47] Bartolomeo Vanzetti took the news very hard. More sensitive than his volatile comrade, he snapped and temporarily lapsed into a psychotic state. Sacco-Vanzetti Defense Committee volunteer lawyer Michael Musmanno told reporters that Vanzetti began shouting in his cell: "I knew it! I knew it! Get the million men! Who is making all that noise?" Vanzetti had also requested that a radio be brought to his cell so that he could broadcast his story to the world.[48] Not long after this incident was reported in the press and on radio, Sacco, Vanzetti, and Celestino Medeiros were again relocated to the condemned cells of Charlestown. The same day that news of the State Supreme Judicial Court's latest decision appeared, the *New York World* devoted its entire editorial page to discussion of the case. "Doubt that Will Not

Down," a lengthy editorial (likely written by Walter Lippmann), argued politely and in great detail that Sacco and Vanzetti should not be executed with lingering doubts about their guilt pricking the national conscience. The *World*'s August 19 editorial was only one of many essays on the case over several weeks, but its extraordinary tone persuaded readers throughout the nation that the death sentences were ill considered and draconian.

The exaction of the death penalty is not finally a judicial question but a question of public policy that has to be settled within the discretion of the executive. The jury at the original trial brought in a verdict of guilty. The presiding judge at the trial had repeatedly denied motions for a new trial. The appellate courts have denied that the rulings of this judge were according to the law. The Advisory Committee concluded that the two men are guilty. But no one has yet passed on the question as to whether the highest interests of the state demand that the two men be executed or that they be imprisoned for life . . . Governor Fuller has stated publicly in another connection that he regards the death penalty as the one form of punishment most calculated to deter the professional criminal. With that opinion we are in sympathy and it is not our practice in clear cases of premeditated murder to plead for clemency. But because we share Governor Fuller's opinion as to the theory of capital punishment we recognize that certain conditions must be fulfilled before the exaction of the penalty can have the deterrent effect, which it ought to have. There must be no doubt in the minds of the community that the condemned had an absolutely unprejudiced trial. There must be no doubt that the condemned is guilty beyond a reasonable doubt. Above all, the circumstances must be such that the condemned dies in the role of a convicted criminal and not in the role of martyr.[49]

The *World*'s passionate editorial was more than a rhetorical entreaty to spare the lives of two wretched and inconsequential anarchists. It also took pain to highlight weaknesses in the prosecution's case: questionable identifications, the alleged bias of the judge, prejudicial questions posed by the prosecutor, an avowedly biased juror, etc. The newspaper also noted that a piece of trial evidence, a cap allegedly belonging to Nicola Sacco that was recovered at the murder scene, had not fitted the defendant's head at the trial. That charge was not new but in the few remaining frantic days of the case, it resurfaced with the impact of a train crash. In the sweltering heat of August 1927, the cap became a metaphor for the entire case: something that had originally appeared convincing until more closely examined.

In England, the *Manchester Guardian* took a slightly different tack, noting that Europeans were appalled at the agonies the prisoners had endured since their arrest in 1920. "Subjection to year after year of alternate hope and despair is a refinement of torture civilization has not yet witnessed since the time of Torquemada, and it is not surprising that the pity, and in some cases the misguided rage, of the world is enlisted in this terrible fight."[50] In Winnipeg, the *Manitoba Free Press* took sharp issue with the

Chicago Tribune, which had recently suggested that foreigners who disagreed with Governor Fuller's decision had no right to seek a new trial or a commutation of sentences. "To foreign onlookers, who have carefully guarded judiciaries of their own, the point of interest in the Sacco-Vanzetti case is the obvious inability of the U.S. Courts to function with authority and efficiency."[51]

Still, as persuasive and eloquent as these editorial arguments were, they almost certainly came too late to have significant impact. By the time the editions containing the editorials reached newsstands, only three days remained until execution night.

It was a waiting game now, and a lucrative one too—executions in the 1920s, like great horse races and prizefights, usually boosted circulation, if only temporarily.

The fact that the executions were an eventuality did not stop the now numerous Sacco-Vanzetti committees and student groups (most were communist affiliated or directed) from working round-the-clock. Nevertheless, the decidedly non-Marxist Sacco-Vanzetti Defense Committee headquarters on Hanover Street was a revolving door of frenetic, nonstop activity. Even at this late date, volunteers still surged through the cramped entrance to be put to work on mimeograph machines or typewriters. Guilt-stricken, off-duty reporters from the *Boston Globe, Boston Post,* and *Boston Herald* proffered their services, making publicity suggestions that had been overlooked by exhausted staff members. All but one of these embattled political constituencies needed each other—anarchist, socialist, labor activist, and liberal.

In the midst of this frantic activity, Katherine Anne Porter reported discovering that the communists no longer had a desire to witness any more eleventh-hour miracles. Porter was not naïve, though; on the contrary, she was a respected intellectual and a well-regarded novelist who would eventually win a Pulitzer Prize. But the realization that she had been used, along with many others, struck her as indecent, a sentiment the communists cavalierly dismissed as bourgeois sentimentalism. As part of their hard-as-nails agenda, a "death-watch" parade was staged in front of the state house in Boston. Here, John Dos Passos was arrested, even though (or because) he had press credentials from the *Daily Worker.* In the last days, though, perhaps the most melodramatic gesture by the Comintern was the use of Luigia Vanzetti, sister of Bartolomeo but really a second-tier stand-in for an ill and elderly Alfred Dreyfus.

Her arrival in New York City, after being detained in France, coincided with the final propaganda push of Willi Münzenberg and James Cannon. Vanzetti was described by dockside reporters as "a quiet little woman in a faded brown traveling cloak, one hand clutching a gold medallion of the Madonna." She could hardly have been more different than her notorious

sibling. A devout Roman Catholic, she had crossed the Atlantic on a personal mission of salvation—to convince Bartolomeo to return to his child-
hood faith before being executed. It was a journey Hollywood screenwriters
could not have exceeded in drama, impact, and, more crucially, timing.
Aldino Felicani, Rosina Sacco, and the famous anarchist Carlo Tresca
greeted Vanzetti at ship-side. All told, 200 people met her, a sizable phalanx
of news media included, as she arrived on the Cunard Line's *Aquitania*.
Photographers popped and newsreel cameras whirred as a trembling, slender, small-boned woman descended the gangplank. Speaking Italian,
Vanzetti told the reporters she only wanted "to see her brother before he
dies." Her one fervent hope was that she would convince him to renounce
atheism and die a reborn Roman Catholic.[52] "I came here to America to see
my brother in the most tragic hour of his life and of terrible suspense to our
family and friends. I came here to bring whatever spirited relief I can, but I
came here with the great hope that this great nation and this great country
in which millions of people have found liberty and happiness will not allow
my brother and Nicola Sacco to die in the electric chair."[53]

Vanzetti's prepared statement, though poignant and sincere, was
eleventh-hour window dressing sponsored by the inflammatory and com-
bative Sacco-Vanzetti Emergency Committee. By now, virtually everyone
at dockside knew this time the executions could not be stopped from being
carried out. Still, it was great political theater, a statement by an ingenuous
victim that gave even the most cynical tabloid reporter sweaty palms and a
racing heartbeat. In fact, Luigia Vanzetti's visit was propaganda *par excellence*. Shortly after arriving, she gave a brief radio address before being
whisked off to Boston to visit her long-departed brother. (Luigia's
attempts at persuading her famous sibling to return to the religious fold
proved unsuccessful.) The next day she addressed a rally, an indescribably
daunting experience for someone who had just days ago left her native
village in Italy. Years later, Katherine Anne Porter recalled a tiny and
intimidated figure speaking to an angry, fist-pumping crowd, thoroughly
terrified by the experience but willing to endure the ordeal to see her
brother a final time.[54] Her appearance partly was arranged to stimulate
sympathy and outrage in the Italian-American community, something that
it largely failed to accomplish. The avowed atheism of her brother and
Sacco did little to help ignite outrage in heavily Roman Catholic and anti-
radical Italian-American communities, or "colonies" as newspapers of the
day described them.

But lacking support from the nation's numerous Little Italys was the
least of it—by now there was little more than a day left. Various U.S.
Supreme Court justices did their best to evade hastily arranged visits from
pleading Sacco-Vanzetti appeals lawyers. Clearly discomfited, Justice
Brandeis declined to hear a request for a stay of execution.[55] (His wife had

been passionately involved with the Sacco-Vanzetti Defense Committee for several years.) Justice Taft, secluded at his summer home in Quebec, also refused involvement, citing the technical disqualification of being on foreign soil. Harlan Stone soon added his name to the list of judicial naysayers and, with that, hope for another stay extinguished like a match in the wind. Acting Attorney General Farnum again insisted the Justice Department had nothing in its files of significance pertaining to Bartolomeo Vanzetti and Nicola Sacco. Speaking in place of his vacationing boss, John G. Sargent, Farnum released a "synopsis" of the thin Sacco-Vanetti file, information culled mostly from field offices in Boston and New York City.[56] He assured reporters that the file only contained "scattered references" to the men—those mostly in connection with an investigation of the Wall Street bombing.

As noted, the file disclosed that a spy had been planted next to Nicola Sacco's cell in Dedham jail. It also revealed, however, that "Massachusetts officials" had asked federal investigators for information on whether or not New York anarchists had received "sudden, large deposits of money" after the 1920 South Braintree murders.[57] Far from clearing the air, though, Farnum's statement only intensified suspicion among Sacco-Vanzetti partisans that the case had been a frame-up from the beginning. A national committee of 300 formed to demand the file's release for public inspection. *New Republic* editor Robert Morss Lovett, University of Wisconsin law professor Alexander Meiklejohn, Stanford University President Emeritus David Starr Jordan, and novelist Zona Gale joined the group.

For the federal government, it was a public relations debacle of the first magnitude. Instead of reassuring skeptics and doubters, a growing number of people wanted to see the contents of the *entire* file. But with a youthful but nonplused Bureau of Information director J. Edgar Hoover tenaciously guarding his files, the request would go unfulfilled.

That the Justice Department did not emphatically refute the conspiracy stories of former Bureau of Investigation agents Letherman and Weyand likely attached undeserved credibility to their accounts. That they were not taken seriously by the Attorney General and had therefore reinforced the Sacco-Vanzetti frame-up thesis cannot be emphasized enough. To make matters worse, Governor Fuller declined the Justice Department's offer to provide his office, or the advisory committee, the Sacco-Vanzetti case files for inspection. Fuller declined to accept the offer, thus passing up a golden counter-propaganda opportunity to dispel the notion that a conspiracy against the anarchists had long been concealed from public view. It was yet another disastrous blunder—one he would come to deeply regret.

The final communist-sponsored rally of the case took place Sunday, August 21. Some 20,000 people were expected to return to crowd Boston Common but police shut the rally down by order of the mayor. The demonstration was then moved to the Scenic Temple on the city's south side, where 1,000 people jammed into the building to hear a series of mostly fiery speeches.[58] After the rally, Luigia Vanzetti and Rosina Sacco left and headed for Charlestown prison. Both Sacco and Vanzetti had just refused the offer of last rites from a Catholic chaplain. Only one day remained. At the state house, the poet Edna St. Vincent Millay met with Governor Fuller. The famous writer, ethereally beautiful with bobbed copper tresses, made quite a contrast to the stuff-shirt sitting stiffly at attention, listening politely, his mind locked in the grip of unassailable executive predetermination. Millay had only recently released a poem she had written about the case, "Justice Denied in Massachusetts."[59] Perhaps with a touch of astringent understatement, a *New York Times* reporter described its tone as "melancholy."

That week, in some instances, the obscure gave way to the absurd. In Washington, D.C., Mrs. Lenora Jones was suspended from her job as a tutor for Capitol pages. News reports said Jones had only recently written to Governor Fuller and offered to take the place of Sacco and Vanzetti on execution night, a request many found extraordinary if not bemusing.[60]

After much experimentation and some misgivings by the major Hollywood studios, sound came to motion pictures to stay in 1927.[61] By then, most Americans were going to local movie theaters several times a week. A popular plot in 1920s gangster pictures was the villain's inevitable death-walk down a long, shadowy corridor to the electric chair. In such movies, the condemned confessed his sins to the obligatory Irish-Catholic priest as he slouched toward eternity, supported by two poker-faced guards, shuffling past the frozen stares of witnesses and the cynical smirks of reporters.

Many in America expected that Sacco and Vanzetti would die much like gangsters in a Hollywood movie. The reality was far more complex, but in some ways life *did* imitate grade B-cinema. For example, there really was an Irish-Catholic priest serving as prison chaplain in Charlestown. And there were many reporters wearing snap-brim hats, chain smoking, waiting for the main event, the political equivalent of the Jack Dempsey-Gene Tunney heavyweight championship fight. The prisoners' heads were shaved, a slit made in one of their trouser legs. They really were served a "special request" last meal and there actually was a direct telephone line hooked up from the governor to the warden's office.

Governor Fuller had been thrust into a dramatic role he had not wanted or welcomed. His state house office became a waiting room for a Whitmanesque assortment of lawyers, celebrities, local politicians, clerics, poets, visiting dignitaries, diplomats, and prominent local citizens seeking commutation for any of a half dozen reasons. On August 22, he heard one last argument for executive clemency from Arthur Hill. By this point, it was strictly a *pro-forma* plea for mercy. The days before the execution were a wild time in Boston, a sort of political Saturnalia—all things status quo turned upside down. Moreover, it was a time that would set the stage and tone for future causes. The last day, August 22, was one that would seep into a multitude of individual memories as one of the most important days of their lives. Another would attach seminal significance to Pearl Harbor Day. A later one would vividly recall the assassination of President Kennedy in 1963. For those in their twenties and thirties in 1927, though, August 22 was a day that would sear their consciences like a branding iron on flesh. For those in Boston, it would never be forgotten, etched into history indelibly and horribly, an American Golgotha of the Jazz Age.

If Boston had been an armed camp in the week prior to execution day, it resembled a small-scale Armageddon on execution day, August 22. Thousands of protesters flooded Boston Common, milling about sweaty, anguished, and politically impotent. The sweltering humidity of a New England August day drenched everyone, intensifying the frustration. An incredulous press watched nervously as the neighborhoods surrounding Charlestown prison were sealed off and encircled by heavily armed contingents of police and plain-clothes detectives.[62] At least 130 demonstrators were arrested—most for nothing more than carrying banners and placards. Police stopped a group of some 300 Sacco-Vanzetti demonstrators from marching to Bunker Hill monument. Mounted state police clopped around on horseback, infuriating the death-watch protesters into feeble shouts and curses and futile backward stumbles. Railroad police and private security swelled the ranks of law enforcement. A police boat patrolled the nearby Charles River. Governor Fuller and Warden William Hendry were determined not to lose the battle of the streets, which they correctly assumed would be controlled by communists. They won handily at the barricades, of course, but the victory came at a terrible price: a loss of moral image and public respect that was not soon restored. It was an expense that no one, least of all Governor Fuller, had reckoned on having to pay.

A common remark about the Sacco-Vanzetti case and the worldwide excitement over it is that interest in it has been wildly exaggerated and influenced by press reports. But if newspapers were to ignore an event which has run round the earth like light, they might as well quit printing. It should clearly be understood that the foreign clamor about a murder trial in Massachusetts is due in part to ignorance of the facts, in part to the eagerness of promoters of social upheaval to capitalize the case for their own destructive purposes. Let it be freely admitted that many radicals, at home as well as abroad, have reached the point where they care nothing about the condemned men except as names to feed and flaunt agitation.[63]

The *New York Times* was largely right—months late in its conclusion but accurate in its analysis. Courtesy of a dying branch of Italian anarchism, the entire experience had eventually become an ideological catapult for international Marxist propaganda. Many Americans, including those at the *Times,* took great offense at the notion of Moscow's ideological foot-soldiers camped out on their courthouse steps making a mockery of justice in major cities throughout the country. Perhaps the oddest thing about it was that a growing number of Americans were equally convinced that the system of justice in this country had failed miserably—in a transparent case of prejudice and local judicial corruption. Sacco-Vanzetti appeals lawyers made eight attempts to stay the executions on August 22. None, of course, succeeded and there was no expectation that they would. At 11 P.M., Governor Fuller told Michael Musmanno he would not stop the executions under any circumstances.[64] Half-way around the world, French communists and various labor organizations made a final plea to American officials in the U.S. Embassy. In Geneva, the mood was ugly—portentously so: A crowd of 5,000 marched through the streets, smashing shop windows owned or operated by Americans. Hotels with large numbers of American tourists attracted a group of angry demonstrators. Theaters showing Hollywood motion pictures, featuring such stars as Douglas Fairbanks and Norma Talmudge, were attacked and the film reels burned in the street. Nevertheless, reaction in Italy was strangely muted. Hope for another eleventh-hour reprieve had not yet entirely evaporated. *Il Tevere,* though, sensed that this time there would be no last-minute miracle: "Agitation, terroristic protests and pressures of all kinds have done nothing but strengthen the U.S. in its position of obdurate and blind resistance."[65] *Papolo di Roma* was somewhat more sanguine: "We believe that in the supreme moment when a decision must be taken the virile courage which defies the opinion of the whole world will give the judges the strength to be weak."[66] Nearer Massachusetts, the *St. Louis Post-Dispatch* assured the governor that executive clemency "would be construed as an act of moral courage."[67] Sacco and Vanzetti and Celestino Medieros once again were prepared for execution. Luigia Vanzetti and Rosina Sacco were allowed three final visits on August 22, the last coming in the early evening. Tearful good-byes were exchanged in front of self-conscious guards.

Boston Common was a roiling mass of youthful humanity; many bore placards and banners as they marched. An armband with stark crimson lettering suddenly was omnipresent that day: "Never Forget: Justice Crucified, Aug. 22, 1927." Luigia Vanzetti and Rosina Sacco also spent an extremely tense hour-and-a-half with Governor Fuller. Newspapers described Vanzetti beseeching the overwhelmed American governor in Italian for her brother's life. Concluding her plea, she asserted that Fuller's name "would be blessed" if he spared the men's lives. The governor patiently listened and then explained that he could not act because his duties "were outlined by the law."[68] Even before that extraordinary final meeting, Fuller had met with Arthur Garfield Hays, Francis Fisher Kane, and Frank P. Walsh, all attorneys from the Citizens' National Committee for Sacco-Vanzetti. The group requested that the governor grant a reprieve until the Justice Department's file on the case could be thoroughly examined. Annoyed and somewhat rattled, Fuller declined to bow to international pressure, instead sticking to his decision and the considered judgment of the advisory committee.

Outside Charlestown prison, a searchlight swept crowds of the curious, some of whom had taken to apartment rooftops for a better view of the unfolding scene below. Strategic cordoning of the neighboring streets by local law enforcement had cut off any chance of a coordinated demonstration. Inside, one hundred reporters waited in a pressroom crammed with dozens of telephones hastily installed for the occasion. Western Union and Postal Telegraph had put in eighteen telegraph wires—four linked directly overseas. Only one journalist was allowed in the death chamber, the improbably named Associated Press reporter W. E. Playfair. In a 1952 newspaper article, Playfair recalled that the most disturbed person in the death chamber that night was Warden Hendry.[69] The first execution began at just after midnight: It was now August 23, technically past the execution date. Medeiros was the first to be led to the execution chamber. A small-time professional criminal, he lived his last hours indulging the final rite of a death-chamber convict: gorging on a specially prepared gourmet meal. Next, Nicola Sacco was put to death. His last words were: "Farewell my wife, my child, and all my friends! Good evening, gentlemen. Farewell, mother." Then, finally in perhaps the most plaintive words of the entire case: "Vive l'anarchia!"

Playfair described the scene in words redolent of 1920s tabloid jazz journalism: "Bing, they stepped on the juice."[70] Bartolomeo Vanzetti was the last to be executed. Popular with the staff and inmates at Charlestown, he graciously shook hands with a tearful Hendry. Vanzetti then made a remarkable statement, one seemingly at odds with the psychological outlook of a guilty man about to be dispatched to eternity: "I wish to forgive some people for what they are now doing to me."[71]

After Vanzetti was declared dead, news about the executions flashed around the world in a matter of hours. In Boston, the Sacco-Vanzetti headquarters closed and its volunteers, some of whom had given six years of their lives to the movement, walked the streets in solitude seeking respite from the crushing burden of failure and grief. Demonstrators in Boston Common and in New York City's Union Square—and in plazas and squares across the country—tidily piled their placards and banners after news of the executions spread. It was as if the pressure had been let out of a huge hot-air balloon. Those that had journeyed to Boston left quickly: Many had run out of both time and money. The city returned to a relative degree of normalcy and its business leaders and city officials could not say often enough how good it felt. The *Boston Herald* actively encouraged this sentiment: "Let us get back to the business and the ordinary concerns of life in the confident belief that the agencies of law have performed their duties with fairness, as well as justice."[72] The *Herald* also pointedly urged that New England retain its "present system of government and existing social order."

It was an editorial example of the minister preaching to the choir. Elsewhere, sentiment ranged from calculated outrage to considered neutrality. The *Cleveland Press* said the executions were a "grievous mistake and a tragic one."[73] The *Chicago Daily News* insisted that "the apostles of world revolution" had seized upon the sincere protest of non-radicals in order to subvert American justice."[74] The *Minneapolis Tribune* decried a "world-wide campaign of violence and intimidation intended to influence the actions of jurists and Governor Fuller."[75] Despite its extensive editorial campaign to have the death sentences commuted, the *New York World* seemed inclined to view Fuller's decision in the most generous light possible but it still felt vaguely troubled: "We may have witnessed a great miscarriage of justice."[76] The *Baltimore Sun* argued that the "world-wide cry of protest" was based on propaganda stoked by blind sentiment.[77] The *Brooklyn Daily Eagle* noted a fact that would pointedly intrude (and embarrass) for years to come: "There has been no review of the evidence in the case by the Massachusetts Supreme Court. The court was only concerned with the legal powers of Judge Webster Thayer to rule as he did."[78] Sounding at least a trifle credulous, the *New York Times* concluded that it had witnessed "consoling proof that a love of justice is still a powerful motive in this country."[79] The *Times* said it was convinced that the case arose out of sincere doubt that was eventually used in the service of "social revolution." The *Milwaukee Journal* asserted that Massachusetts had gotten into trouble not because of anarchism or communism but because "its legal procedure is a hundred years behind the times," and that its trial judges "handed out the death penalty too readily."[80] The *Boston Evening Transcript* described the case as a political photographic negative: a reverse image of the usual trend in American political causes cèlébre. "Massachusetts has narrowly escaped a lynching . . . That it was the community, and not the individual that was to be lynched, in no wise effects the principle of the case."[81]

The radical-minded *Daily Worker* was even more definite in its judgment, which suggested Armageddon: "Sacco and Vanzetti have been murdered. The lifeless bloody bodies of two brave men have been thrown at the feet of the working class, whose companions they were."[82] The *Worker,* however, seized the movement of tragedy to attack the American Federation of Labor and the socialists for betraying Sacco and Vanzetti in their time of need. Writing in the communist newspaper, John Dos Passos interpreted the executions as a violent harbinger of a terrible and swiftly approaching ideological catharsis: the dawn of a Marxist-inspired American revolution. "Sacco and Vanzetti died tonight. The trembling hand of an old man reached for the switch that threw the current of hate, terror and dark into the bodies of two great men, who went to their death with their eyes open to a new sun rising over a festered world. The government lynchers in their silk hats and in their comfortable swivel chairs at their mahogany desks are afraid of the crime they scarcely dared commit. Beyond the horizon, they hear the rumble of marching feet. They know that they are dead stinking corpses, and that Sacco and Vanzetti, whom they kill, are alive—a million men marching on Boston under a fiery sun of the future."[83]

More than any other American intellectual, Dos Passos had taken on the Sacco-Vanzetti case as his crusade. Although he may have suspected even then that Sacco was somehow involved in the crimes for which he was executed, Dos Passos sincerely believed both men had not received fair trials. Many Americans came to agree with him, both within and outside the radical community. In the months following the executions, some in Massachusetts began to develop a posthumous case of guilty conscience. The anarchists had been executed on the basis of evidence that, at least in some states, would not even have drawn a life sentence. Further, the trial judge had been allowed to rule on an appeal alleging his own prejudice. Several major doubts about the case would not be physically eliminated by the electric chair. Alvan Tufts Fuller and his advisors had calculated that in time, concern about whether or not justice in the case had been properly served would dissipate. That proved a spectacularly disastrous assumption: Sacco-Vanzetti would be one of the most remembered, and debated, of all twentieth-century causes célébres.

Predictably, reaction in European nations to the executions was far more hostile than in the United States. In Paris 10,000 demonstrators, some of them from organized gangs of petty criminals, surged through streets and boulevards, overturning café tables and smashing newspaper kiosks to help erect barricades.[84] American tourists in popular nightclubs and brassieres found themselves caught in pitched battles with street fighters. Police and mounted Republican guards protected the American Legion convention, then an annual affair in Paris. In London, there was far less violence but nearly as much outrage, as several thousand streamed through the streets to attend a memorial service at Hyde Park. In Geneva, police used fire hoses to beat back mobs of demonstrators.[85] Shops and stores that sold American goods in various European countries were trashed. Protests and disturbances also were reported in South Africa, Australia, and Portugal.

Hamstrung by Mussolini, the Italian press seemingly reacted more in sadness than anger. Nevertheless, the fascist daily *Il Tevere* blamed the judicial system in the United States.[86] The papal *Osservatore Romano* deplored the idea that Governor Fuller had put "prestige and political decorum" above "right and justice."[87] Rome's *Gironale d'Italia* charged that "this horrible martyrdom is unprecedented in the history of nations." The French press, however, was surprisingly restrained in its commentary.

For example, the *Journal des Debats* scolded the rioters who had ransacked cabarets and nightclubs, menacing patrons and waiters at places such as the *Moulin Rouge.* "One of the most regrettable aspects of the whole sad affair is that the recent agitation contributed to make more inflexible than ever the American judges."[88] *Liberté* seemed to agree, blaming a radical-led campaign that was not so much for Sacco and Vanzetti as it was against American influence and power. "It was they who slowly but surely pushed Sacco and Vanzetti into the electric chair."[89] The Communist daily *L'Humanité* could not have disagreed more. "Class justice has killed Sacco and Vanzetti because they were militant workers, because they were innocent, because the whole world protested, because the dollar is infallible."[90]

In Germany, public opinion was equally divided. The *Morgen Post* noted that the Russian Cheka (state secret police) would have executed "scores" of suspects in such a case without the world ever knowing anything about the affair.[91] The nationalist newspaper *Deutsche Zeitung Tageszeitung* said the state of Massachusetts had refused to "yield to the mob."[92] In Austria, the *Vienna Tagblatt* charged that a "miscarriage of justice had doomed the anarchists."[93]

In London, the *Daily Herald* pointed to the "irreparable harm" done the prestige of the United States throughout Europe. On the other hand, the *Morning Post* editorially defended Governor Fuller in the same tones as many American newspapers. "It is the irony of fate that a procedure that is dilatory from humanitarian motives, and from the determination that no innocent man shall suffer capital punishment can be converted into a slow method of torture."[94] The *Westminster Gazette* noted that seven years of imprisonment and suffering had earned the condemned men grounds for a reprieve.[95]

The funeral for Sacco and Vanzetti began respectably enough but eventually degenerated into a nasty brawl, embarrassing to almost everyone except those involved in the ugly incident. Boston police and city officials had been inveigled into allowing a relatively unrestrained, maudlin, and thoroughly politicized farewell. Sacco and Vanzetti were laid out at Langone Funeral Home in the North End. Their bodies were available for public viewing for three days. Dressed in blue serge suits, white shirts, and figured ties, the two principals of the seven-year political affair of the century appeared less like modern history's most renowned anarchists and more like nondescript shopkeepers who had died young. Most who came to view their bodies had never known or even met in passing Sacco and Vanzetti. Outside, near the funeral home, street vendors sold hot dogs and balloons to neighborhood children and a smattering of curious adults.[96]

The Sacco-Vanzetti Defense Committee kept a fairly tight lid on events until Sunday, the day of the burial. But during the plodding, cross-town funeral procession, protesters frequently clashed with police, hurling

stones and bricks indiscriminately at the conveniently numerous blue uniforms. Along the route of the funeral march, two flower-strewn, horse-
drawn hearses led the way. A cool autumnal day with rolling banks of fog
lent a suitably depressing backdrop. A crowd estimated at 200,000 people
turned out along the twisting, eight-mile, police-approved route, which
stretched from North End Park to Forest Hills Cemetery. Order frequently
broke down along the way. At one point in the procession, mounted police
charged the crowd. Socialists, communists, and anarchists united in street
fighting against the ranks of local law enforcement. By just about any measure of social conscience, it was a disgraceful sight, but thoughts of propri-
ety or respectful deportment were lost that morning in the frenetic shuffle
of unfolding events.

At the funeral chapel there was only one speaker, Mary Donovan. She
delivered the eulogy, describing the executions as "one of the blackest
crimes in the history of mankind."[97] Speaking in a shrill tone of voice
choked with anger, Donovan described Sacco and Vanzetti as victims of
"the crassest plutocracy the world has known since ancient Rome."

After the service, the bodies were cremated.

The total importance of the Sacco-Vanzetti case would not be obvious
for several years. Nevertheless, it ranks as the most enduring cause cèlébre
of the twentieth century, perhaps even greater in impact than the Scottsboro Boys case of the 1930s or the Rosenberg spy case of the 1950s. Still,
in 1927 no one outside of the inner circles of the Comintern even knew
who Münzenberg was. Stalin was well aware of his campaign and was sufficiently impressed to make a fatuous remark about the Sacco and Vanzetti
case proving America was in a state of pre-Revolutionary ferment. While
the Sacco-Vanzetti case would never succeed in bringing America even a
millimeter closer to political revolution and class warfare, it did, however,
irreparably tarnish its image as a just republic that had helped make the
world safe for democracy less than a decade earlier. Its *zeitgeist* had seemingly been altered overnight: The ugly American, a spectral and revolting
image of unfettered insensitivity and arrogance, was born on the back of
this extraordinary, misbegotten case of small-town robbery and murder. It
would not disappear, but, rather, like the Dreyfus case, would gain enduring international stature and political impetus among two generations of
journalists, historians, scholars, college students, and radicals. In this view,
the mythology of America the Beautiful had been exposed as a fraud to a
world now linked by radio and newsreel, a clever political forgery worthy
of the diabolical intrigues of European monarchies. Instead of a nation of
tireless seekers of truth and a beacon for the dispossessed and persecuted,
it was now cast as a misguided continent of bigots and xenophobes, intol-
erant of critics and quite anxious to conceal injustice within the subter-
ranean corridors of a corrupt judiciary and dysfunctional executive
branch. It was a powerful, alluring explanation of a highly complex case

that contained just enough truth to make a conspiracy seem not only possible but also quite likely.

Willi Münzenberg had done a superb job of coordinating the various demonstrations worldwide. In Europe, especially, communists had ample help from their nominal and forsworn ideological enemies: anarchists, socialists, intellectuals, and liberals. The campaign was truly the first linked, global, anti-American campaign of the twentieth century. The fact that it had succeeded against such long odds would not be lost on the Comintern, or its allies, in the years to come. Oddly, though, in America, despite its labors, the Communist Party had derived only the scarcest tangible political benefit from Sacco-Vanzetti. The forced rapprochement between the party in the United States and various radical and liberal constituencies quickly disintegrated after the raucous funeral.[98]

James Cannon would continue to lead the IDL but would eventually be expelled from the party for reasons unrelated to the case. Münzenberg would direct and coordinate another international cause cèlébre, the Scottsboro Boys case, but eventually he would perish in one of Stalin's innumerable purges, a victim of either suicide or execution, depending on one's view. That Americans did not, or refused to, understand the furious undertow of political crosscurrents associated with the case was made clear by *Time* magazine. In it its first and only coverage of the case in its August 28, 1927, issue, the newsmagazine concluded both men died for a "communistic order of mankind."[99]

In fact, Sacco and Vanzetti privately distrusted the international movement conducted in their names. It was a huge compromise for militant anarchists like the Italian Galleanisti in the United States to get into bed with communists and other groups they viewed as ideologically antithetical, if not avowedly hostile to their existence. Viewed from this perspective, it is one of the corkscrew ironies of twentieth-century global causes and movements that Sacco-Vanzetti happened at all. But, then, nowhere else but in the United States could such an obscure, far-fetched propaganda campaign to save two radicals succeed in rousing the wrath and outrage of much of the world's literate population.

Epilogue

23 Agosto 1927
Nicola Sacco   Bartolomeo Vanzetti
Anarchici Innocenti
ASSASSINATI
—*From a fading wall poster commemorating the 75th anniversary of
the executions of Sacco and Vanzetti spotted by the author in
a side street in Florence, Italy, in October 2003*

At the funeral, Mary Donovan described the legacy of Sacco and Vanzetti as a betrayal, a peculiarly tragic American loss of innocence. That Miltonian sentiment—poignant, bitter, cerebral—fitted into the liberal, rather one-dimensional paradigm that defined the case for sixty years. In a way that Donovan could not have realized, arguably Sacco-Vanzetti was more about loss of another type of innocence: manipulation of the news media, various government agencies, and a sometimes credulous public.

Willi Münzenberg could not have asked for a better historical denouement. Nevertheless, from his office in Berlin, the undersized but vibrant propaganda chief could take considerable pride from an international cause that would burn in the minds of the righteously outraged and guilt-stricken for decades. Almost everything went right: the historical timing of the trial, the issue of radicalism gratuitously injected into the transcript, the defense lawyer with his connections to anarchist and labor movements, and the worldwide ascendancy of various radical movements, including those combustibly fratricidal enemies communism, socialism, and syndicalism. Arguably, it was better than good—it was positively made-to-order for the exigencies of modern international propaganda. The only sticking point for Münzenberg and the Comintern was that Sacco and Vanzetti were anarchists. As such, both unquestionably were implacable ideological enemies of the revolution. That took some time and effort to get around, which goes some way to explain why the case was not fully supported by Moscow until late 1926. But by then, Stalin had made that ostensibly flippant comment about America being in a pre-revolutionary stage seemingly triggered by Sacco-Vanzetti. (As he said that, anarchists in the Soviet Union had already been imprisoned and executed for at least several years.)

In the United States by 1927 almost everyone (excepting the rival communist-controlled defense committees) wanted to save the Italians. That developed into a complicating factor that was overcome by the aid of American provincialism, an antiquated state judiciary, and an ambitious governor seemingly committed to a time-honored tradition of presidential nomination: refusing condemned prisoners' requests for executive clemency. (Fuller, though, really did believe in the death penalty and had written a magazine article detailing his convictions on the subject.)

The vast majority of Americans involved in the Sacco-Vanzetti movement were sincere in their words and deeds. Still, they were mostly unwitting pawns in an international board game that assumed that the lives of the two principals were worth far more dead than alive. It was a shattering reckoning for some—many others did not see the connection or ignored its obviousness. Mary Donovan was right, likely in a way *she* had not intended—the Republic had lost its innocence and not without a steep price.

Sometime in 1924, Fred Moore said he learned that one of his clients was definitely guilty and the other possibly guilty. Others allegedly also knew the truth but remained silent for a variety of reasons, not the least of which was an ancient Mediterranean code of honor and silence. Many, including newspaper editorial writers, assumed the case would soon dissolve into the margins of historical obscurity. They could not have been more wrong. In 1927, the British author and syndicated columnist H. G. Wells assumed the case would not depart from the collective consciousness anytime soon. In a *New York Times* column, Wells outlined the reasons for his anger with America's handling of Sacco-Vanzetti. Essentially, Wells thought that from a moral perspective, the United States had badly let the world down. It had become a pariah not because it had falsely convicted two obscure radicals but because it would not admit to having made a tragic mistake. To him, and to many others as well, it was the height of conceit—being conscienceless was far worse than committing any sin of commission.

The question of whether these two Italians were guilty or innocent I made a secondary matter . . . for six years I had heard vaguely about it but had left it alone. It only had been recently that I had been aroused to the realization that it is a case like the Dreyfus case by which the soul of a people is tested and displayed . . . the communist movement had seized upon this trial and made it an occasion for demonstrations and outrages throughout the world. The favorite role of the extreme Red always seems to be that of agent provocateur for reaction. The extreme Red is the curse of creative liberalism. But the misbehavior of excited crowds here and there has nothing to do with the essential offense of the case . . . Europe is not "retrying" Sacco-Vanzetti or anything else. It is saying what it thinks of Judge Thayer. Executing political opponents as political opponents after the fashion of Mussolini or Moscow we can understand, or bandits as bandits but this business of trying and executing murderers as Reds or Reds as murderers seems to be a new and very frightening line for the court of a state in the most powerful and civilized union on earth to pursue.[1]

The title of Wells's column in 1927 was "The Way the World Is Going." If anything, he understood the way the world interpreted the Sacco-Vanzetti case only too well. Wells's latest article on the case had been written and submitted for publication before the executions had occurred. At that time, the editors of the *Times* had declined to publish it. To them, it was the history of the case written small: doing the right thing for the wrong reasons or the wrong thing for the right reasons, nobody quite seemed sure at that point. Nevertheless, the effect of his column was less than salutary for the now-penitent *Times*. It appeared that the nation's most respected newspaper had temporarily censored a powerful critic and then tacitly admitted its own wrongdoing after the fact. Wells smelled like a rose all the way from London, courtesy of American editorial hypocrisy.

It was a brutal lesson in the new post-war propaganda: the engineering of consent anchored by stark cultural symbolism and driven by powerful political imagery. A 4,000-word, meticulously researched and persuasively written article in the *Times* sank into irrelevance in contrast to a simple pen-and-ink poster of two men strapped into an electric chair. A two-sentence press release from an American ambassador faded from memory after hearing a venerable French novelist invoke the name of Alfred Dreyfus. It was as if the terms of the case, steeped in international political tensions, had been rearranged as classical tragedy rendered in strained and, sometimes even farcical, tones. Once launched there was no returning or diverting to another cause or case.

Propaganda had made the Sacco-Vanzetti case almost from start to finish. Fred Moore had played an instrumental role in launching the worldwide campaign to save Sacco and Vanzetti. Moore was shrewd enough to realize that both the art and science of propaganda had changed since the end of the World War. Technology had made life easier for transmitting and staging publicity campaigns, but a new, subtler form of manipulation had emerged in the 1920s: simple, politically sensitive, selectively dishonest, and yet without countervailing information almost impossible to refute. It was a subtle but ingenious refinement of the methodology that had given a huge black eye to the word "propaganda" during World War I. It would later be applied to other cases and causes with varying degrees of success. But the calculus of propaganda in Sacco-Vanzetti, the relatively simple argument of conspiracy and persecution, would set the stage for causes cèlébres for the remainder of the century.

The memory of Nicola Sacco and Bartolomeo Vanzetti did not fade from public memory as many had hoped. Indeed, their legacy endured, calcifying into a hybrid of documentary record and political myth that more than eighty years later is impossible to disentangle. The obvious defects of the Massachusetts state judiciary and the sometimes politically naïve behavior of a well-intentioned committee offered experimental opportunities in North America for international Marxist propaganda—or, rather, for international control of a propaganda campaign that initially was started by a politically heterogeneous cast of far less manipulative and more sincere political actors.

Münzenberg could not have planned any better the final six months of Nicola Sacco's and Bartolomeo Vanzetti's lives. More to the point: He could not have written the epitaph of the two most famous Galleanisti any more dramatically than it unfolded in the United States. The case of the shoemaker and the fisherman quickly became a cautionary political parable about intolerance and bigotry. It was a story that brought tears to high school and college students as they read of the persecution of philosophical anarchists in the *Dictionary of American Biography,* the *Encyclopedia Americana,* or the *Encyclopedia Britannica.* It was the case that launched 10,000 research papers, many coming in the 1960s and 1970s. It was the one cause that radicals and liberals of two very different generations could wholeheartedly agree upon.

After the funeral procession ended, most American newspapers quickly filed the case away, and not with a feeling of considerable relief. International indignation and outrage had been considerable; indeed, at the end, perhaps even greater than during the Dreyfus case. America had wakened with a dreadful hangover and a gargoyle's face the morning after the executions and no amount of editorializing or explanation would soon return it to normalcy. Indeed, the fact that the case had never been a "federal" one kept if from counter-propaganda possibilities that the State Department might have provided. As it was, many federal officials and elected representatives, including President Coolidge, could only sit and watch the case with a mixture of horror and astonishment. Former President, and then current U.S. Supreme Court Justice William Howard Taft, was infuriated with the conduct of Felix Frankfurter. In a letter to Robert Grant (of Governor Fuller's Advisory Committee), Taft vented his spleen in no uncertain terms.

"It is remarkable how (Frankfurter) with his article was able to present so large a body of readers a perverted view of the facts and then through the worldwide conspiracy of communism spread to many, many countries. Our law schools lent themselves to this vicious propaganda."[2]

Many reacted as Taft did but refrained from making public statements or sending off letters to the editor. It was felt, especially in Massachusetts, that further debate would only inflame an already unfortunate situation. If the victor writes the first draft of history, then the Sacco-Vanzetti case appears to have been an instance where the Commonwealth deferred and lost the war of propaganda—the endless and often extraordinary struggle of words, symbols, and images.

William Howard Taft's anger with Felix Frankfurter was a little like a tree falling in the midst of a desolate forest. Next to no one found out about the former president's pique at the Harvard law professor. Nevertheless, Frankfurter's reputation soared; he eventually became an associate U.S. Supreme Court justice and was considered a leading light in liberal American jurisprudence for three decades. He was, however, remembered and revered for his brief but extraordinarily effective contribution to the Sacco-Vanzetti movement. Frankfurter and the many lawyers, scholars, and law school faculty and students that he brought to the case saw to it that the agonizing (and largely stage-managed) final days of the anarchists would not soon be forgotten. Frankfurter's *Atlantic Monthly* article was expanded into a book that was published in 1927.[3] His wife also co-edited a book of selectively edited letters of Sacco and Vanzetti that appeared in 1928.[4] Perhaps more than anything else written about the case, those books shaped the public's image of the case until the early 1960s when Francis Russell's controversial and disputed *Tragedy in Dedham* appeared. In 1928, though, the Sacco-Vanzetti case was just getting its second wind.

> Most murder cases come to an end.
> But as a force in human life the
> case of these two Italians will continue
> for a long time to come.
> —*The Outlook, August 1927*

These prophetic words, written shortly after the executions in 1927, if anything became only too true. Oddly, this long-forgotten news digest magazine placed the executions in a perspective that newspapers and periodicals missed or ignored. "Anarchists and communists and other so-called radicals found common agreement in accepting these two men as symbols of their hostility to the social order. And now that these two men have forfeited their lives for the crime of which they were convicted they will find places in the pantheon of social revolution. With those who worship there it is useless to argue. They rest their case not on reason but on revolution as an object of faith. There are many others, however, whose emotions have been stirred by this case because of their humanitarian interests. Some of these may think of these two executed men as many today think of John Brown—fanatics, perhaps, but victims of a callous and unimaginative social and legal system. Such as these cannot find their emotions easily restored to the normal state."[5]

Perhaps of the thousands of gallons of ink spilled in arguing the Sacco-Vanzetti case, these words go furthest in explaining why it tripped the light-fantastic of an international cause cèlébre. Yet, people were not interested alone in the answer to just one question. They also wanted the answers to many other questions: Why did Governor Fuller let the executions proceed with so many doubts raised about the guilt of the condemned men? Why did Harvard University President Lowell change the wording of the committee's initial draft regarding Vanzetti? Had Frederick Katzmann really made a bribe offer to the defense? Did the Justice Department and the state of Massachusetts conspire to frame Sacco and Vanzetti? Questions such as these would not disappear—indeed, they would arise again and again. The *New Republic* and the *Nation* persisted in analyzing the case from a number of different perspectives. The *New Republic* referred to the case as a "tragedy" two weeks after the executions. The author of a September 1927 article surmised that a grisly end to a torturously confusing case suggested there might be something the Commonwealth did not want to expose to the light of day. Nevertheless, the author was not optimistic about chances of keeping the flame of the cause burning:

If they are not ashamed of what they have done they are certainly uneasy about it. Once they have put an end to the victims they would like also to put an end to the grievance and to the controversy. In cultivating forgetfulness they are, of course, aided by the intrinsic difficulty of keeping the dead alive. Living human beings find it far from easy to remain vividly interested in the affairs of the dead—even though the dead have died in a cause which lives; in that event it is the cause that is kept green rather than the body and spirit of its martyrs. Such is the burden of the great funeral orations of the honored dead, from Pericles to Lincoln. If Sacco and Vanzetti died for a cause (which we doubt) there will be a difference of opinion about what that cause is. Their comrades in anarchy will, of course, do their best to apotheosize them as victims of a ruthless and deliberate class conspiracy; and if the victims themselves in the moments of their last agony cherished a hope, it was that their own blood and the tears of their friends might give abundant nourishment to the cause of anarchy . . . It is equally improbable, though highly desirable that the defense committee will ever be able to establish irrefutably the innocence of Sacco and Vanzetti, and such proof, even if it were forthcoming, would emphasize the tragedy rather than extenuate it.[6]

Katherine Anne Porter established long ago that the far-leftist radical community in America had little or no interest in saving Sacco and

Vanzetti. Communists and anarchists, operating apart and with distinctly separate political agendas, loathed and reviled each other, communicating, when they did, in spasmodic outbursts of mutual hostility and distrust. For the anarchists, the entire seven-year-long episode eventuated into a harsh lesson in the law of unintended consequences. Although they had long held their meetings and rallies in public, Galleanisti operations usually took place in the shadows or in the dead of night. That changed after the police arrested Sacco and Vanzetti and they formed a committee to defend their comrades. The seemingly simple act of closing ranks forced them into a spotlight that was antithetical to their unsubtle *raison d'être*: "health is in you." It was a contradiction in terms the anarchists never quite resolved or figured how to circumvent. On the other hand, the communists undertook their behind-the-scene spoiler role with the single-minded zeal of missionaries in an unexplored wilderness. They also had managed to reap a fertile and enduring propaganda harvest, at the very least for a time in Europe.

In this crucible of competing interests and ferocious ideological crosscurrents, perhaps the least surprising element to emerge was the near complete lack of cooperation and coordination between radical and liberal constituencies in the United States. Perhaps the most surprising thing was the success of many liberals, largely in America, in cobbling together a formidable, if briefly lived, coalition dedicated to keeping Sacco and Vanzetti alive. The chance of saving the anarchists' lives had been calculated as low even by their most sanguine patrons and supporters. When the switch was finally thrown on them, the liberal community disbanded almost immediately and withdrew into a lengthy hibernation. As historian Daniel Aaron notes, the Sacco-Vanzetti case had the unintended effect of disenfranchising liberal solidarity in the United States for many years.[7] It would be a long time before liberals, artists, and intellectuals would again join forces in a political movement. Never again would a cause cèlébre sap a single ideological group of its vitality the way the Sacco-Vanzetti case had in the United States.

But many beyond those who tried to save Sacco and Vanzetti came to think that a grave injustice had been committed—as do a good many today. Others were just as convinced the affair amounted to nothing more than the convergence of political opportunism and blanket social protest. In the wake of the executions, *Time* magazine published the plea of a Philadelphian, John Trimble: "For God sake do not canonize two saints for future generations of Reds."[8]

For its part, the *New Republic* blamed the nearly forgotten and long-dismissed Sacco-Vanzetti jury. The public opinion journal said that the panel had been prejudiced against the defendants before the trial even began. Now the United States would have to absorb the "horror and censure of the world."[9] That was not true. Many Americans felt they still did not have to accept anything that came from across the ocean anymore.

These people thought, if nothing else, the process was now reversed, with Europe waiting for direction from its now fabulously prosperous old colonies. Relatively few in the United States in 1927 were willing to listen to advice or take admonishment about the case. The whole matter was filed away under a collective "best soon forgotten." All but a handful of opinion journals and a Sacco-Vanzetti memorial committee dutifully followed that line. Edna St. Vincent Millay cogently summarized the moral conflict in a December 1927 essay in the *Outlook* magazine. St. Vincent Millay had been the *ex officio* poet laureate of the movement. The executions had scarred her soul and badly shaken her faith in American political and legal institutions. Devoid of bitterness, she nonetheless reminded the conscience-stricken that the ghosts of two honest men could not be swept under the carpet as easily as dust. "For you long to return to your gracious world of a year ago, where people had pretty manners and did not raise their voices, where people whom you know, whom you entertained in your houses, did not shout and walk the streets vulgarly carrying banners, because two quite inconsequential people, two men who could not even speak good English, were about to be put forever out of mischief's way. Do let us forget, you say: after all what does it matter?"[10]

More elegiac than remonstrative, St. Vincent Millay's words nonetheless summarized the experiences of most liberals as well as various radicals. Some day, the truth would emerge and on that day there would be a terrible reckoning worthy of an Old Testament parable. Most of those on the defense committee had kept the faith for years and would continue to do so. Gardner Jackson made sure that the committee bulletin continued. A magazine called the *Lantern* also published articles on the case.[11] There were periodic references to it in the opinion journals and books. The *New York Times* finally ran H. G. Wells's *lese majesty* essay on the case in mid-October 1927. For a several months it was as if everyone had agreed to silence, to simply forget. Gradually, painful reminders surfaced that Bartolomeo Vanzetti and Nicola Sacco went to their deaths asserting their innocence. The magazine *Survey* published an article by *New York Times* labor reporter Louis Stark. Author of a 1922 series on the Sacco-Vanzetti case, Stark put a telescope on the doubts surrounding the guilt of the anarchists.[12] He also unburdened his conscience about Harvard President Lowell's refusal to release the minutes of the advisory committee's investigation of the case to the press. Lowell, of course, feared that the press would sensationalize the findings favorable to the defense and that they then would become so much grist for the communist propaganda mill.

Stark referred to Boston in the weeks prior to the executions as "a vast whispering gallery."[13] The most persistent rumors that swept through restaurants and newspaper offices "were that Sacco and Vanzetti could not have committed the South Braintree crimes." Stark pointed to the hypothesis of former Bureau of Information agents Letherman and Weyand that "professional highwaymen" committed the crime. This, of course, reinforced the Morelli gang theory of Herbert Ehrmann *cum* Celestino Medieros. Stark's point was that Bartolomeo Vanzetti and Nicola Sacco had been victims of bias three times: before a jury, before the advisory committee, and then before Governor Fuller. Such was not completely the case, at least in each instance, but the appearance and inevitability of conspiracy would persist for more than half a century.

In the final months of the case, Governor Fuller and Harvard University's President Lowell plainly distrusted the press. Trial prosecutor Frederick Katzmann and Judge Thayer had been suspicious of the press for years. Much has been made of the fact that many newspaper reporters knew of the prosecution's collaboration with the Justice Department in the Sacco-Vanzetti case. News media scholar Ben Bagdikian has asserted that journalists of the 1920s had failed to act as a "balance wheel" in not speaking out on behalf of the Italian anarchists.[14] Perhaps. While this criticism is true to a point, it also fails to distinguish between what reporters suspected and what they really knew. Indeed, no reporter wrote of a conspiracy between the Justice Department and Katzmann because none could identify one. Katzmann had asked the Justice Department for information on Sacco and Vanzetti but that was the documented extent of the collaboration. While Katzmann may have acted deplorably as a prosecutor, nonetheless, there is no extant historical evidence indicating his involvement in a plot to frame Sacco and Vanzetti.

Judge Thayer's and Katzmann's actions and words during and after the trial were arguably more than enough to warrant the suspects a new trial. That was the issue that caused such angst among reporters who followed the case. But nothing could be published about either Katzmann's or Thayer's judicial and extra-judicial conduct. Everything that reporters learned had reached their ears second- or third-hand and could not be reliably confirmed. Like Captain Dreyfus, Sacco and Vanzetti almost certainly deserved a second trial. Unlike Dreyfus, though, both men had declined to reveal the full truth of their experiences, whatever they might have been. Likely very few reporters who covered the trial thought Sacco and Vanzetti totally innocent. Most, of course, knew by then that at the least both had had links for years to the Galleanisti. Many did consider them victims of a biased judge and jury. The number of journalists who thought them victims of prejudice increased dramatically by Spring 1927 but, then again, by then many in the general population were thinking the same thing. Most reporters were not even remotely familiar with details of the case or the trial beyond what meager clip-files could provide. Reporters declined to write about their opinions of the case because of professional and ethical considerations and because their editors were well aware of the more stringent libel laws of the time. While discussing their experiences covering the case, a number of Boston reporters gave colleagues the unmistakable impression that Judge Thayer, Governor Fuller, and the Lowell Committee had all realized for some time that Sacco and Vanzetti were innocent. Such was not the case, but the powerful propaganda of 1926 and 1927 had inflated several poor political judgments in Massachusetts into a sustained mythology of conspiracy that, at least on the surface, seemed only too well to fit the facts of the case. Even if you felt Sacco and Vanzetti were guilty as charged, their trial, to many Americans, appeared as a terrible stain on judicial history. In November 1927, sociologist John Dewey addressed this issue in a *New Republic* article, "Psychology and Justice."[15] Dewey analyzed, in part, the action of the advisory committee on the basis of class distinctions and suggested its members had cast a blind eye to evidence strongly suggesting the trial had been less than scrupulously fair.

The February 1928 *Atlantic Monthly* published William G. Thompson's recollection of his final conversation with his clients. Most of that talk, conducted at Charlestown state prison, was with an animated Bartolomeo Vanzetti.[16] He reassured Thompson that both he and Sacco were innocent. (Vanzetti also said he was innocent of the Bridgewater robbery conviction.) Thompson asked Vanzetti to issue a statement discouraging displays of public violence after his death. Vanzetti would not issue such "sweeping advice," although he noted that he personally opposed violence against women and children.

It was tacit acknowledgment that both men were members of a militant radical organization and not necessarily the mythopoeic coffeehouse radicals their defenders often portrayed them as being. Still, the *Monthly* piece was only the first public suggestion that Sacco and Vanzetti were less than the "canonized saints" that the anguished letter-writer inveighed against in August 1927. The dark irony that Vanzetti likely was innocent of both the Bridgewater and South Braintree crimes afflicts the muse of history with a corkscrew-like dilemma. Vanzetti almost certainly was innocent, but in protecting his anarchist brethren he likely helped perpetrate a propaganda fraud as formidable as anything seen in World War I.

Almost a century ago, U.S. Senator Hiram Johnson said that truth was the first casualty of war. For the Galleanisti, secrecy was the first and last order of the day, war or peace. Their silence allowed the false legacy of Sacco and Vanzetti, a myth artfully constructed by Fred Moore, to flourish and perpetuate. A famously outraged poem by Malcolm Cowley, "For St. Bartholomew's Day," succinctly explained the twentieth-century celebrity defining cause cèlébre martyrdom.

> Beyond the chair, beyond the bars,
> of day and night your path lies free
> yours is an avenue of stars
> march on, O dago Christs, while
> we march on to spread your name
> abroad like ashes in the winds of god.[17]

Alvan Fuller's political career was also scattered to the winds. He declined to stand for reelection for governor in 1928. Before the executions, Fuller was a rumored dark-horse candidate for president of the United States. Nevertheless, his political star quickly set at the Republican national convention that year.[18] A conservative-leaning populist, Fuller was used to governing from a blend of instinct and conscience, but in Sacco-Vanzetti he had been badly overmatched in an unforeseen battle with a monolithic international cause. Although thin-skinned and egotistical, Fuller was unfairly blamed for the moribund judicial system that allowed Sacco and Vanzetti to take place. Nevertheless, he ignored his more temperate friends' advice to commute the death sentences to life in prison and paid a price that exacted a penalty he never quite fathomed: a political reputation shattered on the rocks of history.

In late October 1928, the *Outlook and Independent* magazine published a two-part series on Bartolomeo Vanzetti. The news magazine claimed that a small-time hoodlum named Frank Silva, and not Vanzetti, was guilty of the Bridgewater crime.[19] Silva, who was paid for the revelation, obliged investigative reporter Silas Bent with an affidavit outlining his participation in the 1919 crime. Protected by an expired statue of limitations, Silva named several others as members of the Bridgewater gang. (Vanzetti was not among their number.) Silva's story, unlike that of Celestino Medeiros, had a reasonable degree of credibility. Moreover, Bent used the services of investigators to check the accuracy of Silva's claims. The *Outlook* concluded that Vanzetti was innocent, at least of the Bridgewater crime. It editorially urged the public to renew its interest in the case. "To open a closed case is hard enough; but it is still harder to reopen a closed mind. Why not forget? Because in the South Braintree case it was not only Sacco and Vanzetti, but also our administration of justice that was on trial. If that has not failed us, then we should know it. We cannot afford to regard any miscarriage of justice as a closed case. As we value the future safety of society, our own safety and the safety of our children, we must be ready to listen and learn."[20]

In truth, practically no one in the United States was listening and certainly no compelling lesson had been learned. Only the *New Republic* endorsed the *Outlook*'s editorial, although it, too, was uncertain about the South Braintree crime.[21] In any event, the revelation had almost no impact and was ignored by the mainstream press. The presidential election of 1928 assured that the case would not be re-examined by anyone any time soon. Outside of the Sacco-Vanzetti memorial committee and the Boston anarchist community, hardly anyone else cared. Shortly after the *Outlook*'s series appeared, the Massachusetts Bar Association recommended changes in the state judiciary based on experiences involved with Sacco-Vanzetti.[22] Surprisingly, none would occur for more than a decade.

Sacco-Vanzetti would not disappear. It came to haunt the American political psyche, an anguished presence hovering above the nation's conscience like an incubus at the witching hour. In a 1929 the *Nation* article, "The Power of Two Ghosts," Gardner Jackson vowed that the defense committee would struggle to vindicate the reputations of the executed men. Many former members did just that, attending annual services and meetings and publishing articles and books on the case. In 1928, Jackson and Marion Denham Frankfurter published *Letters of Sacco and Vanzetti,* and Upton Sinclair, his roman á clef, *Boston.* Eugene Lyons's *The Life and Death of Sacco and Vanzetti* made it into print before Christmas 1927. In 1931, Osmond K. Fraenkel presented *The Sacco-Vanzetti Case,* the first truly non-partisan book-length evaluation of America's most famous cause cèlébre.[23] Defense lawyer Herbert Ehrmann published *The Untried Case: The Sacco-Vanzetti Case and the Morelli Gang* in 1933. John Dos Passos's celebrated trilogy of novels, *U.S.A.,* featured a segment in *The Big Money* that contained a searing portrait of the case. Michael Musmanno published *After Twelve Years* in 1937, a fascinating if somewhat exaggerated memoir of his assistance to William G. Thompson in the final months of the case. Eleven years followed before another book on the case appeared. In 1948, Edumund Morgan and G. Louis Joughin introduced the first edition of *The Legacy of Sacco and Vanzetti.* Their book stimulated renewed debate on the case. In this extensive and even-handed evaluation of the Sacco-Vanzetti history, the authors sympathized with the view that the anarchists did not receive a fair trial, while casting a jaundiced eye upon the notion of martyrdom.

By this time, many believed that "the shoemaker and the fisherman" had been nothing less than persecuted foreign radicals caught up in reactionary backlash of the Palmer raids. Countless poems, a half-dozen plays, and eight novels about the men reinforced this image.

Fred Moore's unsubstantiated claim to Upton Sinclair that Sacco was guilty and Vanzetti possibly guilty made a belated appearance in a 1953 issue of the *Journal of Social Science.* The same year, novelist Howard Fast's *The Passion of Sacco and Vanzetti* related that case to the Rosenberg cause cèlébre of 1950–1953. In 1958, psychiatrist and author Ralph Colp, Jr. wrote two separate essays about the mental breakdowns of Sacco and Vanzetti for the *Nation.* The accounts were based on until-then unavailable records of both men's hospitalizations.[24]

Max Eastman recounted in a 1961 issue of the *National Review* that Carlo Tresca had told him in 1942 that Sacco was guilty and Vanzetti innocent. The same year, Tom O'Connor disputed the prosecutor's case against the anarchists in a review of Robert Montgomery's *The Murder and The Myth.*[25] In a law review article, O'Connor challenged the book's credibility, noting it was based on a case without a solid foundation in fact. Investigative journalist Fred J. Cook asserted in a December 1962 review of Francis Russell's *Tragedy in Dedham* that the author ignored the fact that neither of the fingerprints of Sacco nor Vanzetti were recovered from the "bandit car" used in the South Braintree robbery.[26] Michael

Musmanno also took Russell to task in a March 1963 review in the *New Republic.* By then a prominent Pennsylvania judge, Musmanno excoriated Russell for alleged misquotations, misrepresentations, and the appropriation of hearsay evidence. He also criticized ballistics tests done on the Sacco handgun in 1961 as unreliable and inadmissible in court.[27] In 1963, Ben Bagdikian claimed in the *New Republic* article that the Morelli gang, not Sacco and Vanzetti, had committed the South Braintree crime.[28]

In 1969, Herbert B. Ehrmann published *The Case that Will Not Die: Commonwealth vs. Sacco and Vanzetti.* An answer to Montgomery's and Russell's books on the case, among other things the author noted Sacco had an alibi for his whereabouts on the day of the crime.[29] Kathernine Anne Porter's slender volume on the case, *The Never Ending Wrong,* was released in 1977—the fiftieth anniversary of the Sacco-Vanzetti executions—as was Roberta Strauss Feurelicht's book, *Justice Crucified.*

Porter and Feurelicht helped reopen debate on the case and Massachusetts' Governor Michael S. Dukakis re-ignited the long-dormant controversy in Summer 1977 when he proclaimed a Sacco-Vanzetti Memorial Day, noting there was "severe doubt" surrounding the men's convictions. A future presidential candidate (in 1988), Dukakis's action evoked the gratitude of surviving sibling Vencenzia Vanzetti but in turn annoyed a new generation of Massachusetts Republicans and succeeded in angering the family of long-dead Alvan Fuller.[30]

Luigi Galleani died a recluse in Italy, surrounded by Mussolini's security agents. Anarchism withered in the 1930s and was all but dead by World War II. The Sacco-Vanzetti case had started a fund-raising venture by Galleanisti intent on freeing two countrymen. What happened, of course, was something very different. The Sacco-Vanzetti case muscled its way into history, making possible at least two other American causes celèbrés, the Rosenberg and Scottsboro Boy cases, and indirectly influenced the outcome of the Mooney case, which concluded in 1939. But more than that, it eventually made many Americans realize that they were no longer disparate parts of a remote nation that could ignore at will international protest and outrage. In the eyes of most of the nations of the world, America had let the symbolic torch of freedom slip from its preeminent grasp. The cultural and political insularity provided by the Atlantic Ocean had vanished forever on the backs of two of the most unlikely figures in our history. Perhaps the greatest irony of this most intensely public case is that both of its central figures may have taken to the grave secrets that could well have saved them from execution.

Notes

PREFACE

1. Harold D. Lasswell, *Propaganda Technique in the World War* (New York: Peter Smith, 1938), p. 2.

2. Richard S. Lambert, *Propaganda* (London: Thomas Nelson and Son Ltd., 1938), p. 7.

3. Ibid., p. 7.

4. Daniel J. Czitrom, *Media and the American Mind: From Morse to McLuhan* (Chapel Hill, N.C.: University of North Carolina Press, 1982), p. 123.

5. Lasswell, *Propaganda Technique*, p. 9.

6. Edward L. Bernays, *Propaganda* (New York: Liverright Publishing Corp., 1928), p. 9.

7. Ibid., p. 20.

8. Lambert, *Propaganda*, p. 131.

9. Serge Chakotin, *The Rape of the Masses: The Psychology of Totalitarian Political Propaganda* (New York: Haskell House Publishers, Ltd., 1971), pp. 170–171.

10. Egal Feldman, *The Dreyfus Affair and the American Conscience: 1893–1906* (Detroit, Mi.: Wayne State University Press, 1981), pp. 86–88; Betty Schechter, *The Dreyfus Affair: A National Scandal* (Boston: Houghton Mifflin, 1965), p. 208.

11. Schechter, *Dreyfus Affair*, p. 208.

12. Feldman, *Dreyfus Affair and American Conscience*, p. 89.

13. Warren I. Susman, *Culture as History: The Transformation of American Society in the Twentieth Century* (New York: Pantheon Books, 1984), p. 8.

14. Richard Hofstadter, "The Paranoid Style in American Politics," *Harper's*, November, 1964, pp. 79–86.

CHAPTER 1

1. Bartolomeo Vanzetti, "Awaiting the Hangman: A Journalistic Conspiracy of Quietness," quote from the Official Bulletin of Defense Committee, Sacco-Vanzetti case papers, Drawer 131, Box 177-3, reel 21, Harvard Law School (HLS).

2. Richard V. Ouhahan, "Senator Curtis Named for VP on First Ballot with 1,052 Votes to 34; Hoover Promises Real Relief to Farmers," *New York Times,* June 16, 1928, p. 2.

3. *New York Times,* June 16, 1928, p. 2.

4. "Bandits Kill Guard, Shoot Paymaster, Steal $16,000," *Boston Daily Globe,* April 16, 1921, p. 1.

5. Paul Avrich, *The Haymarket Tragedy* (Princeton, N.J.: Princeton University Press, 1984), pp. 391–394.

6. Frederick Trautman, *The Voice of Terror: A Biography of Johann Most* (Westport, Ct.: Greenwood Press, 1980), p. 129.

7. Henry David, *The History of the Haymarket Affair: A Study in the American Social Revolution and Labor Movements* (New York: Russell and Russell, 1958, 2nd ed.), p. 528.

8. David, *History of the Haymarket Affair,* p. 530.

9. Nunzio Pernicone, *Italian Anarchism: 1864–1892* (Princeton, N.J.: Princeton University Press, 1993), pp. 258–259.

10. Paul Avrich, *Sacco and Vanzetti: The Anarchist Background* (Princeton, N.J.: Princeton University Press, 1991), p. 50.

11. Ibid., p. 99.

12. Ibid., p. 103.

13. Ibid., p. 137.

14. Ibid., pp. 140–141.

15. "Midnight Bombs For Officials in 8 Cities," *New York Times,* June 3, 1919, p. 1.

16. Julian F. Jaffe, *Crusade Against Radicalism: New York During the Red Scare, 1919–24* (Port Washington, N.Y.: Kennikat Press, 1972), p. 1; Stanley Cohen, *A. Mitchell Palmer: Politician* (New York: Columbia University Press, 1963), pp. 217–245; William Preston, *Aliens and Dissenters: Federal Suppression of Radicals, 1903–1933* (Cambridge, Mass.: Harvard University Press, 1963), pp. 208–220, 221–222.

17. Donald Johnson, *The Challenge to American Freedoms: World War I and the Rise of the American Civil Liberties Union* (University of Kentucky Press, 1963), pp. 11–20.

18. "Red's Death Plunge, 14 Stories, Bares Long Bomb Trail," *New York Times,* May 4, 1920, p. 1.

19. Ibid., p. 1.

20. Ibid., p. 1.

21. "Bandits Kill Guard, Escape with $27,000," *New York Times,* April 16, 1920, p. 18.

22. Ibid., p.18.

23. "Parmenter, the Second Victim of Bandits, Dead," *Boston Evening Globe,* April 16, 1920, p. 1.

24. "Find Bandits in West Bridgewater," *Boston Sunday Globe,* April 18, 1920, p. 2.

25. G. Louis Joughin and Edmund M. Morgan, *The Legacy of Sacco and Vanzetti* (Chicago: Quadrangle Books, 1948), p. 6.

26. Francis Russell, *Sacco and Vanzetti: The Case Resolved* (New York: Harper Row Publishers, 1986), p. 58.

27. Ibid., p. 58.

28. Ibid., p. 58.

29. Ibid., p. 59.

30. "Police Obtain Clue to More of Bandit Gang," *Boston Herald,* May 8, 1920, p. 1.

31. Ibid., p. 1.

32. Ibid., p. 1.

33. Ibid., p. 1.

34. Ibid., p. 1.

35. Joughin and Morgan, *Legacy of Sacco and Vanzetti,* p. 456.

36. Russell, *Sacco and Vanzetti,* p. 73.

37. Joughin and Morgan, *Legacy of Sacco and Vanzetti,* p. 456.

38. Russell, *Sacco and Vanzetti,* p. 73.

39. Ibid., p. 73.

40. Joughin and Morgan, *Legacy of Sacco and Vanzetti,* p. 458.

41. Russell, *Sacco and Vanzetti,* p. 76.

42. Joughin and Morgan, *Legacy of Sacco and Vanzetti,* p. 439.

43. William Young and David Kaiser, *Postmortem: New Evidence in the Case of Sacco and Vanzetti* (Amherst, Mass.: University of Massachusetts Press, 1985), p. 38.

44. Joughin and Morgan, *Legacy of Sacco and Vanzetti,* pp. 8–9.

45. Ibid., pp. 8–9.

46. Eugene Lyons, *Assignment in Utopia* (New York: Harcourt, Brace and Co., 1937), p. 32.

47. Quoted in Dorothy Gallagher, *All the Right Enemies: The Life and Murder of Carlo Tresca* (New Brunswick, N.J.: Rutgers University Press, 1988), p. 79.

48. Young and Kaiser, *Postmortem,* p. 38.

49. "Vanzetti Convicted in Plymouth Court," *Boston Herald,* July 2, 1920, p. 5.

50. Ibid., p. 5.

51. Bartolomeo Vanzetti, *Background of the Plymouth Trial,* Boston: Road to Freedom Group, 1927. Fromkin Collection, Golda Meir Library, University of Wisconsin-Milwaukee. This pamphlet was widely distributed after Sacco and Vanzetti were sentenced in April 1927.

52. "Vanzetti Convicted in Plymouth Court," *Boston Globe,* July 2, 1920, p. 5.

53. "Twelve Years for Vanzetti Bandit," *Boston Daily Globe,* August 17, 1920, p. 11.

54. Russell, *Sacco and Vanzetti,* p. 94.

55. Lyons, *Assignment,* p. 32.

56. Ibid., p. 13.

57. Eugene Lyons, *The Life and Death of Sacco and Vanzetti* (New York: International Publications, 1927), pp. 30–31.

58. Russell, *Sacco and Vanzetti,* p. 97.

59. Ibid., p. 97.

60. Lyons, *Assignment,* p. 32.

61. David Felix, *Protest: Sacco and Vanzetti and the Intellectuals* (Bloomington, Ind.: Indiana University Press, 1965), p. 20.

62. Lyons, *Assignment,* p. 22.

63. Robert H. Montgomery, *Sacco-Vanzetti: The Murder and the Myth* (New York: Devin-Adair Co., 1960), p. 69.

64. Russell, *Sacco and Vanzetti,* pp. 13–14.

65. Roberta Strauss Feuerlicht, *Justice Crucified: The Story of Sacco and Vanzetti* (New York: McGraw-Hill Book Co., 1977), pp. 196–198.

66. "Court Interpreter Held for Hearing," *Boston Globe,* January 17, 1921, p. 2.

67. "Katzmann Denies He Knows Mrs. DeFalco," *Boston Daily Globe,* February 2, 1921, p. 1.

68. Russell, *Sacco and Vanzetti,* p. 16.

69. Montgomery, *Sacco-Vanzetti,* p. 70; the letter cited is reproduced on pp. 72–74.

70. Ibid., pp. 69–70.

71. John Nicholas Beffel, "Eels and the Electric Chair," *New Republic,* December 29, 1920, pp. 127–129.

72. Ibid., p. 129.

73. Lyons, *Life and Death,* p. 71.

74. "Pick Three Jurors in Paymaster Trial," *Boston Herald,* June 1, 1921, p. 1.

75. "Sacco and Vanzetti Murder Trial Jury Isolated," *Boston Herald,* June 5, 1921, p. 1.

76. "Jury at Scene of Murder of Paymaster," *Boston Herald,* June 7, 1921, p. 1.

77. Elizabeth Glendower Evans, "Foreigners," *New Republic,* June 8, 1921, pp. 44–46.

78. "Reds Will Defend Alleged Slayers," *New York Times,* May 30, 1921, p. 22.

79. Elizabeth Ellam, "Mooney Case of New England Now on Trial at Dedham," *Boston Herald,* June 12, 1921, p. 9.

80. Russell, *Sacco and Vanzetti,* pp. 12–13.

81. *Boston Herald,* June 12, 1921, p. 9.

82. Ibid., p. 9.

83. Felix, *Protest,* p. 61.

84. James Joll, *The Anarchists* (Boston: Little, Brown & Co., 1964), p. 222.

CHAPTER 2

1. "Is Identified as Murder Car in Sacco Case," *Boston Herald,* June 9, 1921, p. 1.

2. Frank Sibley, "Neal is Witness in Payroll Murder," *Boston Globe,* June 8, 1921, p. 3.

3. *Boston Herald,* June 9, 1924, p. 4.

4. Ibid., p. 1.

5. "Girl Points to Sacco as Man She Saw in Car After Murder," *Boston Herald,* June 10, 1921, p. 1.

6. Ibid., p. 1.

7. Cited in Felix, *Protest,* p. 62.

8. "Sacco Stands When Witness Identifies Him," *Boston Herald,* June 12, 1921, p. 1.

9. Ibid., p. 1.

10. "Saw Vanzetti in Murder Car," *Boston Herald,* June 14, 1921, p. 1.

11. "Sacco Smiles at Accusers," *Boston Herald,* June 15, 1921, p. 1.

12. Ibid., p. 1.

13. Ibid. William Tracy's last name appears in some newspaper articles spelled as "Tracey"; similarly, Louis De Barardinis's last name in some articles is sometimes misspelled "De Barradinos."

14. "State Finishes Testimony in Bandit Murder," *Boston Herald,* June 17, 1921, p. 1.

15. Ibid., p. 1.

16. "Bullet-Torn Murder Car Used by Bandits Inspected by Jury," *Boston Herald,* June 17, 1921, p. 1.

17. Ibid., p. 10.

18. "'Liar' Shouts Vanzetti to Police Witness," *Boston Herald,* June 18, 1921, p. 1.

19. "Widow of Slain Men Fails to Identify Gun," *Boston Herald,* June 21, 1921, p. 1.

20. Ibid., p. 1.

21. "Experts Pick Murder Pistol," *Boston Herald,* June 22, 1921, p. 2.

22. Ibid., p. 1.

23. "Says Sacco and Vanzetti Not in Bandits Car," *Boston Herald,* June 23, 1921, p. 1.

24. "Are Not Bandits Witnesses Say," *Boston Herald,* June 26, 1921, p. 3.

25. "Says Vanzetti and Sacco Not the Slayers," *Boston Herald,* June 25, 1921, p. 1.

26. *The Sacco-Vanzetti Case; Transcript of the Record of the Trial of Nicola Sacco and Bartolomeo Vanzetti in the Courts of Massachusetts and Subsequent Proceedings, 1920–1927.* (Edited by Charles C. Burlingham and Bernard Flexner.) Six volumes; I–V, and supplemental volume. New York: Holt and Co., 1929. Trial record, I: pp. 1,418–1,419. (Herein referred to as trial record).

27. Trial record, p. 1,378.

28. "Vanzetti to Go on Trial Today," *Boston Herald,* June 30, 1921, p. 3.

29. Trial record, p. 2,266 a–c.

30. Ibid., pp. 1,701–1,702.

31. Ibid., p. 1,759.

32. Frank P. Sibley, "Sacco Faces Sharp Grilling on Murder," *Boston Daily Globe,* July 7, 1921, p. 1.

33. Trial record, p. 1,858.

34. Ibid., p. 1,866.

35. Ibid., p. 1,877.

36. Bartolomeo Vanzetti, "Awaiting the Hangman," reel 21 (HLS).

37. Sacco-Vanzetti Case Papers," Drawer 131, Box 172-2, reel 4, p. 1 (HLS).

38. Sibley, "Evidence Finished: Defense Rests at Dedham," *Boston Daily Globe,* July 12, 1921, p. 1.

39. "American Verdict Free of Prejudice, Is Demanded," *Boston Evening Transcript,* July 13, 1921, p. 6.

40. Ibid., p. 6.

41. "Katzmann Scores Defense," *Boston Evening Transcript,* July 14, 1921, p. 4.

42. Ibid., p. 4.

43. Frank P. Sibley, "Real Issue Identity Says Judge Thayer," *Boston Evening Globe,* July 14, 1921, p. 1.

44. "Jury Gets Case," *Boston Evening Transcript,* July 14, 1921, p. 4.

45. Sibley, "Sacco and Vanzetti Found Guilty of Murder," *Boston Daily Globe,* July 15, 1921, p. 1.

46. The *Standard-Times* article is reprinted in *Commonwealth vs. Sacco and Vanzetti,* Robert P. Weeks, ed. (Englewood Cliffs, N.J.: Prentice-Hall, Inc., 1958), pp. 263–270.

47. Ibid., p. 268.

48. *Boston Daily Globe,* July 15, 1921, p. 3.

CHAPTER 3

1. Clarence R. Skinner, "The Sacco-Vanzetti Case," *Survey,* August 16, 1921, p. 584.

2. Arthur Warner, "Sacco and Vanzetti—a Reasonable Doubt," *Nation,* September 28, 1921, pp. 343–345.

3. Ibid., p. 343.

4. Samuel Spewack, "Kindle Red Uprising From Murder Trial," *Milwaukee Journal,* November 20, 1921, p. 1.

5. Ibid., p. 1.

6. Ibid., p. 1.

7. Spewack, "Appeal to Save Lives of Reds Stirs World Unrest," *Milwaukee Journal,* November 21, 1921, p. 1.

8. Ibid., p. 1.

9. Ibid., p. 2.

10. Ibid., p. 1.

11. Ibid., p. 2.

12. Spewack, "Italian Reds Fight for Comrades Facing Death," *Milwaukee Journal,* November 22, 1921, p. 2.

13. Spewack, "Reds' Protests Circle the World," *Milwaukee Journal,* November 25, 1921, p. 27.

14. Ibid., p. 27.

15. "The Anarchists and the Ambassador," *Literary Digest,* November 5, 1921, p. 1.

16. Anatole France, "To the People of America," *Nation,* November 23, 1921, p. 586.

17. Ibid., p. 586.

18. "More Sacco Propaganda," *New York Times,* November 25, 1921, p. 28.

19. "White Terror and Red Terror," *The Outlook,* November 2, 1921, pp. 334–335.

20. Eugene Lyons, "Italians in American Courts," *Survey,* November 12, 1921, pp. 237–238.

21. "Our Communist 'Martyrs' Disturbing the World," *Literary Digest,* December 10, 1921, pp. 32–40.

22. "Denies Motion for Trial," *Boston Sunday Globe,* December 25, 1921, p. 1.

23. Ibid., p. 12.

24. "Red Unions Defeat Rank and File Rule," *New York Times*, January 1, 1922, p. 6.

25. Ibid., p. 6.

26. Louis Stark, "Are Sacco and Vanzetti Guilty?" *New York Times*, March 5, 1922, p. 3.

27. Ibid., p. 3.

28. Ibid., p. 3.

29. Joughin and Morgan, *Legacy*, p. 229.

30. For example, see Anthony Capraro Collection, Box 2, "Sacco and Vanzetti Atlanta Investigation," Correspondence and Literature, 1922–1963, Extensive Correspondence with Angelino Mole. Immigration History Research Center (IHRC), University of Minnesota, Twin Cities.

31. "Raps Italian Reds on Sacco-Vanzetti," *New York Times*, March 21, 1922, p. 5.

32. Ibid., p. 5.

33. Ibid., p. 5.

34. Howard L. Stebbins, "The Sacco-Vanzetti Case," *The American Bar Association Journal*, November, 1922, p. 8.

35. Letter from Earl Browder to Fred H. Moore, September 3, 1924, Fred H. Moore Collection, Boston Public Library, Rare Book Collection.

36. "Sacco and Vanzetti Must Die—Judge Thayer," *Daily Worker*, October 3, 1924, p. 1.

37. Leon A. Harris, *Upton Sinclair: An American Rebel* (New York: Thomas Crowell, Co., 1975), p. 246; also see William A. Bloodworth, Jr., *Upton Sinclair* (Boston: Twayne Publishers, 1977), pp. 115–116.

38. "Chief Counsel Quits Defense of Sacco," *New York Times*, November 9, 1924, p. 29.

39. Ibid., p. 29.

CHAPTER 4

1. "Vanzetti Removed to Insane Hospital," *New York Times*, January 3, 1925, p. 15.

2. "Sacco-Vanzetti Protest," *New York Times*, March 2, 1925, p. 7.

3. Stephen Koch, *Double Lives: Spies and Writers in the Secret Soviet War of Ideas Against the West* (New York: Free Press, 1994), p. 31.

4. Ibid., p. 31.

5. Letter from James P. Cannon to Eugene V. Debs, July 15, 1925, Box 3, Folder 1, State Historical Society of Wisconsin (SHSW). Cannon informed Debs that the ILD was "the defender of every worker persecuted for his activities in the class struggle without any exceptions and without regard to his affiliations."

6. Letter from James P. Cannon to Eugene V. Debs, May 27, 1926, Box 3, Folder 1 (SHSW).

7. For a trenchant account of this experience see Katherine Anne Porter, *The Never Ending Wrong* (Boston: Little, Brown and Co., 1977), p. 18; also see Joan Givner, *Katherine Anne Porter: A Life* (New York. Simon & Schuster, Inc., 1982), pp. 193–194.

8. Koch, *Double Lives*, p. 34.

9. Herbert B. Ehrmann, *The Untried Case: The Sacco-Vanzetti Case and the Morelli Gang* (New York: Vanguard Press, Inc., 1960), pp. 35–36.

10. Ibid., p. 37.

11. Ibid., p. 30.

12. Ibid., p. 37.

13. Ibid., pp. 44–46.

14. Ibid., pp. 65–66. Dudley P. Ranney was District Attorney in charge of the Sacco-Vanzetti case.

15. Russell, *Sacco and Vanzetti*, pp. 166–167.

16. Weeks, *Commonwealth v. Sacco and Vanzetti*, pp. 205–206.

17. Ibid., p. 206.

18. "Sacco's Last Plea for Life is Denied," *New York Times*, May 13, 1926, p. 10.

19. "Vanzetti Appeals to Workers," *Daily Worker*, May 21, 1926, p. 1.

20. Ibid., p. 1.

21. "Paris Reds Champion Sacco and Vanzetti," *New York Times*, June 4, 1926, p. 13.

22. "Reichstag Members Urge Sacco Retrial," *New York Times*, July 8, 1926, p. 19.

23. See Felix, *Protest*, pp. 174–175; Koch, *Double Lives*, pp. 35–36.

24. Koch, *Double Lives*, p. 36.

25. Felix, *Protest*, p. 175.

26. Richard Frost, *The Mooney Case* (Palo Alto, Calif.: Stanford University Press, 1968), pp. 288–293; Curt Gentry, *Frame-Up: The Incredible Case of Tom Mooney and Warren Billings* (New York: W.W. Norton and Co., 1967), pp. 230–231.

27. Robert Louis Hoffman, *More Than a Trial: The Struggle Over Captain Dreyfus* (New York: Free Press, 1980), p. 17.

28. Ibid., p. 18.

29. "The Sacco-Vanzetti Case," *New Republic*, June 9, 1926, pp. 75–76.

30. Marion Denham Frankfurter and Gardner Jackson, eds., *The Letters of Sacco and Vanzetti* (New York: Viking, 1928), p. 201.

31. Theodore Draper, *American Communism and Soviet Russia: The Formative Period* (New York: Viking Press, 1960), pp. 181, 279–280.

32. "Herrick Receives Two Death Threats," *New York Times*, July 27, 1926, p. 1.

33. Felix, *Protest*, p. 140.

34. Roland Gibson, "Sacco-Vanzetti Case Has Three Moves Left," *New York Times*, September 12, 1926, IX, p. 14.

35. "Sees Federal Plot to Convict Sacco," *New York Times*, September 16, 1926, p. 10; "Says Make of Car Has Significance," *Boston Evening Globe*, September 16, 1926, p. 1; "Charge Defense Not Diligent," *Boston Evening Globe*, September 17, 1926, p. 1.

36. "Sacco Hearing Ends With Bitter Attack," *New York Times*, September 18, 1926, p. 36; "Will Require Weeks for Sacco Decision," *Boston Evening Globe*, September 18, 1926, p. 1.

37. Joughin and Morgan, *Legacy*, p. 183.

38. *New York Times*, September 16, 1926, p. 10.

39. Bartolomeo Vanzetti, "Awaiting the Hangman," Drawer 131, Box 177 (HLS), reel 21.

40. *New York Times,* September 16, 1926, p. 10.

41. "The Department of Justice and the Sacco-Vanzetti Case," *New Republic,* Septembr 29, 1926, pp. 150–153.

42. Ibid., p. 153.

43. Russell, *Sacco and Vanzetti,* pp. 179–180.

44. Ibid., pp. 179–180.

45. Felix Frankfurter, *The Case of Sacco and Vanzetti,* p. 178.

46. "Defense Takes Offensive in Sacco Hearing," *Daily Worker,* September 16, 1926, p. 1; "Medeiros Gave Confession in Danger of Life," *Daily Worker,* September 17, 1926, p. 2; "State's Case Shows Up Weak in Sacco Trial," *Daily Worker,* September 18, 1926, p. 1; J. Louis Engdahl, Sacco Defense Evidence Was Withheld," *Daily Worker,* September 20, 1926, p. 1.

47. Engdahl, " 'Guilty' Charge Hurled Against U.S. Government in Sacco-Vanzetti Case," *Daily Worker,* September 30, 1926, p. 2.

48. Engdahl, "The Underworld of Crime Knew the Real Criminal in Sacco-Vanzetti Case," *Daily Worker,* October 2, 1926, p. 2.

49. Engdahl, "Morelli Gang Was Suspected but Crime Was Charged Against Sacco, Vanzetti," *Daily Worker,* October 4, 1926, p. 2; Engdahl, "Convict Rejects Offer of U.S. to Aid Betrayal of Sacco and Vanzetti," *Daily Worker,* October 6, 1926, p. 2.

50. Engdahl, "Truth is Trickling Thru in Spite of Every Effort of the New England Gang," *Daily Worker,* October 19, 1926, p. 2.

51. Koch, *Double Lives,* p. 34.

52. "New Trial to Sacco, Vanzetti: Appeal to Be Made," *New York Times,* October 24, 1926, p. 1; "Final Fight for Sacco, Vanzetti," *Boston Daily Globe,* October 25, 1926, p. 1.

53. "Final Fight for Sacco, Vanzetti," *Boston Daily Globe,* October 25, 1926, p. 17.

54. *New York Times,* October 24, 1926, p. 17.

55. Koch, *Double Lives,* pp. 37–38.

56. Engdahl, "The Struggle to Save the Life of the Daily Worker Is Part of the Growing Fight to Save the Lives of Sacco and Vanzetti," *Daily Worker,* October 26, 1926, p. 1.

57. Official Bulletin of Defense Committee, Drawer 131, Box 177-3, reel 21, (HLS); the date of *The Herald* editorial of Bullard is October 26, 1926.

58. "Fuller at Peace in Paris Suburb," *New York Times,* November 15, 1926, p. 6.

59. "Sacco-Vanzetti Protests in France," *Boston Daily Globe,* November 1, 1926, p. 1.

60. *New York Times,* November 15, 1926, p. 6.

61. Ibid., p. 6.

62. "Sacco-Vanzetti Attorneys File Bill of Exceptions for New Trial," *Daily Worker,* October 30, 1926, p. 1.

63. "10,000 Unionists in Sacco Protest," *New York Times,* November 18, 1926, p. 25; "Paris Lawyers Seek Fuller To Aid Sacco," *Boston Daily Globe,* November 18, 1926, p. 36.

64. William Manchester, *Disturber of the Peace: The Life of H. L Mencken* (New York: Harpers and Brother, 1951), p. 213.

65. Daniel Aaron, *Writers on the Left: Episodes in American Literary Communism* (New York: Harcourt, Brace & World, Inc., 1961), p. 170.

66. John Dos Passos, *The Best Times: An Informal Memoir* (New York: American Library, 1966), p. 170.

67. Quoted in Shelley Fisher Fishkin, *From Fact to Fiction: Journalism and Imaginative Writing in America* (Baltimore, Md.: Johns Hopkins University Press, 1985), p. 177.

68. Dos Passos, *Best Times,* p. 169.

69. "Governor Extends Respite to Medeiros to April 27," *Boston Evening Transcript,* January 19, 1927, p. 9; "Confession of Sacco Wins Third Reprieve," *New York Times,* January 20, 1927, p. 48.

70. "Sacco-Vanzetti Case Argued in Supreme Court," *Boston Evening Transcript,* January 1, 1927, p. 12.

71. Ibid., p. 12.

72. "French Police Guard Our Embassy in Paris as Sacco and Vanzetti Agitation Flares Up," *New York Times,* March 1, 1921, p. 1.

73. Ibid., p. 1.

74. Frankfurter and Jackson, *Letters,* p. 163.

75. Ibid., p. 120.

76. Ibid., p. 151.

77. See Russell, *Sacco and Vanzetti,* p. 133.

78. "Red Cause Assailed," *New York Times,* December 14, 1926, p. 45.

79. "Three Massachusetts Bandits Die in Chair for Killing of Watchman in Car Barn Hold-up," *New York Times,* January 6, 1927.

80. J. Louis Engdahl, "Congress Does Not Hear Demand for the Release of Sacco and Vanzetti," *Daily Worker,* February 25, 1927, p. 2.

81. "Sacco-Vanzetti Appeal Overruled," *Boston Evening Transcript,* April 5, 1927, p. 1; "Sacco and Vanzetti Lose in Supreme Court," *Boston Evening Globe,* April 5, 1921, p. 1; "Long History of Sacco-Vanzetti Case," *Boston Evening Globe,* April 5, 1927, p. 1.

82. Ibid., p. 1.

83. Felix Frankfurter, "The Case of Sacco and Vanzetti," *Atlantic Monthly,* March, 1927, p. 431.

84. Ibid., p. 428.

CHAPTER 5

1. Benjamin Gitlow, *I Confess: The Truth About American Communism* (New York: E. P. Dutton & Co., 1940), pp. 471–472.

2. Trial record, p. 4,895; "Sacco and Vanzetti Sentenced," *Boston Evening Globe,* April 9, 1927, p. 1; "Sacco and Vanzetti Must Die in July; Denounce Judge as He Sentences Them: Defense Maps Plans for New Appeal," *New York Times,* April 10, 1927, p. 1.

3. Ibid., *New York Times,* April 10, 1927, p. 1.

4. Trial record, p. 4,897.

5. Ibid., p. 4,897.

6. Ibid., p. 4,897.

7. "Vanzetti Blames Hysteria of Wartime for Sentence," *New York Times,* April 10, 1927, p. 8.

8. *Boston Evening Globe,* April 4, 1927, p. 1; "Must Die Week of July 10," *Boston Evening Transcript,* April 9, 1927, p. 1.

9. "Judge Says He has Nothing to Fear," *New York Times,* April 11, 1927, p. 8.

10. Ibid., p. 8.

11. Ibid., p. 8.

12. Ibid., p. 8.

13. "One-Hour Strike and Union Square Meeting Planned Here as Sacco-Vanzetti Protest," *New York Times,* April 10, 1927, p. 1.

14. Ibid., p. 1.

15. *New York Times,* April 11, 1927, p. 8.

16. Ibid., p. 8.

17. "Legislature Urged to Uphold an Inquiry on Sacco, Vanzetti," *New York Times,* April 12, 1927, p. 1.

18. "The Sacco-Vanzetti Case," *Milwaukee Journal,* April 12, 1927, p. 10.

19. The editorials are cited in Joughin and Morgan, *Legacy,* p. 263.

20. Ibid., p. 263.

21. Ibid., p. 264.

22. Ibid., p. 264.

23. "They Shall Not Die! They Shall Be Freed!" *Daily Worker,* April 11, 1927, p. 1.

24. *The Times,* April 14, 1927, p. 13.

25. Joughin and Morgan, *Legacy,* p. 263.

26. Ibid., p. 257.

27. "Resolution Asks Inquiry," *New York Times,* May 10, 1927, p. 9.

28. Drawer 131, Box 177-3, reel 23 (HLS).

29. Ibid., reel 23.

30. Quoted in *Literary Digest,* April 23, 1927, p. 6.

31. Ibid., p. 6.

32. Ibid., p. 6.

33. Louis Stark, "Facts in Sacco-Vanzetti Case," *New York Times,* April 17, 1927, viii, p. 3.

34. "Sacco-Vanzetti," *New Republic,* April 20, 1927, p. 237.

35. George Kirchwey, "Sacco-Vanzetti, *Nation,* April 20, 1927, pp. 415–416.

36. "Sacco Refuses to Sign Final Appeal to Governor Fuller," *Boston Evening Transcript,* May 5, 1927, p. 6.

37. "Sacco-Vanzetti World Protest Swamps Massachusetts Governor," *Daily Worker,* April 13, 1927, p. 1.

38. "Says Judge Thayer Did Confuse Issue," *New York Times,* April 22, 1927, p. 16; "Says Judge Thayer Abhorred Two Men," *Boston Daily Globe,* April 22, 1927, p. 1.

39. "Professors of Law Urge Sacco Inquiry," *New York Times,* May 10, 1927, p. 9.

40. Joughin and Morgan, *Legacy,* p. 232.

41. Albert J. Gordon, "Fuller Weighs the Case of Sacco and Vanzetti," *New York Times,* May 28, 1927, viii, p. 4.

42. "Nor Friend Nor Foe Can Save Fuller," *New York World,* May 15, 1927, p. 2.

43. "Professors of Law Urge Sacco Inquiry," *New York Times,* May 10, 1927, p. 9.

44. "Pistol Expert Called in Sacco Inquiry," *New York Times,* May 19, 1927, p. 29.

45. *New York World,* May 15, 1927, p. 2.

46. Philip D. Strong, "Expect to Die, Stay Cheerful," *Milwaukee Journal,* May 13, 1927, p. 5; "Victory in Death Seen by Sacco and Vanzetti," *New York World,* May 13, 1927, p. 15.

47. Ibid., p. 15.

48. Ibid., p. 15.

49. Weeks, *Commonwealth v. Sacco,* p. 227.

50. *New York Times,* May 28, 1927, viii, p. 4.

51. "Dynamite Sent to Governor Fuller," *Milwaukee Journal,* May 15, 1927, p. 6; "Dynamite for Governor Fuller Seized at Burlington," *Boston Evening Globe,* May 14, 1927, p. 1.

52. "Sacco Board 'Would Embarrass' Fuller," *Boston Evening Globe,* May 14, 1927, p. 1; "Fuller Sees Juror in Sacco Inquiry," *New York Times,* May 14, 1927, p. 17.

53. Joughin and Morgan, *Legacy,* p. 300.

54. Ibid., p. 264.

55. "Sacco-Vanzetti Emergency Meeting Tomorrow Night," *Daily Worker,* June 23, 1927, p. 1.

56. "Sacco and Vanzetti Shall Not Die," *Daily Worker,* June 6, 1927, p. 7.

57. Katherine Anne Porter, *The Never Ending Wrong* (Boston: Little, Brown and Co., 1977), p. 18; Givner, *Porter,* pp. 193–194.

58. "Sacco-Vanzetti U.S. Conference is Demanded Now," *Daily Worker,* May 27, 1927, p. 1.

59. Francis Russell, *Tragedy in Dedham: The Story of the Sacco-Vanzetti Case* (New York: McGraw-Hill Book Co., 1971, pp. 337–338.

60. Koch, *Double Lives,* p. 32.

61. F. Lauriston Bullard, "Bay State is Cleft by Cause Cèlébre," *New York Times,* June 26, 1927, ii, p. 2.

62. Bruce Bliven, "In Dedham Jail: A Visit to Sacco and Vanzetti," *New Republic,* June 22, 1927, pp. 121–122.

63. "Dramatic Editor of Life in Sacco-Vanzetti Review," *Boston Evening Transcript,* July 13, 1927, p. 1.

64. John Paul Diggins, *Mussolini and Fascism: The View from America* (Princeton, N.J.: Princeton University Press, 1972), p. 272; also see Philip V. Cannistraro, "Sacco, Vanzetti and the Anarchists: The Transatlantic Context," *Journal of Modern History,* March 1996, pp. 31–62; Patrick J. Gallo, *Old Bread, New Wine: A Portrait of Italian Americans* (Chicago: Nelson-Hall, 1981, pp. 146–147.

65. "Sacco Aides Losing Hope," *Milwaukee Journal,* July 24, 1927, p. 1.

66. "Fuller at Scene of 2 Murders," *Boston Daily Globe,* July 27, 1927, p. 1; "Governor Fuller Visits Scene of Murder," *New York Times,* July 27, 1927, p. 25.

67. Ibid., p. 25; "Sacco-Vanzetti Report Filed," *Boston Daily Globe,* July 28, 1927, p. 1.

68. "Dreyfus May Come to Sacco Appeal," *Boston Daily Globe,* July 28, 1927, p. 1; "Famous Dreyfus Case Recalled by His Interest in Sacco Affair," *Boston Daily Globe,* July 28, 1927, p. 9; "Dreyfus May Come on Sacco Mission," *New York Times,* July 28, 1927, p. 8.

69. "Letter Tells of Despair at Fate," *New York Times,* July 31, 1927, p. 1.

70. "Picket Hearst Newspapers," *Daily Worker,* July 25, 1927, p. 2.

71. "Fuller Gives Day to Sacco Report," *New York Times,* August 1, 1927, p. 10.

72. "2,000 for Sacco 'Capture' City Hall," *New York World,* August 1, 1927, p. 1.

73. Arthur Weinberg and Lila Weinberg, *Clarence Darrow: A Sentimental Rebel* (New York: G. P. Putnam's Sons, 1980), p. 354.

74. "Sacco and Vanzetti Must Die Says Fuller," *New York World,* August 4, 1927, p. 1.

75. Ibid., p. 1.

76. Aldino Felicani, "Sacco-Vanzetti: A Memoir," *Nation,* August 14, 1967, pp. 108–112.

CHAPTER 6

1. "Sacco and Vanzetti Must Die Says Fuller—Decision is Backed by Inquiry Committee," *New York World,* August 4, 1927, p. 1.

2. Felix, *Protest,* p. 254.

3. *New York World,* August 4, 1927, p. 1.

4. "Massachusetts Stands the Test," *Boston Evening Transcript,* August 4, 1927, p. 12.

5. "The Sacco-Vanzetti Case," *Literary Digest,* August 13, 1927, p. 9.

6. Ibid., p. 9.

7. Ibid., p. 9.

8. *New York Times,* August 27, 1927, p. 4.

9. "Reaffirming the Guilt of Sacco and Vanzetti," *Literary Digest,* August 20, 1927, p. 6.

10. Ibid., p. 6.

11. Ibid., p. 6.

12. *Literary Digest,* August 13, 1927, p. 9.

13. *Literary Digest,* August 20, 1927, p. 7.

14. Ibid., p. 6.

15. "Governor Fuller's Decision Has Brought Both Denunciation and Approval From All Parts of the World," *New York World,* August 5, 1927, p. 1; "Tremendous Response to Decision," *Boston Evening Transcript,* August 4, 1927, p. 1; "Bishop Lawrence Praises Governor for his Decision," *Evening Transcript,* August 7, 1927, p. 10.

16. *New York World,* August 5, 1927, p. 1; "Violent Speech and Acts Noted all Over the World," *Boston Evening Transcript,* August 4, 1927, p. 10. Vanzetti was halted in France temporarily for reasons not fully explained in news accounts of the time. According to a report in an American newspaper, the steamship company she traveled with would not yet permit her to set sail. Reportedly, Vanzetti held a temporary visa from the U.S. State Department.

17. Ibid., p. 2.

18. "Fascist Organ Terms Sacco End 'Shameful,'" *New York Times,* August 5, 1927, p. 1.

19. Felix, *Protest,* p. 172.

CHAPTER 7

1. Dale Kramer, *Heywood Broun, A Biographical Portrait* (New York: Current Books, 1949), p. 176

2. Russell, *Sacco and Vanzetti,* p. 139.

3. Quoted in the *Official Bulletin of the Sacco-Vanzetti Defense Committee,* May 15, 1927, p. 4 (SHSW.)

4. Ronald Steel, *Walter Lippmann and the American Century* (Boston: Little, Brown and Co., 1980), p. 229.

5. "The Lowell Committee Report," *New York World,* August 8, 1927, p. 10.

6. "Mercy," *New York World,* August 10, 1927, p. 12.

7. Kramer, *Broun,* p. 173: Edwin Emery and Michael Emery, *The Press and America: An Interpretive History of the Mass Media,* 6th ed. (Englewood Cliffs, N.J.: Prentice Hall, 1988), p. 368.

8. Kramer, *Broun,* p. 175.

9. Ibid., p. 175.

10. Ibid., p. 175.

11. Ibid., p. 177.

12. Quoted in Joughin and Morgan, *Legacy,* p. 287.

13. Ibid., p. 287.

14. Kramer, *Broun,* p. 179.

15. "Judge Denies Reds' Petition," *Milwaukee Journal,* August 8, 1927, p. 1.

16. Ibid., p. 1.

17. "An Appeal to Mr. Coolidge," *St. Louis Post-Dispatch*, July 12, 1927, p. 20.

18. "Three Cities Terrorized by Bombings," *Milwaukee Journal,* August 6, 1927 p. 1.

19. Edna St. Vincent Millay, "Fear," *Outlook,* November 9, 1927, pp. 293–310.

20. "Files Sacco Plea, Seeking New Trial," *New York Times,* August 7, 1927, p. 1.

21. "Chicago Police Fire on Sacco Mob of 4,000," *Boston Evening Transcript,* August 10, 1927.

22. Marion Meade, *Dorothy Parker: What Fresh Hell Is This?* (New York: Penguin Books, 1989), p. 180.

23. "Reds Defense Group Asks La Follette Aid," *Milwaukee Journal,* August 9, 1927, p. 1.

24. "Borah Wants Secret Files Made Public, Refuses to Sign Petition," *Boston Daily Transcript,* August 11, 1927, p. 1.

25. "British Urge Mercy for Doomed Men," *New York Times,* August 10, 1927, p. 4.

26. "Family of Sacco Still Trusts in U.S. Justice," *Milwaukee Journal,* August 11, 1927, p. 1.

27. "Says Bullet Came From Sacco's Pistol," *New York Times,* August 10, 1927, p. 5; "How the Sacco Bullet Was 'Finger Printed,'" *Boston Evening Transcript,* August 9, 1927, p. 10.

28. "Communist International in Plea to Help Save Sacco and Vanzetti from Chair," *Daily Worker,* August 8, 1927, p. 1.

29. Ibid., p. 1.

30. "Start March on Boston Today to Picket Prison," *Daily Worker*, August 9, 1927, p. 1.

31. "Reds Get Respite, Win New Legal Tilt," *Milwaukee Journal*, August 11, 1927, p. 1.

32. Ibid., p. 1.

33. Laurence J. Cahill, "Why Did it Come To Boston?" *Boston Evening Transcript*, August 16, 1927, p. 14.

34. Drew Pearson, "Red Sentences Affects Trade," *Milwaukee Journal*, August 14, 1927, p. 3.

35. Ibid., p. 3.

36. "One Plain Moral," *New York Times*, August 14, 1927, p. 8.

37. "Let's Keep Our Heads," *Milwaukee Journal*, August 15, 1927, p. 6.

38. "Nothing in Files Bearing on the Vanzetti Case," *Boston Evening Transcript*, August 11, 1927, p. 1.

39. Ibid., p. 1.

40. "Sacco Breaks Fast When Facing Force," *New York Times*, August 16, 1927, p. 1.

41. Louis M. Lyons, "Bomber's Attempt to Kill McHardys Fails," *Boston Daily Globe*, August 17, 1927, p. 1; "State High Court Hears Plea; Bomb Wrecks Home of Juror in Case," *New York Times*, August 17, 1927, p. 1.

42. "Powers Hapgood Gets Six Months on Riot Charge," *Boston Evening Transcript*, August 16, 1927, p. 1.

43. *New York Times*, August 17, 1927, p. 1; "Expect Decision Soon on Sacco Exceptions," *Boston Daily Globe*, August 17, 1927, p. 1.

44. Ibid., *Boston Daily Globe*, August 17, 1927, p. 1.

45. Mike Gold, "Boston Prepares for a Lynching," *Daily Worker*, August 15, 1927, p. 4.

46. "Turn on the Light," *Daily Worker*, August 17, 1927, p. 1.

47. "Sacco, Vanzetti Lose in State Supreme Court," *St. Louis Post-Dispatch*, August 19, 1927, p. 1. "Sacco and Vanzetti Lose in the Supreme Court," *Boston Daily Globe*, August 19, 1927, p. 1.

48. Ibid., p. 1.

49. "Doubt that Will Not Down," *New York World*, August 19, 1927, p. 12.

50. "The Last Chance," *Manchester Guardian*, August 20, 1927, p. 16; also see "More Death-Watch Marchers Arrested Near State House," *Boston Evening Transcript*, August 20, 1927, p. 1; "Sunday Meetings on Common Prohibited," *Boston Daily Globe*, August 20, 1927, p. 11.

51. Manitoba *Free Press*, August 27, 1927, p. 11. The editorial is signed with the initials T.B.R.

52. "Miss Vanzetti Here as Sister, Not Propagandist," *Boston Globe*, August 19, 1927, p. 11; "Vanzetti's Sister Hastens to Boston," *New York Times*, August 20, 1927, p. 4.

53. Ibid., *New York Times*, August 20, 1927, p. 4.

54. Porter, *Never Ending Wrong*, pp. 38–39.

55. "Brandeis Declines to Act; Sacco Counsel Now Seek Justice Stone on Last Day," *New York Times*, August 22, 1927, p. 1.

56. "Government Has No Sacco-Vanzetti Files," *Boston Evening Transcript,* August 22, 1927, p. 4.

57. Ibid., p. 4.

58. Felix, *Protest,* p. 226.

59. "Poem by Miss Millay of Sacco and Vanzetti," *New York Times,* August 22, 1927, p. 2; "Doom of Sacco and Vanzetti Stirs Edna St. Vincent Millay," *New York World,* August 22, 1927, p. 2.

60. *New York World,* August 22, 1927, p. 2.

61. See J. Douglas Gomery, "The Coming of the Talkies: Invention, Innovation and Diffusion," in *The American Film Industry,* Tino Balio, ed. (Madison, Wis: University of Wisconsin Press, 1976), pp. 193–211.

62. "Demonstration in Sacco Case," *Boston Evening Globe,* August 22, 1927, p. 1; "Boston Besieged; Scores Arrested," *New York Times,* August 23, 1927, p. 1.

63. "Justified Concern," *New York Times,* August 21, 1927, p. 8.

64. "Fuller Hears Petitions," *New York Times,* August 23, 1927, p. 1.

65. "Rome Newspapers Await Executions," *New York Times,* August 21, 1927, p. 19; John L. Balderston, "London Stages Big Protest on Sacco," *New York World,* August 22, 1927, p. 2.

66. *New York World,* August 22, 1927, p. 2.

67. "The Last Day," *St. Louis Post-Dispatch,* August 22, 1927, p. 20.

68. "Medeiros, Sacco, Vanzetti Died in Chair This Morning," *Boston Daily Globe,* August 23, 1927, p. 1; *New York Times,* August 23, 1927, p. 1.

69. Felix, *Protest,* p. 233.

70. Ibid.; also see Jeannette Marks, *Thirteen Days* (New York: Albert and Charles Boni, 1929), p. 6.

71. *New York Times,* August 23, 1927, p. 2.

72. Joughin and Morgan, *Legacy,* p. 325.

73. "The Execution of Sacco and Vanzetti," *Cleveland Press,* August 24, 1927, p. 8.

74. "Red Agitators and the Law's Delay," *Chicago Daily News,* August 24, 1927, p. 8.

75. "A Futile Use of Intimidation," *Minneapolis Tribune,* August 24, 1927, p. 14.

76. "Press Comment on the Sacco-Vanzetti Executions," *Nation,* September 14, 1927, p. 252.

77. Ibid., p. 252.

78. Ibid., p. 252.

79. "Some Left-Over Morals," *New York Times,* August 24, 1927, p. 22.

80. "The Sacco-Vanzetti Challenge," *Milwaukee Journal,* August 27, 1927, p. 16.

81. *Boston Evening Transcript,* August 24, 1927, p. 12.

82. "Sacco and Vanzetti Murdered," *Daily Worker,* August 24, 1927, p. 1.

83. John Dos Passos, "They Fear Their Own Crime," *Daily Worker,* August 24, 1927, p. 5.

84. "10,000 Fight Paris Police Over Sacco; Embassy Menaced," *New York World,* August 24, 1927, p. 1; "Sacco Disorders in Paris," *Times* (London), August 26, 1927, p. 1.

85. "London Crowd Charged by Police; Riot at Geneva," *Milwaukee Journal,* August 24, 1927, p. 2.

86. "Sacco Death Stirs Press of Europe," *New York World,* August 24, 1927, p. 2.

87. *Milwaukee Journal,* August 24, 1927, p. 2.

88. "Sacco Agitators Censured Abroad," *New York Times,* August 24, 1927, p. 2.

89. Ibid., p. 2.

90. Ibid., p. 2.

91. *New York World,* August 24, 1927, p. 2.

92. Ibid., p. 2.

93. Ibid., p. 2.

94. *New York Times,* August 24, 1927, p. 2.

95. Ibid., p. 2.

96. "Throngs View Bodies of Sacco and Vanzetti," *New York Times,* August 26, 1927, p. 8.

97. "Sacco and Vanzetti Followed by 7,000 in Boston Funeral," *New York Times,* August 29, 1927, p. 4.

98. "Red Collection Not Turned In," *Milwaukee Journal,* August 28, 1927, p. 1.

99. "Radicals," *Time,* August 29, 1927, pp. 9–10.

EPILOGUE

1. H. G. Wells, "Wells Speaks Some Plain Words to U.S.," *New York Times,* October 16, 1927, iv, p. 3.

2. Joughin and Morgan, *Legacy,* p. 308.

3. Felix Frankfurter, *The Case of Sacco and Vanzetti: A Critical Analysis for Lawyers and Laymen* (Boston: Little, Brown, 1927).

4. Marion Denham Frankfurter and Gardner Jackson, eds. *The Letters of Sacco and Vanzetti* (New York: Viking, 1928).

5. "A Trial of the Law," *Outlook,* August 31, 1927, p. 562.

6. "Penalties of the Sacco-Vanzetti Execution," *New Republic,* September 7, 1927, p. 57.

7. Aaron, *Writers on the Left,* pp. 169–173.

8. "Radicals," *Time,* August 29, 1927, p. 10.

9. *The New Republic,* August 31, 1927, p. 278.

10. Edna St. Vincent Millay, "Fear," *Outlook,* November 11, 1927, p. 293.

11. Joughin and Morgan, *Legacy,* p. 313.

12. Louis Stark, "The Grounds for Doubt," *Survey,* October 21, 1927, pp. 38–41, 55–57.

13. Ibid., p. 39.

14. Ben Bagdikian, *The Media Monopoly* (Boston: Beacon Press, 1983), viii.

15. John Dewey, "Psychology and Justice," *New Republic,* November 27, 1927, pp. 9–12.

16. William G. Thompson, "Vanzetti's Last Statement," *Atlantic Monthly,* February, 1928, pp. 254–257.

17. Malcolm Cowley, "For St. Bartholomew's Day," *Nation,* August 22, 1928, p. 172.

18. *New York Times,* June 16, 1928, p. 2.

19. "Frank Silva's Story," *The Outlook and Independent,* October 31, 1928, p. 1,055; Silas Bent, "Checking Up the Vanzetti Story," November 7, 1928, p. 1,096.

20. "Bridgewater and After," *Outlook and Independent,* November 14, 1928, p. 1,163.

21. "Vanzetti Was Innocent," *New Republic,* November 7, 1928, pp. 317–318.

22. F. Lauriston Bullard, "Proposed Reforms Echo of Sacco Case," *New York Times,* December 11, 1926, p. 12.

23. Osmond K. Fraenkel, *The Sacco-Vanzetti Case.* In the American Trials Series (New York: Knopf Publishers, 1931).

24. Ralph Colp, Jr., "Bitter Christmas: A Biographical Inquiry into the Life of Bartolomeo Vanzetti," *Nation,* December 27, 1958, pp. 485–500; Colp, "Sacco's Struggle for Sanity," *Nation,* August 16, 1958, pp. 65–70.

25. Tom O'Connor, "The Origins of the Sacco-Vanzetti Case," *Vanderbilt Law Review,* June, 1961, pp. 987–1,006; also see Barry C. Reed, "The Sacco-Vanzetti Case: The Trial of the Century," *American Bar Association Journal,* August, 1960, pp. 867–872.

26. Fred J. Cook, "The Missing Fingerprints," *Nation,* December 29, 1962, pp. 442–451.

27. Michael Musmanno, "Was Sacco Guily?" *The New Republic,* March 2, 1963, pp. 25–30; for a 1974 panel discussion in which several surviving Sacco-Vanzetti Defense Committee members and Nicola Sacco's grandson, Spencer Sacco, confront Russell regarding alleged discrepancies in his book, *Tragedy in Dedham,* see transcript of the conference held in Boston (IHRC), Miscellaneous Italian Collection, Box 2.

28. Ben Bagdikian, "New Light on Sacco-Vanzetti," *New Republic,* July 13, 1963, pp. 13–17.

29. Herbert B. Ehrmann, *The Case that Will Not Die: Commonwealth vs. Sacco and Vanzetti* (Boston: Little, Brown and Co., 1969), pp. 375–388; also see Ehrmann, "Sacco and Vanzetti: The Magnetic Point and the Morelli Evidence," *Harvard Law Review,* January 1960, pp. 571–596.

30. Israel Shenker, "Sacco-Vanzetti Case Is Evoking Passions 50 Years After Deaths," *New York Times,* August 23, 1977, p. 33.

Select Bibliography

Aaron, Daniel. *Writers on the Left: Episodes in American Literary Communism.* New York: Harcourt, Brace and World, Inc., 1961.

Avrich, Paul. *The Haymarket Tragedy.* Princeton N.J.: Princeton University Press, 1984.

———. *Sacco and Vanzetti: The Anarchist Background:* Princeton, N.J.: Princeton University Press, 1991.

Bernays, Edward L. *Propaganda.* New York: Liveright Publishing Corp., 1928.

Bloodworth, William A., Jr. *Upton Sinclair.* Boston: Twayne Publishers, 1977.

Chakotin, Serge. *The Rape of the Masses: The Psychology of Totalitarian Propaganda.* New York: Haskell House Publishers, Ltd., 1971.

Cohen, Stanley. *A. Mitchell Palmer: Politician.* New York: Columbia University Press, 1963.

Czitrom, Daniel J. *Media and the American Mind: From Morse to McLuhan.* Chapell Hill, N.C.: University of North Carolina Press, 1982.

David, Henry. *The History of the Haymarket Affair: A Study in the American Social Revolution and Labor Movements,* 2nd ed. New York: Russell and Russell, 1958.

Diggins, John Paul. *Mussolini and Fascism: The View from America.* Princeton, N.J.: Princeton University Press, 1972.

Dos Passos, John. *The Best Times: An Informal Memoir.* New York: American Library, 1966.

Draper, Theodore. *American Communism and Soviet Russia: The Formative Period.* New York: Viking Press, 1960.

Ehrmann, Herbert B. *The Untried Case: The Sacco-Vanzetti Case and the Morelli Gang.* New York: Vanguard Press, Inc., 1960.

————. *The Case That Will Not Die: Commonwealth vs. Sacco and Vanzetti*. Boston: Little, Brown and Co., 1969.

Emery, Edwin, and Emery, Michael. *The Press and America: An Interpretive History of the Mass Media*, 6th ed., Englewood Cliffs, N.J.: Prentice Hall, 1988.

Feldman, Egal. *The Dreyfus Affair and the American Conscience: 1893–1906*. Detroit, Mi.: Wayne State University Press, 1981.

Felix, David. *Protest: Sacco, Vanzetti and the Intellectuals*. Bloomington, Ind.: Indiana University Press, 1965.

Feuerlicht, Roberta Strauss. *Justice Crucified: The Story of Sacco and Vanzetti*. New York: McGraw-Hill Book Co., 1977.

Fishkin, Shelley Fisher. *From Fact to Fiction: Journalism and Imaginative Writing in America*. Baltimore, Md.: Johns Hopkins University Press, 1985.

Fraenkel, Osmond K. *The Sacco-Vanzetti Case*. New York: Russell, 1969.

Frankfurter, Felix. *The Case of Sacco and Vanzetti: A Critical Analysis for Lawyers and Laymen*. Boston: Little, Brown, 1927.

Frankfurter, Marion Denham, and Jackson, Gardner, eds. *The Letters of Sacco and Vanzetti*. New York: Viking, 1928.

Frost, Richard H. *The Mooney Case*. Palo Alto, Calif.: Stanford University Press, 1968.

Gallagher, Dorothy. *All the Right Enemies: The Life and Murder of Carlo Tresca*. New Brunswick, N.J.: Rutgers University Press, 1988.

Gallo, Patrick J. *Old Bread, New Wine: A Portrait of the Italian Americans*. Chicago: Nelson-Hall, 1981.

Gentry, Curt. *Frame-Up: The Incredible Case of Tom Mooney and Warren Billings*. New York: W.W. Norton and Co., Inc., 1967.

Gitlow, Benjamin. *I Confess: The Truth about American Communism*. New York: E.P. Dutton & Co., 1940.

Gomery, J. Douglas. "The Coming of the Talkies: Invention, Innovation and Diffusion." In *The American Film Industry,* Tino Balio, ed. Madison, Wis.: University of Wisconsin Press, 1976.

Harris, Leon A. *Upton Sinclair: An American Rebel*. New York: Thomas Crowell, Co., 1975.

Hoffman, Robert Louis. *More Than a Trial: The Struggle Over Captain Dreyfus*. New York: Free Press, 1983.

Jaffe, Julian F. *Crusade Against Radicalism: New York During the Red Scare, 1919–24*. Port Washington, N.Y.: Kennikat Press, 1972.

Johnson, Donald. *The Challenge to American Freedoms: World War I and the Rise of the American Civil Liberties Union*. Lexington, Ky.: University of Kentucky Press, 1963.

Joll, James. *The Anarchists*. Boston: Little, Brown & Co., 1964.

Joughin, G. Louis, and Morgan, Edmund, M. *The Legacy of Sacco and Vanzetti*. Chicago: Quadrangle Books, 1964.

Koch, Stephen. *Double Lives: Spies and Writers in the Secret War of Ideas Against the West*. New York: Free Press, 1994.

Kramer, Dale. *Heywood Broun: A Biographical Portrait*. New York: Current Books, 1949.

Lambert, Richard S. *Propaganda*. London: Thomas Nelson and Son Ltd., 1938.

Lasswell, Harold D. *Propaganda Technique in the World War.* New York: Peter Smith, 1938.

Lyons, Eugene. *Assignment in Utopia.* New York: Harcourt, Brace and Co., 1937.

———. *The Life and Death of Sacco and Vanzetti.* New York: International Publications, 1927.

Manchester, William. *Disturber of the Peace: The Life of H. L. Mencken.* New York: Harper and Brothers, 1950–51.

Marks, Jeannette. *Thirteen Days.* New York: Albert and Charles Boni, 1929.

Meade, Marion. *Dorothy Parker: What Fresh Hell Is This?* New York: Penguin Books, 1980.

Montgomery, Robert H. *The Murder and the Myth.* New York: Devin-Adair, Co., 1960.

Pernicone, Nunzio. *Italian Anarchism: 1864–1892.* Princeton, N.J.: Princeton University Press 1993.

Porter, Katherine Anne. *The Never Ending Wrong.* Boston: Little, Brown and Co., 1977.

Preston, William. *Aliens and Dissenters: Federal Suppression of Radicals, 1903–1933.* Cambridge, Mass.: Harvard University Press, 1963.

Russell, Francis. *Sacco and Vanzetti: The Case Resolved.* New York: Harper and Row Publishers, 1986.

———. *Tragedy in Dedham: The Story of the Sacco-Vanzetti Case.* New York: McGraw-Hill Book Co., 1962.

Schechter, Betty. *The Dreyfus Affair: A National Scandal.* Boston: Houghton Mifflin, 1965.

Steel, Ronald. *Walter Lippmann and the American Century.* Boston: Little, Brown and Co., 1980.

Susman, Warren I. *Culture as History: The Transformation of American Society in the Twentieth Century.* New York: Pantheon Books, 1984.

Trautman, Frederick. *The Voice of Terror: A Biography of Johann Most.* Westport, Conn.: Greenwood Press, 1980.

Weeks, Robert P., ed. *Commonwealth vs. Sacco and Vanzetti.* Englewood Cliffs, N.J.: Prentice-Hall, Inc., 1958.

Weinberg, Arthur, and Weinberg, Lila. *Clarence Darrow: A Sentimental Rebel.* New York: G.P. Putnam's Sons, 1980.

Young, William, and Kaiser, David. *Post Mortem: New Evidence in the Case of Sacco and Vanzetti.* Amherst, Mass.: University of Massachusetts Press, 1985.

PRIMARY DOCUMENTS

Anthony Capraro Collection. "Sacco and Vanzetti Atlanta Investigation," Correspondence and Literature, 1922–1963. Box 2; Miscellaneous Italian Manuscript Collection, Spencer Sacco panel discussion. Box 2 Immigrant Historical Research Center, University of Minnesota. Twin Cities Campus.

Bulletin of the Sacco-Vanzetti Defense Committee. May 1927. (SHSW).

Letter from Earl Browder to Fred H. Moore, September 3, 1924. Fred H. Moore Collection, Boston Public Library. Rare Book Collection.

Letter from James P. Cannon to Eugene V. Debs, July 15, 1925, Box 3, Folder 1. State Historical Society of Wisconsin (SHSW). James P. Cannon Collection.

The Sacco-Vanzetti Case; *Transcript of the Record of the Trial of Nicola Sacco and Bartolomeo Vanzetti in the Courts of Massachusetts and Subsequent Proceedings, 1927.* Edited by Charles C. Burlingham and Bernard Flexner. Six volumes; I-V and supplemental volume. New York: Holt and Co., 1929.

Vanzetti, Bartolomeo. *Awaiting the Hangman: A Journalistic Conspiracy of Quietness.* Quoted in the Official Bulletin of Defense Committee. Sacco-Vanzetti Case Papers. Drawer 131, Box 177-3, reel 21. Harvard Law School.

———. *Background of the Plymouth Trial.* Boston; Road to Freedom Group, 1927. Fromkin Collection, Golda Meir Library. University of Wisconsin–Milwaukee.

PERIODICALS

"The Anarchists and the Ambassador." *Literary Digest.* November 5, 1921.

Bagdikian, Ben. "New Light on Sacco-Vanzetti." *New Republic.* July 13, 1963.

Beffel, John Nicholas. "Eels and the Electric Chair." *New Republic.* December 29, 1920.

Bent, Silas. "Checking Up the Vanzetti Story." *Outlook and Independent.* November 7, 1928.

Bliven, Bruce. "In Dedham Jail: A Visit to Sacco and Vanzetti." *New Republic,* June 22, 1927.

"Bridgewater and After." *Outlook and Independent.* November 14, 1928.

Colp, Ralph, Jr. "Sacco's Struggle for Sanity." *Nation.* August 16, 1958.

———. "Bitter Christmas: A Biographical Inquiry into the Life of Bartolomeo Vanzetti." *Nation.* December 28, 1958.

Cook, Fred J. "The Missing Finger Prints." *Nation.* December 20, 1962.

Cowley, Malcolm. "For St. Bartholomew's Day." *Nation.* August 22, 1928.

"The Department of Justice and the Sacco-Vanzetti Case." *New Republic.* September 29, 1926.

Dewey, John. "Psychology and Justice." *New Republic.* November 27, 1927.

Evans, Elizabeth Glendower. "Foreigners." *New Republic.* June 8, 1921.

Felicani, Aldino. "Sacco-Vanzetti: A Memorial." *Nation.* August 14, 1967.

"Frank Silva's Story." *Outlook and Independent.* October 31, 1928.

Frankfurter, Felix. "The Case of Sacco and Vanzetti." *Atlantic Monthly,* March 1927.

Hofstadter, Richard. "The Paranoid Style in American Politics." *Harper's.* November, 1964.

Kirchwey, George. "Sacco-Vanzetti." *Nation.* April 20, 1927.

Lyons, Eugene. "Italians in American Courts." *Survey.* November 12, 1921.

Millay, Edna St. Vincent. "Fear." *Outlook,* November 9. 1927.

Musmanno, Michael. "Was Sacco Guilty?" *New Republic.* March 2, 1963.

New Republic. August 31, 1927.

"Penalties of the Sacco-Vanzetti Execution." *New Republic.* September 7, 1927.

"Press Comment on the Sacco-Vanzetti Executions." *Nation.* September 1, 1927.

"Radicals." *Time.* August 29, 1927.

"Reaffirming the Guilt of Sacco and Vanzetti." *Literary Digest.* August 20, 1927.

"Sacco-Vanzetti." *New Republic.* April 20, 1927.

"The Sacco-Vanzetti Case." *Literary Digest.* August 13, 1927.

Skinner, Clarence R. "The Sacco-Vanzetti Case." *Survey.* August 16, 1921.

Stark, Louis. "The Grounds for Doubt." *Survey.* October 21, 1927.

Thompson, William G. "Vanzetti's Last Statement." *Atlantic Monthly.* February 1928.

"A Trial of the Law." *Outlook.* August 31, 1927.

"Vanzetti Was Innocent." *New Republic."* November 7, 1928.

Warner, Arthur. "Sacco and Vanzetti—a Reasonable Doubt." *Nation.* September 28, 1921.

"White Terror and Red Terror." *Outlook.* November 2, 1921.

NEWSPAPERS

Boston Daily Globe
Boston Evening Transcript
Boston Herald
Chicago Daily News
Cleveland Press
Duluth Herald
Hartford Times
Le Monde (France)
Macon Telegraph
Manchester (England) *Guardian*
Manitoba (Canada) *Free Press*
Milwaukee Journal
Minneapolis Tribune
New York Daily Worker
New York Times
New York World
Springfield Republican
St. Louis Post-Dispatch
Times (London)

LAW REVIEWS AND JOURNALS

Cannistraro, Philip, V. "Sacco, Vanzetti and the Anarchists: The Transatlantic Context." *The Journal of Modern History,* March 1996.

Ehrmann, Herbert B. "Sacco and Vanzetti: The Magnetic Point and the Morelli Evidence." *Harvard Law Review,* January 1966.

O'Connor, Tom. "The Origins of the Sacco-Vanzetti Case." *Vanderbilt Law Review,* June 1961.

Reed, Barry C. The Sacco-Vanzetti Case: The Trial of the Century." *American Bar Association Journal,* August 1960.

Stebbins, Howard L. "The Sacco-Vanzetti Case." *American Bar Association Journal,* November 1922.

Index

About the Author

JOHN F. NEVILLE is a freelance writer who holds a Ph.D. from the University of Minnesota. He has worked as a freelance newspaper and magazine reporter and as a public relations writer. His first book, *The Press, the Rosenbergs, and the Cold War* was published by Greenwood in 1995.